# Rice Roots

## THE VIETNAM WAR:
## TRUE STORIES FROM THE DIARY
## OF A U.S. COMBAT ADVISOR

Robert R. Amon Jr.

**RICE ROOTS**

**THE VIETNAM WAR:
TRUE STORIES FROM THE DIARY
OF A U.S. COMBAT ADVISOR**

Copyright, 2020
Robert R. Amon Jr.

No text or images in this book
may be used or reproduced in any
manner without written permission
of the copyright holder.

All Rights Reserved

Cover layout and interior pages
layout by Capri Porter.

Printed in the United States of America

ISBN: 978-1-7347007-1-8

Published by
Legacies & Memories
St. Augustine, Florida
www.LegaciesandMemoriesPublishing.com

For More Information About This Book,
or to Contact the Author, Please Visit:
**www.RiceRoots.com**

## DEDICATION

This book is dedicated to the memory of Charles H. Emery and to all who choose to wear the uniform of our country. They so love our values and way of life that they're willing to give up their todays for others' tomorrows.

"Rejoice, O young man, in thy youth."

Ecclesiastes 11:9

## CONTENTS

Dedication...iii

Contents...vii

Lexicon...ix

Foreword...xi

Introduction...xiii

Maps...xiv-xv

Prologue...xix

CHAPTER ONE
**'On My Honor'...1**

CHAPTER TWO
**'Rice Roots'...14**

CHAPTER THREE
**The 168 Company...39**

CHAPTER FOUR
**'Trời Ơi!... Trời Ơi!'...70**

CHAPTER FIVE
**To Hell in a Handbasket...102**

CHAPTER SIX
**'Nasty'...127**

CHAPTER SEVEN
**Sitting Ducks...158**

CHAPTER EIGHT
**Blackest of Days...195**

CHAPTER NINE
**Brownwater Navy...207**

CHAPTER TEN
**Old Guy, New Guy...240**

CHAPTER ELEVEN
**Return to Hóa Quản Village...267**

Epilogue...297
Acknowledgements...301
References...304
Contact the Author...307

# LEXICON

AK-47: Kalashnikov 7.62x39mm assault rifle, 30-round magazine
ARVN: Army of the Republic of (South) Vietnam
ASAP: As Soon As Possible
B-40: Shoulder-held rocket-propelled grenade launcher
B-52: Jet-powered, long-range, Boeing Stratofortress bomber
BAR: Browning Automatic Rifle
BOQ: Bachelor Officer's Quarters
CPT: The rank of Captain (O3)
CHARLIE: Derived from VC, "Victor Charlie" phonetically
CHINOOK: Boeing CH-47 double-bladed helicopter
CIB: Combat Infantryman's Badge
COL: The rank of Full Colonel (O6)
CONEX: 8'x8' steel container made by Container Express Company
CORDS: Civil Operations and Revolutionary Development Support
DEROS: Date of Effective Return from Overseas
EER: Enlisted Efficiency Report
ETA: Estimated Time of Arrival
FNG: Fucking New Guy
GEN: The rank of General (O7 and above)
HUEY: U.S. Army Bell UH-1D helicopter
JUMP WINGS: U.S. Army Parachutists Badge
KIA: Killed in Action
LT: The rank of Second Lieutenant (2LT - O1) or First Lieutenant (1LT - O2)
LTC: The rank of Lieutenant Colonel (O5)
M1-M2: .30 caliber carbines, WWII and Korean War vintage
M3 Grease Gun: .45 caliber WWII-Era submachine gun
M16: Adaptation of the AR-15 rifle, firing 5.56x45mm rounds
M60: Belt-fed U.S. machine gun firing 7.62x51mm rounds
M79: 40mm grenade launcher

MACV: Military Assistance Command, Vietnam
MAJ: The rank of Major (O4)
MAT: Mobile Advisory Team
MEDCAP: Medical Civic Action Program
MEDIVAC: Medical evacuation by helicopter
MPC: Military Payment Certificates
NCO: Non-Commisioned Officer
NVA: North Vietnamese Army
OCS: Officer Candidate School
OER: Officer Efficiency Report
PBR: Patrol Boat, River
PFs: Popular Forces (platoon-sized units)
POW: Prisoner of War
PSDF: Peoples' Self-Defense Force
PSP: Perforated Steel Planking
RD Cadre: Revolutionary Development Cadre
REMF: Rear Echelon Mother Fucker
RFs: Regional Forces (company-sized units)
RPG: Rocket-Propelled Grenade
RTO: Radio Telegraph Operator (radio man)
SFC: Sergeant First Class
SITREP: Situation Report
UH-1D: U.S. Army Bell UH-1D helicopter
VC: Viet Công (Vietcông), "Victor Charlie" phonetically
WIA: Wounded in Action

# FOREWORD

By Col. Bill Stanberry, U.S. Army, Retired

I had never known a soldier who kept a diary every day for a year while in combat, especially one living in an insecure mud-walled revetment with four other soldiers. These soldiers were embedded among South Vietnamese troops and civilians with uncertain loyalties who were surrounded and frequently captured or killed by the enemy. This very dangerous environment is the setting for this story. The year was 1969, and the soldier maintaining a daily log of events was First Lieutenant Robert Amon.

I learned that there was such a diligent journal-keeper exactly fifty years after the fact, when I got a call from Lieutenant Amon informing me that he was writing a book. Because I was his commanding officer and mentioned throughout, he was asking permission to use my name. I remembered Lt. Amon as being the best of the best team leaders in Kiến Giáng Province, where I was senior advisor to the province chief.

After reading the manuscript and examining his weathered, age-worn diary, I agreed to his request to use my name. Moreover, his relation of events, of which I had personal knowledge, is remarkably factual and unblemished by any exaggeration to make himself a hero. The authenticity of this book, written by using the lead-in of his daily diary entries, persuaded me to enthusiastically offer to endorse his book.

Lt. Amon reported to me in Rạch Giá, the provincial capital city, on February 12, 1969, for an infantry assignment with a Military Advisory Team (MAT). I observed during my interview that he had an unusually clear grasp of the pacification concept of "winning the hearts and minds" of the community and religious leaders, the military, and the people whom he was to advise and support. This mission differed from that of conventional military units in Vietnam whose major mission was to destroy the enemy and provide security in a designated area of operation.

I assigned Lieutenant Amon to MAT 88, a five-man team embedded with usually less than sixty mostly untrained recruits who were often equipped with weapons inferior to those of the VC. The team was on the edge of the U-Minh Forest, an uncontested VC hideout in South Vietnam's Delta. His team was housed in a crude shelter in an outpost surrounded by a mud berm and moat. Their primary means of communication was through an interpreter.

In his role as advisor to the military, Lt. Amon participated in almost daily patrols and weekly night ambushes. Lt. Amon's effectiveness and noteworthy progress made MAT 88 the site to which I sent all senior officers and other official VIP visitors to see how pacification could be successfully accomplished.

Bob Amon's interesting style of handwritten diary entries followed by extremely well-written narration results in the most unembellished, authentically believable story by this modest, unsung hero working at the "grass roots" level in a book aptly titled "Rice Roots." This book should be read by military officers and history scholars to understand precisely how pacification can be an effective strategy. To that end, I highly recommend *Rice Roots* as required reading at the United States Army War College in Carlisle, Pennsylvania.

## INTRODUCTION

This book is a true story, based on a diary that I kept while serving as a combat advisor to the South Vietnamese Army in 1969. I have made every effort to preserve the exact truthfulness and accuracy of the circumstances, locations and situations as they occurred. This was possible through my original diary entries, information contained in letters I sent home, in preserved combat topographical map coordinates and in over 500 photos in my possession.

Most conversations in this memoir are, out of necessity, based on recollection. But to the best of my ability, I know you will be able to capture the moment.

Other factual information was obtained through declassified United States Army files and previously published works as referenced, as well as personal interviews with my former commander, Colonel Bill Stanberry, conversations with Helen Emery, and the much-appreciated input from my wife, Carolyn (Zgutowicz) Amon, who accompanied me to Hóa Quản Village on my return trip to Vietnam.

The book is formatted with short and dated *italicized diary entries*, followed by my narration in regular text. Occasional reference material within the text is identified with numbered superscript following the text referenced, as on page eight, for example: "nearly half the entire number of Americans killed during the fifteen-year period of the Vietnam War."[1] These numbered sources can be found in the back of the book under "References."

You will also occasionally notice a small superscript letter like this one on page fifty-two: *Heard gunfire about a half mile away, near the pagoda.*[C] The small letters refer to actual locations on the two topographical combat maps furnished on the following two pages.

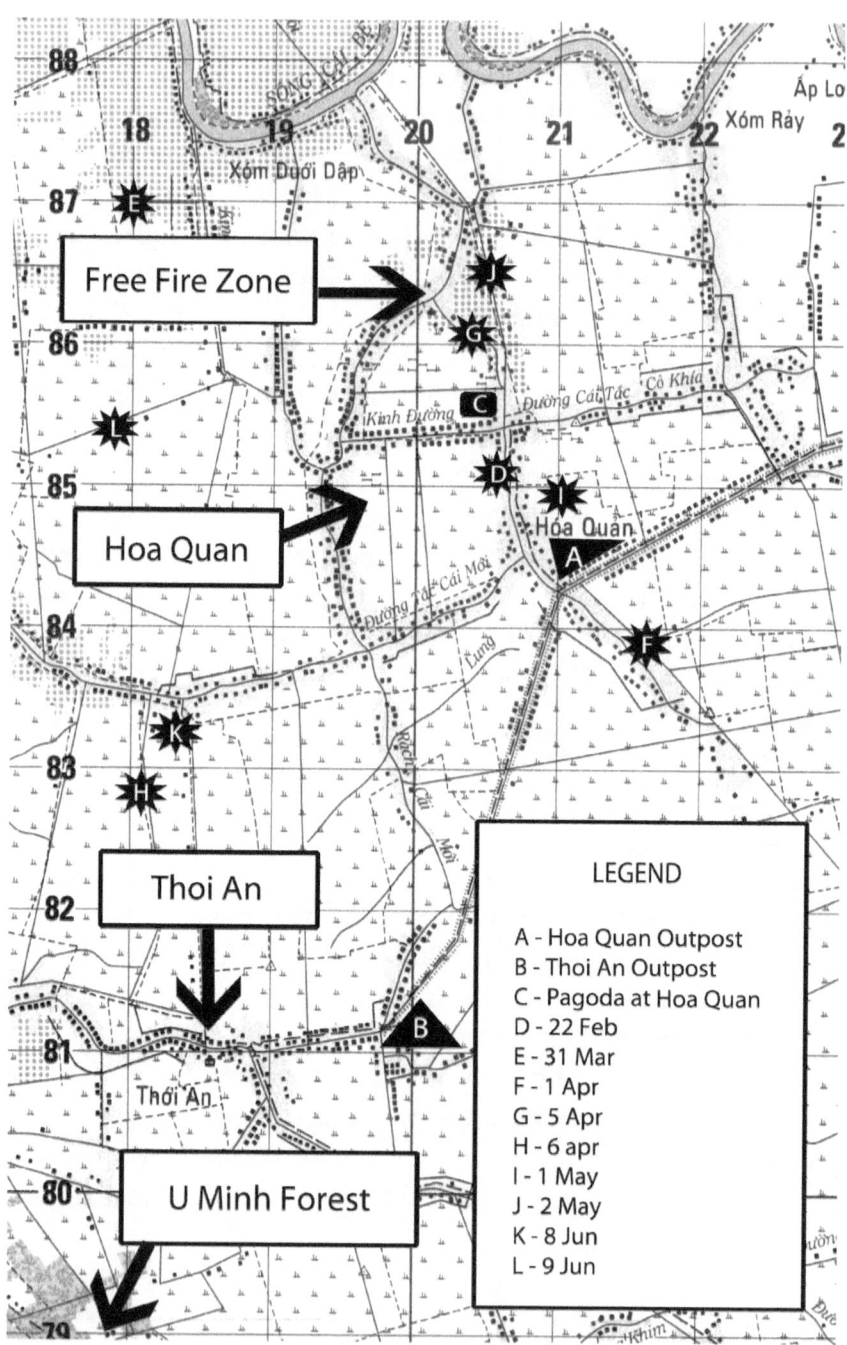

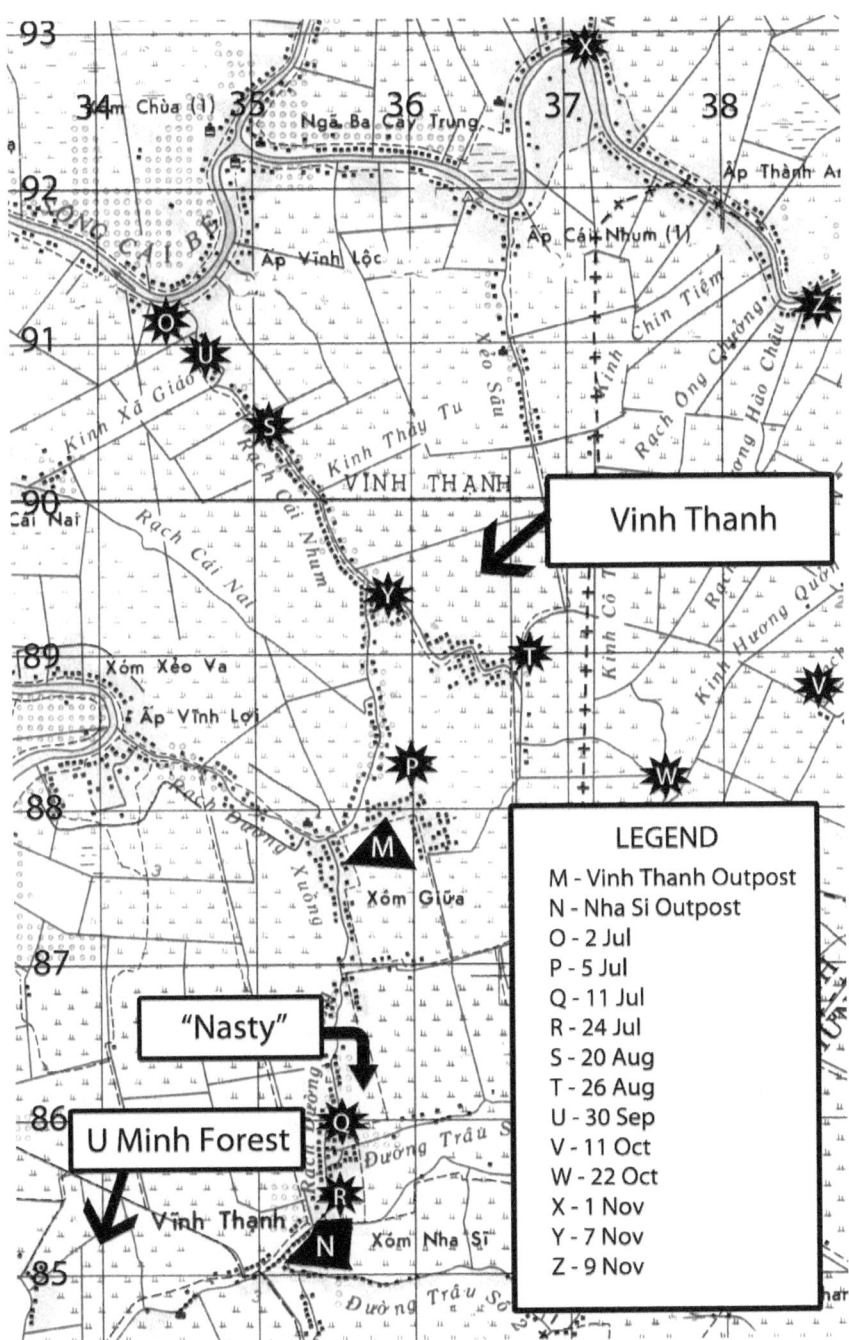

# Rice Roots

## THE VIETNAM WAR:
## TRUE STORIES FROM THE DIARY
## OF A U.S. COMBAT ADVISOR

## PROLOGUE

Everybody thought Chuck Emery was an orphan. Even his Buffalo State College classmates thought so. It was easier and less painful for Chuck to let them all think that. And besides, it was better than the awful truth.

They had an inkling that he had been bounced around in a number of foster homes in New York, but the subject was usually mercifully dropped whenever his formative years were mentioned. He was much too nice a fellow to put through having to explain the details. And that suited him fine.

Friends remember him washing and ironing classmates' chinos and madras shirts to earn some spending money. Everyone liked the lovable young man for his wit and sense of humor and his ability to openly and unconditionally accept people for who they were.

Then there was the older woman in his life, Miss Shirley McGill from Stevens Point, Wisconsin, who many remember he mentioned often. He referred to Shirley as his friend, but she seemed to be much more than that. She's the one who had been a mentor to him back in the old New York neighborhood when he was growing up. In those days, she lived in the vicinity of the NYC foster homes he and his sister had been shuffled between since the age of nine. And since the foster homes were all in the same general area, he became the adopted boy of the entire neighborhood because of his outgoing personality.

And within that world he developed a confident, self-sufficient, NYC toughness. But his disarming, boyish grin and happy-go-lucky demeanor won many hearts, including Shirley's. She soon became more of a mother to him than his own.

Even his U.S. Army records listed no parents - only Shirley McGill's name. He had written "none" on line thirteen on the NOK (Next of Kin) form where one would normally list their mother and father. Then he wrote Shirley's name and address on the next line, identifying the relationship as "friend," and signed the form at the bottom. The Army had absolutely no record of either a mother or a father in any of their personnel files on him. It dove-tailed perfectly with the college ruse.

He was twenty and in his sophomore year when he left Buffalo State. His six-month scholarship had run out and college would have to wait. Besides, there were more important things to do. There was a war on and the United States needed college-age infantry officers. The recruiter on campus told him, based on his accumulated credits, that he had a good shot at being accepted into the U.S. Army's Officer Candidate School. He was going to be somebody. He was going to make something of himself. He was going to be a United States Army officer!

There were people in a distant land, a little-known country called Vietnam, who very much needed our help to remain free, and that appealed to him in a big way. He would finally have a sense of purpose to his life. Something he could latch onto. A calling. He could finally make a difference while leaving all traces of his dark, unpleasant, unloved childhood behind.

The year was 1966 and things were heating up over there. Time to get a move on. Shirley McGill didn't like the idea very much, but she gave him her blessing anyway. By June, he left his Buffalo State jacket and a handful of the meager personal belongings of his youth behind with her, and promised to write as often as possible. Shirley promised to write even more often than that.

Maybe now he wouldn't have to explain all this foster-home business to any of the college boys he had been hanging out with, or any of the real reasons why he had to grow up that way. And certainly not to someone like myself. Men preparing themselves for war don't concern themselves with anyone's past. They're only concerned with what lies ahead.

By the time I met him, the two of us were immersed in only one thing, the business of learning how to stay alive. And that chance meeting had a profound influence on my life.

CHAPTER ONE

# 'On My Honor'

JANUARY 9, 1969

I nervously rang the front doorbell.

It was the home of Mayo Parks, a friend with whom I had walked to school since the age of ten. As kids, we played neighborhood softball and were in the same Boy Scout Troop. Our paths to this point had been similar since boyhood, and at the ripe age of twelve we both went to the 1957 Boy Scout Jamboree at Valley Forge, Pennsylvania. The theme on our neckerchiefs was "Duty, Honor and Country," and featured a silhouette of George Washington on bended knee.

During the summers at Camp Winnebago, Troop 34 always excelled. Along with Billy Scott, Don Garrido, Mayo and others, we passed the twenty-one merit badges required for the rank of Eagle. Scouting stressed leadership training and sharpened our outdoor skills. We learned to be self-sufficient, to rely on and believe in ourselves. Together, with scout signs up, we recited "The Scout Oath" hundreds of times in a time best captured by Norman Rockwell: "On my honor, I will do my best, to do my duty, to God and my country." It was a great time to be growing up. The '50's were the Wonder Bread years, the fun-filled Hoola Hoop years. They were also the prelude to the unexpected, unwanted, bastard decade: the 1960's, with all its racial turmoil, social unrest and escalation of the Vietnam War.

After college, Mayo and I both joined the Army to become second lieutenants and paratroopers. He completed Airborne Training just before me and was sent to the famed 101st Airborne Division in Vietnam.

On this day in early January of '69, while home on leave, my mother told me Mayo Parks had been wounded and was also home, but he was on medical leave, recuperating. Mayo's mom said he had been asking to see me before I shipped out for Vietnam. Not having seen Mayo in the seven years since high school graduation, I raced over to Westover Road that same afternoon and waited until Mrs. Parks appeared at the door. She graciously escorted me to their back porch.

Mayo appeared before me now, hobbling on crutches. His thigh and calf on one side were half the size of the other. The once-athletic build I remembered was out of balance, atrophied through inactivity and operations. I stood to help him, but he would have none of it as he maneuvered himself into a chair.

As only Mayo could tell it, when he got to Vietnam, he became a platoon leader with the 101st. In a battle in the A Shau Valley in 1968, a North Vietnamese machine gunner noticed Lieutenant Parks trying to direct some of his men to maneuver to the side of the enemy to outflank them. The din and chaos of the battle prevented Mayo's men from hearing him, so he stood up to motion to them, presenting the gunner with an opportunity to hit an American officer. The machine gunner nailed Mayo with four rounds, knocking him off his feet and backward into a ditch full of water, where he almost drowned. His platoon, meanwhile, was taking so many casualties that the man of highest rank still unscathed was a buck-sergeant E-5. Medics were all busy and unavailable, so the sergeant called another unit working in the area and was able to borrow a medic from the other outfit to come to the aid of his dying platoon leader.

When the medic from the other unit arrived at the ditch, he was stunned! The dying officer he had been summoned for was none other than Mayo Parks! The medic's name was Tommy Wands, a young man we had both known who had grown up two doors from Mayo on Westover Road in Linden, NJ. Neither Tommy nor Mayo had heard from one another since high school, unaware that the other was even in Vietnam, much less in the same area. Amazed, Tommy found himself kneeling over the kid with whom we all played softball every summer!

Overcoming his astonishment, Tommy worked on Mayo, staying with him, personally escorting him onto the medivac. He insisted of the crew chief that the lieutenant be given four IVs to replace the blood loss while in route to the field hospital. Mayo's description of how Tommy saved his life that day rendered me speechless. But Mayo had a humorous way of recanting things, and he grinned and laughed while he told me what happened.

And it was as if I were still talking to my fellow Boy Scout about some funny camping trip incident instead of the near-death horror of him being shot that day. He continued his antics until we both wound up howling, like it was a story he was making up about somebody else. And we were kids again.

"Hey listen, Bob," he said with a grin. "I'm telling you, man, you know what they say about keeping your ass down in war? Well (giggle), it's true! I'm serious, man (chuckle), don't stand up, whatever you do (ha-ha). I'm not shittin' ya Bob, really, no joke, keep your ass down (chuckle)."

It stuck in my mind.

One of the four .30 caliber machine gun bullets which knocked Mayo down that day smashed into his knee cap. The worst of his wounds, he would walk with a limp for the rest of his life and resort to the use of a cane, enduring reconstructive operations and countless therapy sessions. He had been lucky.

On January 9, 1969, with eleven days remaining before reporting to Travis Air Force Base in route to the Republic of Vietnam, I wondered what changes this place had in store for all of us. Mayo had made it home, albeit wounded. My best friend, Eagle Scout Don Garrido, was already there with the Marines up near Da Nang. And I was on my way.

We were all fresh out of college. We were all eager to serve our country. We all proudly volunteered. I remember hoping Vietnam was not going to find a way to leave it's ugly, indelible mark on all of us.

I knew I was about to become a part of this era, an eye-witness participant. "I need to take pictures and record this year," I told myself, "this might be worth writing about some day." On January 9th I drove over to the Menlo Park Shopping Center looking for a diary to take with me to Vietnam. In the Hallmark Card Store next to Bamberger's, I was drawn to a little diary with an olive-green cover that simply read "DIARY 1969." It was just what I was looking for. It was perfect.

JANUARY 10, 1969
Diary Entry:
*Kathy and John getting ready for the wedding. Went to the rehearsal at the Reformed Church.*

I hadn't seen my relatives since my own wedding a year prior, after I had completed Officer Candidate School and volunteered to be a paratrooper. With brand-new gold bars on my shoulders and silver jump wings on my chest, I signed into the 82nd Airborne Division at Ft. Bragg, North Carolina in March of 1968.

Now, I was home on leave from Fort Bragg, with orders to report to Vietnam in just ten days. The sight of me at Kathy and John's wedding prompted lots of questions from my relatives.

"What's it like jumping out of airplanes?"

"When are you leaving for Vietnam?"

"Do you know what your assignment will be yet?"

The Super Bowl was only three days away and my leave time was waning quickly. I was trying to make the best of enjoying the holiday time with my family and friends before departing for Vietnam. I wasn't overly uneasy or afraid of going to Vietnam, but I did feel uncomfortable about my family being uneasy and worrying about me - awkward beyond words.

JANUARY 12, 1969
Diary Entry:
*Super Bowl III: NY Jets beat the Baltimore Colts, 16-7.*
I remember sitting on my dad's back porch, drinking beer

with him and watching Super Bowl III. My Uncle Jim, a lawyer and a B-17 bomber pilot in World War II, lived in Baltimore and was a huge Colts fan. Prior to the game, he had called my dad to entertain the possibility of a friendly little wager.

"Sure," Dad said.

"So how many points do you want me to give you, Bob?" Jim asked, knowing the Jets were eighteen-point underdogs.

"I don't need any," Dad said. "Namath guaranteed the Jets are gonna win it outright!"

After the game that evening, I remember my dad getting on the phone with Uncle Jim and rubbing in the victory! What a great afternoon! It took my mind off where I was heading.

JANUARY 19, 1969
Diary Entry:

*Packed up most of my things. Very bad day. Tomorrow I go to Vietnam and leave my family and all these pleasant times behind. Hard to imagine what will happen in the next year.*

The day before leaving was actually worse than leaving. I didn't know what to say to anyone, especially to my wife. There wasn't anything to talk about. Nothing would change what was to be. I just wanted to get on with it.

JANUARY 20, 1969
Diary Entry:

*10:00 a.m.: Flight to Travis AFB. Not a bad flight. My family said goodbye this morning. I love them all but now I have no choice but to go.*

I really don't remember anything about this morning except for a flashback at Newark Airport: I stepped out into the cold, deciding not to look back, and walked across the tarmac and up the stairway into the airplane. Once in my seat, I had second thoughts about not wanting to see them one more time. I might never see them again! I tried looking through the window at the airport, but couldn't see my wife or any of my family.

JANUARY 21, 1969
Diary Entry:
*TWA jet just reached Hawaii sometime during morning. Still morning. Landed at Wake, crossed the International Date Line - is now Wednesday morning. Touched down at Biên Hòa Airbase in Vietnam.*

JANUARY 23, 1969
Diary Entry:
*Arrived at 90th Replacement Battalion yesterday afternoon. Ran into James, McAlister, Peebles and two others from OCS class. Some guys pulled out for 101st and 173rd Airborne. These guys in the rear areas have it made. Some don't even know there is a war here.*

JANUARY 24, 1969
Diary Entry:
*My name still isn't on the list of assignments. James and Peebles left to fly helicopters in the Mekong Delta. That is what they wanted because it's flat. Good luck boys ...*

*I got my assignment - MACV, Military Assistance Command, Vietnam. They want me to go to Advisor School. I don't know what the advisors do.*

*Got on truck at 3:00 p.m. Sun is hot, very hot - no breeze. The Vietnamese don't seem to mind it. Arrived at the Advisor School one-half hour later. I'm still in a secure area. I hear explosions in the distance.*

Military Assistance Command, Vietnam (MACV), was a household word in Vietnam. MACV (pronounced Mack-Vee) exercised almost complete control over the entire theater of operations in Vietnam. The MACV patch, worn on the left shoulder, was red and yellow, the official colors of the government of South Vietnam.

The MACV patch was commonly associated with every "Chairborne Ranger" staff officer that ever pranced the air-conditioned corridors of the "Pentagon East," the MACV Headquarters in Saigon.

There was one exception, however: U.S. combat military advisors "in the field" in South Vietnam who wore the MACV patch on their shoulders were a different breed.

MACV combat advisors were the first to arrive in Vietnam and the last to leave before Saigon fell in 1975. As early as 1959, during Eisenhower's presidency, U.S. military advisors were being inconspicuously embedded with South Vietnamese troops in the field, in most cases at considerable risk to themselves.

The first groups of Americans to die in Vietnam during those early years were all U.S. combat advisors being the early forerunners of the later, more popularized, 12-man Special Forces Green Beret Teams. One needs only to visit the Vietnam Veterans' Memorial in Washington to read the names of those earliest of advisors to die in Vietnam. They're easily found, they're at the very beginning of the gradually ascending chronological list of over 58,000 names etched in granite on "The Wall" in that quiet park off of Constitution Avenue.

## JANUARY 25, 1969
Diary Entry:

*Processed into MACV Advisor School. A captain assigned me to work in IV Corps--Mekong Delta, as an infantry advisor to the South Vietnamese.*

*Damn - damn lousy assignment. Very low rice land with numerous rivers, canals, and VC. Ran into some guys coming back from hospitals in Japan. Field duty sounds pretty rough. They've been humping it all the time - no showers, eating C-rations all the time.*

Advisor School started Monday morning and would last twelve days, with eight hours of class a day and one hour of language lab at night. There were four basic subjects - weapons, tactics, leadership and Vietnamese language. Upon graduation, advisors were being assigned to five-man American Advisory Teams all over Vietnam, embedded with the South Vietnamese troops they were advising.

By the end of 1967 the war had claimed the lives of 20,057 men.

But in 1968 alone, an additional 16,899 Americans were killed. And in 1969, another 11,780 would die. The death figures for 1968 and 1969 therefore totaled 28,679. Escalating weekly reports of the numbers killed climbed to triple digits, making those two years the highest casualty period during the war and accounting for nearly half the entire number of Americans killed during the fifteen-year period of the Vietnam War.[1] The height of daily U.S. casualties in South Vietnam was occurring, ironically, as I was preparing to go into "the field" in an infantry combat "slot!"

I had no way of knowing these statistics at the time, but I was looking down the barrel of a cannon. To make matters worse, having to tell my family I was going to the Mekong Delta was not a good thing to be writing home about either.

Back home, most military families had already heard about the U-Minh Forest in the Delta. The U-Minh had been referred to militarily as "triple canopy," a term used to describe the fact that the lowest of vegetation, growing to a height of five or six feet, is covered by a second "canopy" of small trees. Both of these are shaded by a third canopy of growth provided by the largest of trees. From the air, it is impossible to see anything but a green carpet.

Because of the dense cover the U-Minh Forest provided, it was the home of the most persistent of Vietcông units and even some North Vietnamese Army (NVA) regular units. It provided sanctuary for Basic Training Camps for new Vietcông replacements, hospitals, rest areas for battle-weary NVA regulars and a safe place to bring captured Americans for interrogation.

During what was to become my entire year in the field in 1969, I can't remember one South Vietnamese incursion or U.S. invasion into the U-Minh Forest. It was considered off-limits; impenetrable. The locals told stories about the old days, when the French were in Vietnam, before they unraveled in the debacle at

Diện Biên Phư. The French sent a battalion of crack paratroopers into the U-Minh in the '50s to "clean it out" and dislodge the communists. The Foreign Legionnaires went into the U-Minh on a Friday and were never heard from again. Not one radio message, not one piece of equipment recovered, not one article of clothing found. Nothing. Such was the reputation of the U-Minh Forest, and we had heard about it all the way back to Ft. Bragg.

As safe a sanctuary as the U-Minh Forest was for communist guerilla insurgents, it was a conventional military tactician's worst nightmare. This was America's first guerilla war, and we were caught flat-footed. Conventional maneuvers were still very effective against the main-force NVA regulars in the north. Effective, that is, if a commander could catch them in the open and trap them into fighting conventionally.

But the elusive Vietcông in the Delta were an enemy that defied conventional tactics. Nowhere in General William Westmoreland's Vietnam was the terrain more suitable to the hit and run, hide and seek tactics of the clandestine Vietcông. And no place in Westmoreland's Vietnam was the terrain more obstinately resistant to the tactical maneuvers of the '60s military mind than the Mekong Delta and its U-Minh Forest.

There are relatively few roads in the Delta. Tanks, armored personnel carriers (M-113's) and all mechanized artillery pieces were useless. Water tributaries, commonly referred to as canals, connect major rivers and crisscross all land areas. In effect, they are "roads." These canals are virtually impossible to control after nightfall. During the dry season they were difficult, but not impossible to traverse by smaller sampan. But during the wet season, they swelled to become a maze of intricate "highways" between villages. "Highways" on which to transport ammunition. "Highways" that can't be bombed, mined, or patrolled. Uncontrollable, uncontested Vietcông highways.

The Ho Chi Minh trail, as we know today, consisted of not one trail, but thousands of "trails," including every road, river, canal and foot path from North Vietnam to Saigon. Many of them came down through the Mekong Delta.

No, the area I was going to in the Mekong Delta was not a coveted duty assignment for me, especially as an infantry advisor and particularly in January of 1969. But making the best of it was the order of the day, and a good place to start was with a positive letter to my folks back home.

JANUARY 26, 1969<br>Letter Home:

*Dear Folks,*

*Hope everything is okay back home! Advisor School starts tomorrow and I'm in a safe area for now. We're going to be learning Vietnamese. We're going to be assigned to infantry slots because they are short of infantry lieutenants in the field.*

*I'll be living with South Vietnamese units and accompanying them on all their daytime patrols and night ambushes. I don't know how I wound up with this job but it is considered the most essential U.S. effort in this stage of the war. I think it will be a long 12 months but I have developed a feeling to where I would like to help the Vietnamese help themselves. Food is pretty good here.*

*They're going to keep us busy learning Vietnamese, but I'll write again when I get a chance.*

*Love, Bob*

JANUARY 26, 1969<br>Diary Entry:

*Slept in. Last chance to enjoy myself. Many infantry, artillery, and armor combat branch officers attending the school. Don't like what I hear about the Mekong Delta. A lot of VC strongholds. One almost resigns oneself to being hit at least once while down there.*

*This work will be interesting though. The South Vietnamese very much want and need our help. My assignment will be in Kiến Giáng Province. The U.S. 9th Infantry Division is operating between there and Saigon.*

On this date I found out my assignment: Kiến Giáng

Province. Drawing Kiến Giáng with its U-Minh Forest was like drawing the "old maid." But I wouldn't have been happy being confined to a desk job or a supply tent for my tour of duty. I hadn't come to Vietnam for that. I wanted to see the real war, I wanted to know what it was really like. I was tired of seeing the United States "pussyfooting" around in Vietnam. In my mind, the only thing worse than going to Vietnam was going to Vietnam and not taking part in getting it over with. "What an adventure this is going to be!" I thought.

Was I in over my head? Did I bite off more than I could chew? I don't know. Gotta get some sleep and go to class in the morning.

JANUARY 27, 1969
Diary Entry:

*0630 a.m.: Up and shaved.*

*0730 a.m.: Started classes on Vietnamese language. Also had classes on RF and PF forces. Regional Forces operate in company sweeps looking for Vietcông. Popular Forces work at platoon level.*

*Vocabulary is hard to pick up. We get 40 words a day to learn - attend class till 7:30 sometimes 8:30 pm- not too much time for personal study to learn the words.*

I knew little of South Vietnam's Regional Forces (RFs) and Popular Forces (PFs). Regional Force and Popular Force units were ground troops assigned to a specific village area or "district" within the province from which they had been recruited. In effect, they were district militia, locally recruited "guard." The RFs and PFs were responsible for hunting down local Vietcông and protecting the villages (and the hamlets within the villages) within their districts. They were often under-trained and under-equipped to fight their usually better-equipped counterparts.

JANUARY 28, 1969
Diary Entry:
*0730: Attended classes on the mission of MAT - (Mobile*

*Advisory Team) to RF/PF forces in Vietnam. We will be expected to go along on operations and night ambushes with the South Vietnamese. We will be assigned to 5-man teams and sometimes might not see big American units unless they are passing through.*

*Had 2-hour class on the M-1 carbine. This is an old U.S. rifle which is outdated in our Army but currently used by South Vietnamese forces against NVA and V.C. Most of them don't have the M16 rifle yet.*

By Tuesday morning I had a pretty clear picture of what my job was going to be in Vietnam. Mobile Advisory Teams (MATs) consisted of five men, each being responsible for a specific area of expertise, a compact version of the twelve-man Green Beret teams. The composition of a MAT team was as follows: one team leader, an assistant team leader (both junior officers), a heavy weapons NCO (non-commissioned officer), a light weapons NCO and a medic. Each team was assigned one South Vietnamese interpreter.

The MAT team stayed in the field 100% of the time, at no time being allowed to rotate back to a "rear" area. One team member could be absent from the team, but only with permission from headquarters. Team strength was allowed to drop to a total of four men therefore, provided there remained at least one medic and one officer in charge.

I began to get the impression that this job was going to be complicated and difficult. It didn't take me long to imagine the enormity of the role: advise troops already in combat. Show them how to be better. Help them win, and do it with no practical experience of my own!

I felt that the Army had prepared me well, however. Or maybe I had prepared myself well. My Eagle Scout, leadership-building days in the Boy Scouts and countless hours spent outdoors and on rifle ranges gave me some self-assurance. I chose to think positively, to look forward to being an advisor, confident that I would do my best. And this time at Advisor School was going to be my last opportunity to get ready.

Freedom was in the air at the Advisor School in South

Vietnam in early 1969. Back home, on college campuses, one would never know it. But the chimes of freedom were flashing all around us as we readied ourselves to go out into the field and help the South Vietnamese people defend themselves against a communistic way of life.

CHAPTER TWO

# 'Rice Roots'

JANUARY 29, 1969
Diary Entry:
*Up at 6:15 - starting to get into the swing of things. It doesn't take anyone too long to get into a pattern. Had breakfast with Chuck Emery, Don Loveless and Dave Jones - all 1st Lieutenants. All of us are going to IV Corps. Chuck is going to An Xuyên - from what we hear there are many VC there too.*

Chuck Emery and I became instant friends five days prior as we picked out our bunk locations upon arrival at Advisor School. The 9th Infantry Division combat patch on his right shoulder and the Combat Infantryman's Badge on the front of his fatigues caught my attention.

At first, I had settled on a bunk near a screened window, about midway down the long plywood box we'd be calling home for the next three weeks. But I noticed he chose a bunk near the door.

"Closer to the bunker," he said, looking in my direction.

"Okay," I thought, "the rocket attacks." I immediately moved my gear to the bunk next to his by the door. I found myself impressed by this individual, by his common sense, enthusiasm and sense of humor. Chuck was an unmarried 1st lieutenant, a product of infantry OCS at Ft. Benning. He wore glasses, stood over six feet tall and was from Long Island, New York. He had arrived in Vietnam in late September 1968 and was sent to the 9th Infantry, but when the opportunity to become a combat advisor and work with South Vietnamese troops presented itself, he jumped at the chance. He was truly eager to make a difference at their level.

I was still wearing my gold 2nd lieutenant bars, and although Chuck was slightly younger than me, he was infinitely "older" in Vietnam experience. Three months is an eternity in the field. He was street-wise beyond his years, and because he technically still outranked me, I think our relationship went a little like: "I'll take you under my wing." We spent the next fourteen days studying, eating, drinking beer together and preparing ourselves to become advisors.

JANUARY 30, 1969<br>Diary Entry:

*Had classes on medical subjects, supporting fire, weapons, RF/PF offensive operations and of course, language. Get two hours a day and an hour of lab at night. Food is good.*

*This is like R&R for some guys who have been humping it with the infantry. Gives them a chance to relax and clear up jungle rot.*

The mix of men at Advisor School was fascinating. Except for Chuck Emery, who already had a little time in Vietnam, Lieutenants Loveless, Jones, Gozia, Youngblood and myself were all new "in-country." Fresh meat from "The Real World." The FNGs, the Fuckin' New Guys. The six of us were the "Delta Guys," all of us headed to IV Corps.

Most of the others in our classes already had combat time in Vietnam. Many of them, including Chuck, had already been awarded the Combat Infantrymen's Badge (CIB), given only to those who had been assigned to an infantry unit for a minimum of thirty days and had engaged in at least one firefight. Most had seen more combat than that. The CIB was fitting: a silver rifle on a blue background, encased by a silver wreath.

The combat veterans' fatigue shirts also carried the unit designation patches of the outfits they had served in, giving each one a "combat personality." They stood in formation next to us in the morning. They ate lunch in the mess hall at the next table. All of them had personalities inseparable from their recent assignments. They had been selected to be advisors because they had been exemplary soldiers. They laughed about their extreme physical discomforts, about close calls and "body counts" imposed on them by former commanders. They spoke amongst themselves about buddies killed, dumb military decisions, freak accidents and "contact" with the enemy. They shared a common air about them, all individuals, yet somehow, all the same person because of what they had experienced. They were already "Vietnam Veterans" in my eyes even though they hadn't gone back to the States yet.

I didn't fit in with them - I had no CIB. I wore brand new, almost shiny, unlaundered jungle fatigues with no combat patch on my right shoulder. Most of us had no stories; we weren't even sun-tanned. We hung out with the other new lieutenants, not wanting to be, yet sensing that we were, outsiders. We asked questions of one another: "What state are you from?" The veterans asked questions of no one. They didn't want to know where anyone was from. It didn't matter.

We talked about college, about baseball, about growing up. They had no interest in that. They very often spoke in three-word sentences. When we were near them, we kept our mouths shut, trying to pick up something, anything. What was it like? If they thought you were eavesdropping, they would stop talking and stare directly across the table at you until you had to turn your eyes away. We were virgins.

One day, at the end of a class on RF/PF operations, the instructor finished up by asking if there were any questions. One of the seasoned combat veterans raised his hand and said, "Yeah, I got a question: How do I get a job as an instructor here?" The entire class laughed.

Maybe someday I could fit in with them. Maybe I'd wind up having my own "combat personality" and be able to communicate the way they did... make friends of other vets without asking a lot of questions the way they did... trust one another, instantly, the way they did... bond with other combat vets the way they did. Maybe, some day, I could be like them.

JANUARY 31, 1969
Diary Entry:

*6:30: Up and attend Vietnamese class. Trung Úy De is the instructor. He's an excellent Vietnamese officer and a very funny guy.*

*In the afternoon attended classes on the M1 carbine (an old outdated WWII weapon), also M16 and M79. Went to lab and then to the officer's club. "O" club is usually crowded with rear area troops who get drunk every night.*

The Vietnamese instructors at the Advisor School had been educated in Saigon and spoke excellent English. The very much "Americanized" Trung Úy De (1st Lieutenant De) became our favorite instructor because of his liberal use of American slang and profanity. Obviously, he had been exposed to more than just an English language dictionary. Chuck and I howled as De put on his little one-man skits.

At the end of each skit came his words of wisdom: "You tell counterpart he full of shit if he want you to ride back from operation in sampan. Everyone want to ride in sampan, easy way. Bullshit on sampan ride, *beau-coup* dangerous! You tell him he no get helicopter to go see girlfriend." Then he pointed at one of the NCOs in the front row: "And what about you, *Trung Sí*, you go see girlfriend lately?"

By day, Chuck and I learned Vietnamese customs, religions and mores. In the evening, we sat in air-conditioned trailers set up as mobile study halls. Rows of desks lined both walls, divided by partitions, and each advisor sat during "language lab" wearing earphones while listening to the constant drone of Vietnamese conversation. Because many of the noncoms had served previously with American infantry units, a certain re-education was also taking place for them. Our role was not only to help in a military capacity, but to help win the "hearts and minds" of the Vietnamese civilians in the villages.

Chuck Emery and I talked about this often. We were becoming convinced that Vietnam could be free of communism if the United States paid more attention to winning the hearts and minds.

"We can win this war," Chuck said, "but we won't win it by bombing the shit out of them. I think we're on to something here with this advisor stuff. This war has to be won at the village level, as advisors, by working directly with the people and troops in the villages."

"I think you're right, Chuck," I said, "it has to be at the grass roots level."

"Rice roots," he smiled, "at the rice roots level."

"Yeah Chuck, I guess we're both gonna see this war at the 'Rice Roots.'"

By now, I was really getting into Vietnamese vocabulary, proper pronunciation and word usage. Chuck was better at weapons training, so we helped each other. What I lacked in weapons knowledge, I made up for in language, and vice-versa. After language lab, with a thirst that wouldn't quit, Chuck and I set out for the "Officer's Club," a room no larger than 15 x 20, with a 13" Magnavox TV above the bar. We knew this was to be the last of our training and that we'd soon miss even the simple comforts of this room: the ice in our drinks, the screens on the windows, and the security of a large military base. We'd soon be headed for "the field."

### FEBRUARY 1, 1969
### Diary Entry:

*Today I'm supposed to make 1st Lieutenant but the Army is about 2 weeks behind time. Had language class with Trung Úy De again and studied air support. Also had class on light machine gun. More language lab at night.*

Weapons training consisted of becoming familiar with all of the weapons that the Regional and Popular Force troops were using in the field. We had already been told that our fully automatic M16 rifle, so common in American rifle companies,

# 'Rice Roots'

was a scarce commodity in RF companies and PF platoons. Only the best Vietnamese RFs had them and most others couldn't be "trusted" with them.

We were going to be training the Vietnamese on older weapons which were state-of-the-art in their day in WWII, but by 1969 were not even in the lineup. We were told not to expect much of anything when it came to working with the Vietnamese.

It seemed odd to Chuck and me that by this stage of the war, with all the emphasis on helping them fight this war on their own, they were being issued relatively ineffective weapons. If the United States could commit *us* to the effort, why wasn't more modern weaponry being distributed to the South Vietnamese?

We never once imagined the level of mistrust and lack of confidence afforded the RFs and PFs by American higher command, which was their real reason for the lack of issuance of better weapons. Only after putting ourselves on the line in the field would we discover what a great tactical blunder this was; a real obstacle to achieving our goals and winning.

### FEBRUARY 3, 1969
### Diary Entry:

*More classes on language and RF/PF personnel. They have a bad problem with morale in some of their units. Some are not paid on time or in the right amounts. It is understandable why they are not efficient.*

*Went to the weapons department with Chuck after lab and disassembled and assembled various weapons - .30 caliber machine gun, M1 carbine, BAR, M79 grenade launcher.*

Lieutenant Emery and I both felt positive about our assignments and had a feeling of pride. We felt that we would be doing our part in what we were certain would be the ultimate history of the war - enabling the South Vietnamese troops to become self-sufficient and take over entirely as U.S. forces pulled out.

I felt very uneasy on February 3rd because I didn't know all the weapons well enough to assemble and disassemble them in the allotted time. Tomorrow would be a weapons test for us, and at dinner I was continually asking Chuck questions about this machine gun, that bolt mechanism, etc. I was probably driving him nuts.

All I could think about was if a weapon jammed and I couldn't fire it, I'd be in trouble. I wanted to know all the weapons thoroughly, to be able to pop the cover off, know why it's jammed, fix it, reload it, and have it work again. Saying I was trained on it wouldn't be good enough. There wouldn't be any excuses after this. I had to know these weapons, period.

And then there were the stories. Stories in advisor class about Vietnamese outposts being attacked in the middle of the night and being overrun. "Overrun" was a nice way of saying annihilated. There had been incidents of American advisors in remote jungle outposts with little or no access to artillery, tanks, gunships and bombers, finding the units they were advising incapable of fighting off larger VC or NVA units. We were to have an "evacuation plan," a pre-arranged escape and evasion route in this event, to flee with the South Vietnamese out of the outpost for the safety of the closest American unit.

Chuck sensed my anxiety, because I wouldn't stop asking him questions at dinner. Finally, he said, "For God's sake, Bob, alright already! We're going over to the weapons shed after supper and I'm gonna give you a hand."

So it was, on that night of February 3, 1969, he worked with me side by side in the weapons shed. By the light of an overhead light bulb dangling by its cord, two hot and sweaty figures swatted flying insects while handling the oily, dusty weapons of war. Over and over again, he watched as I disassembled and reassembled all of the weapons I was unsure of.

There are people who come into your life that affect you for the rest of your life. When my head hit the pillow that night I slept well, reassured and thankful that Chuck had helped me. I don't think I told him how much his help meant to me. I probably just said "Thanks," but I will always remember how unselfishly 1st Lieutenant Charles H. Emery Jr. helped me that night when I needed it the most. I knew I was prepared and ready on the weapons, as evidenced in my next diary entry.

### FEBRUARY 4, 1969
### Diary Entry:

*Had weapons test. Very easy. Had to take apart and assemble all the weapons authorized to the Vietnamese.*

*Went out to firing range at 09:30 and fired the BAR and .30 cal and M79 - plus the M1 carbine. Good weapons, but some are outdated.*

*More language lab that night.*

### FEBRUARY 5, 1969
### Diary Entry:

*0730: Class on RF/PF logistical support.*

*0930: Went out to firing range near Dĩ An and fired off some demolitions - made homemade defense explosives to ward off attacks.*

*1330: Had class on intelligence-including Vietcông infrastructure. More language and lab from 7:30 to 8:30 p.m.*

If an advisor was lucky enough, he might be assigned a rifle company attached to a large, well-fortified provincial or district compound. But most of us were going to smaller compounds called "outposts." We would be living in these outposts with one RF company (60 men) or a PF platoon (20 men). The outposts were no larger than fifty meters across at the widest point, and were quite literally mud forts. The forts were hand-dug from a rice paddy at strategic locations in contested Vietcông areas. The location of these forts could disrupt the VC and inhibit their movement, possibly at the intersection of several canals.

The mud from the rice paddy was shoveled up out of a straight trench and piled alongside the trench, forming a straight mud wall parallel to the trench called a "berm." The trench would then be intentionally flooded with the water from the rice paddy, forming a moat. The moat was perhaps ten feet deep and again as wide, forming another barrier. The berm was patted and smoothed with Vietnamese shovels and back-breaking labor until it was shaped straight and level, notched at intervals for firing positions.

Almost all outposts were shaped in the configuration of a triangle, with one entrance or "front gate" located along one of the sides. The front gate was the only section of berm with a pass-through opening. Because the front gate provided easy run-through access, the front gate was the most vulnerable area. A well-aimed B-40 rocket could knock out the machine gun bunker located there, and, if two of the three machine guns located at the corners of the triangle could be silenced, the front gate could be effectively assaulted and breached.

My February 5th diary entry records attending a class at 9:30 a.m. at the firing range in which we were being taught how to make "homemade defense explosives to ward off attacks." The instructors explained that helping the South Vietnamese make homemade booby traps out of hand grenades would show them how to use their ingenuity to defend themselves. Obtaining barbed wire "might be a problem" from time to time because of poor South Vietnamese supply channels due to low-priority. We'd all need to be resourceful as advisors, not being able to count on our U.S. supply chain to fill our needs.

That was all well and good, but Chuck and I were realizing that we were going to be put in the middle of the weaning process: no barbed wire, no M16s, little air support, little artillery support, no armored vehicles, living in mud forts with berms and moats, and now using "homemade defense explosives," booby traps to ward off attacks through "front gates."

I started to feel like we were going back in time, back to a time when warfare was more primitive. Back in time to when ancient hordes of Mongolian warriors swept down upon Vietnam. Thousands of years ago, didn't the Vietnamese defend themselves in the same manner - Mongolian tribesmen attacking their mud forts across moats and berms and "front gates" and being repulsed by their homemade weapons? And we were going to advise them on how to do this stuff? Weren't they already masters at this?

Why not just take away the lousy M1 rifles as well and issue everyone bows and arrows? Better yet, let's make our own! It was going to be an adventure alright!

FEBRUARY 7, 1969
Diary Entry:

*0730 Hrs.: Class on Revolutionary Development Cadre - this is a team that helps with civilian medical facilities and sanitation in the villages. They help the people. We are told to keep a look out for these teams and work with them.*

*Had a class on VC organization and tactics. They have all the equipment we do - some even carry captured M16s. They shouldn't be underestimated.*

FEBRUARY 7, 1969
Letter Home:

*Hi Folks,*

*I made 1st Lieutenant yesterday. They had a ceremony formation outside and the colonel from the school pinned my silver bar on. I'm really enjoying this easy life in the rear area. Will write again when I get to my MAT team.*

*Love, Bob*

Revolutionary Development Cadre ("RD Cadre") were armed civilian teams of Vietnamese under the operational control of Civil Operations and Revolutionary Development Support (CORDS). The black pajama-clad RD Cadre were trained as pacification workers at Vung Tau and sent into contested areas to work closely with the village chief, the People's Self Defense Force (PSDF), the local RF and PF forces and American advisors, should they be working in that village.

RD Cadre teams were an excellent concept. RD Cadre moved in after a Regional Force Company felt they had sufficiently eliminated the majority of the Vietcông in the area, or had caused them to "*Chieu Hói*" (surrender). The RD Cadre would then be directed by the newly elected village chief to perform whatever civilian projects needed to be done to reconstruct the village or improve village life. If a home had been damaged, they would help repair it. If the Vietcông had burned down a schoolhouse, the RD Cadre would obtain some wooden poles and cut some nipa palm leaves for thatching to restore it. Town meeting halls could be rebuilt, village offices constructed and foot bridges erected to provide access to the trade area in the center of the village. This rejuvenated the commercial flow of goods and services into a village center once again. These teams had the capability of breathing life back into a village: capitalism at its most embryonic stage.

But the Vietcông despised the RD Cadre, who disrupted their dominating communist control of the village. Also, because some of the RD Cadre had been former Vietcông, the VC saw them as traitors and defectors who were now being paid by the U.S. to help promote capitalism and democracy. The RD Cadre were often attacked and killed by the Vietcông, and it was going to be our job to protect them and enable them to perform their mission.

FEBRUARY 8, 1969
Diary Entry:

*Up at 6:30. Went to a skit on RF/PF support operations. Very good. Immediately afterward most of the guys pulled out for their areas of assignment to the different MAT teams. The IV Corps Mekong Delta men stayed behind: Chuck, Don, Dave and myself, as well as a few others like Gozia and Youngblood. Tomorrow we will fly to Cần Thơ, so tonight we get crocked. Everybody has a good time. Got to bed at 10:45. All my gear is mostly assembled.*

Saturday was "graduation day" at the Advisor School as Chuck and I were summoned in to fill out the sobering NOK (Next of Kin) notification forms in case anything happened to us while in the field.

This was followed by the last of Trung Úy De's skits demonstrating the ideal American-Vietnamese relationship: The advisor wanting to help and see results, his counterpart accepting the help and agreeing to bring results, each exhibiting enormous amounts of patience. We all laughed at the simplistic scenario.

"Yeah, right," Chuck said.

After lunch, at our final formation at 1 p.m., everyone was told to "listen up" as instructions were given as to which trucks were going where and what times they would be "saddling up." By 2 p.m. the place was in transition again. The bunks where everyone had slept were now stripped clean. New guys were walking in, duffle bags over their shoulders and sheets under their arms, commenting, "I'm grabbing me a bottom bunk," and, "I'm goin' over here next to the screen, more breeze," followed by, "Yeah, good idea, man this fucking place is hot."

The stench of diesel fuel permeated the now dust-filled air as the large, olive drab, 2 1/2-ton trucks (deuce-and-a-halfs) pulled in with the new guys and pulled out with our old classmates, now advisors. They were going to places other than the Mekong Delta, places with strange-sounding names like Hué, Dalat, Pleiku and Kontum.

Addressing the back end of one of the departing deuce-and-a-half's, one of our Delta guys blurted out, "Hey, you guys going up to Two Corps, we heard there's lot'sa Charlie up there (Vietcông - VC – 'Victor Charlie')."

Someone yelled back, "Hey, screw you Four Corps, at least we ain't goin' to the Delta. You guys are gonna have wet asses your whole tour. You best keep those wet asses down!"

"Yeah, you too!" was our reply. One of them, waving his hand, yelled back, "Take care of yourself, man. See you around."

Of course, we knew we'd never see any of those guys again. But on February 8, 1969, I thought enough of them to record their departure in my diary. We were not to know what their assignments would be or what fate they would encounter while performing the difficult task of advising and helping the South Vietnamese units they'd be reporting to. And even though they knew there was a war going on, they had no way of knowing that in early 1969, the Vietnam War was a raging inferno. None of us did.

Chuck and I packed up our duffle bags, padlocked the ends shut, and left them on our bunks to mark our spots. One more visit to the O-Club, the only bar on campus, was in order, and the remaining six of us "Delta Guys" intended to avail ourselves of a final salute.

Checking in at Tan Son Knut for our flight to Can Tho.

### FEBRUARY 9, 1969
Diary Entry:

*0930: Chuck and I left the security of the Dĩ An/ Biên Hòa/ Long Binh complex and were driven by truck to Tan Son Nhut Airbase. The ride took about 45 minutes. Checked in at airport and took off for Cần Thơ at about 1400. Sat next to Chuck and took pictures of the Mekong River as we moved further into Charlie country. Saw dotted outposts and bomb craters from air. Many small villages. Arrived at Cần Thơ, IV Corps nerve center. Checked into the Bassac Hotel downtown. Guards at the gate and wire all around.*

The Bassac Hotel in downtown Cần Thơ was our first real taste of the flavor of Vietnam. Unlike the Quonset huts we had slept in at the military installation at Dĩ An, the Bassac was a converted civilian hotel in the heart of the city. The hotel obviously borrowed its name from the Bassac River, the major offshoot of the Mekong River.

In its heyday, the Bassac must have really been a showplace. But as I focused on the facade more closely, it looked like bullets had etched pock-marks into the masonry. Yes, the front wall of the old Bassac told the tale of a city and country under siege one more time. Actually, this gave the hotel the necessary ambiance we were looking for on our first night away from the confines of a military base. Our adventure was coming alive!

"This place is pretty cool," Chuck said, as the driver came to a stop in front of the Bassac. A four-foot wall made of green sandbags encircled the entrance, out to a radius of thirty feet from the front doorway. Barbed wire climbed toward the sky, supported by poles embedded amongst the sandbags. In the center of this barricade was the "front gate" to the hotel, a two-man, sandbagged bunker position covered by a thatched roof of nipa palm. The scene was a quick reminder that the Vietcông took a particular interest in BOQs (Bachelor Officer Quarters), and that the Tet holiday was fast approaching. Sitting on the sandbags were two ARVN guards, one with a rifle lying next to him. The other, with a banana in his hand, gave us a salute without standing up or even trying to figure out what to do with the banana. He was the higher-ranking of the two and wore a QC armband on his fatigues, the equivalent of the U.S. Army MP (Military Police) armband.

"They look sharp, huh?" I murmured sarcastically to Chuck. We grabbed our duffle bags out of the jeep, threw them onto our shoulders, and walked past the gate into the hotel. Both ARVNs interrupted their chattering to acknowledge us again with a nod and a smile. We practiced our Vietnamese with a "*Cháo ông*" (Hello), and they replied, "*Cháo, Trung Úy.*" Once inside, we wandered around the hallways for a while, unable to find anyone in charge who could tell us where our sleeping quarters were. We finally returned to the bunker out front for some guidance, still humping our duffle bags over our shoulders in the intense, over-the-top heat.

After unsuccessfully trying to communicate in our newly-learned Vietnamese (this actually became quite funny), we resorted to the use of pantomime and hand signals, and the smiling QC pointed up to the roof of the hotel. There we might be able to find out where our room was.

"*Cám ón ông,*" (Thank you) I said, as we humped our duffle bags back through the entranceway and up the stifling stairwell to the top floor in the sweltering, sticky heat of late afternoon.

The top floor of The Bassac Hotel was a bar. We dropped our belongings on the floor next to our barstools and ordered beers while observing cliques of American civilians arriving for Happy Hour. We imagined them to be news reporters, office workers, civilians in charge of construction projects, whatever. In Vietnam, civilians always seemed to out-rank military people, regardless of rank.

The people in this bar that night had obviously seen hundreds of 1st lieutenants come and go, and several of our attempts at making small talk were largely ignored. A heavyset guy on the other side of Chuck was wearing a flowered Hawaiian shirt, and he spun his bar stool around to put his back to us, not interested in having small talk with any newly-arrived junior officers.

Chuck excused himself to find out from them who was in charge, so we could get a couple of bunks to sleep in. But Chuck's insolence at having interrupted their partying was more than the portly, flower-shirted one could bear.

"There is no one 'in charge,' *lieutenant,*" he snarled. "You'll have to wait for Sergeant Barrows, who'll probably be along shortly... at which time he'll undoubtedly assign you a room," he snapped. Rolling his eyes, he turned his back to us once again, and continued his ever-important conversation with the others.

Even before Chuck and I had left the states for our assignments in Vietnam, we had both heard of the term REMF. It was yet another acronym. In 1960s Vietnam, no one spoke English if they could use an acronym. In a world gone acronymically berserk, someone in the Army created this one, a mockery of all the others. REMF stood for Rear Echelon Mother Fucker, a denigration of the very people in the rear areas who have nothing better to do all day than create these acronyms in the first place.

Taking another swig of my Hamm's beer, I said to Chuck, "Is it my imagination, or do these people have a case of the ass? They don't even know there's a freaking war going on. They've really got it made."

Chuck turned his face toward my shoulder, away from the Hawaiian-shirted fat guy at the bar, and leaned closer to me. When I looked into his eyes past the late-day glare in his glasses, he had a big grin on his face.

"Yeah," he said, "but would you really want to be stationed here? Think about it. How'd you like to spend the rest of your tour in this rear area dealing with these REMF assholes every night?" Both of us began howling and pounding the bar to the obvious disapproval of the REMFs, who now suspected they were the object of our laughter.

### FEBRUARY 10, 1969
### Diary Entry:

*Up at 06:00. Went into Eakin Compound and received briefings on almost every phase of military and civilian programs.*

*After our briefings, I returned to the Bassac Hotel with Chuck Emery. Had dinner in a Vietnamese restaurant. The food wasn't too bad.*

Chuck and I awoke early. We had a "briefing" at 0800 out at Eakin Compound, the Advisory Headquarters for the entire Mekong Delta, and we didn't want to be late. If we hustled, we could make the chow line at the mess hall. We both knew we only had a few more hot meals left before departing for the "field." We hitched a ride on a passing jeep.

The only respite one gets from the heat in Southeast Asia is in the early morning, before the sun gets another crack at burning off the damp, cool morning dew. This process doesn't take more than half an hour, and we enjoyed the cool, breezy ride in the open jeep, knowing that soon there would be no relief from the heat. I had never experienced anything quite like that first early morning ride in the streets of that overcrowded Vietnamese city.

Downtown Can Tho – February, 1969.

Our eyes took in the aura of Cần Thơ awakening to a new day: the laundry hanging from the windows, the fish, eels, ducks and vegetables being put on display in the open-air store fronts. The early morning chores were being done, and with the many motor scooters buzzing around, the gray smoky exhausts mixed with all the other foul smells of the city.

We climbed out of the jeep and found ourselves standing in front of a six-foot high plywood sign with bold letters on it announcing "EAKIN COMPOUND." The early morning chill had a chance of disappearing until we read the inscription dedicating Eakin Compound: "TO THE MEMORY OF CAPTAIN HOWARD M. EAKIN JR., U.S. ARMY, KILLED IN ACTION IN AN XUYÊN PROVINCE, REPUBLIC OF VIETNAM, 5 JUNE 1963."

"I wonder if he was an advisor?" I said, my eyes scanning the "killed in action" part again as the morning chill still inexplicably traversed my spine with the arriving heat.

"Probably," Chuck replied. "I would guess by the date, he had to be."

Many years later, I discovered what happened to Captain Eakin. Ray Bows writes, "Captain Eakin voluntarily accompanied Vietnamese Army units on their combat operations. On 5 June 1963, Captain Eakin volunteered to guide the pilot of a CH-21 helicopter evacuating an American soldier from a combat operation near Rạch Giá (ironically, where I was headed). The helicopter was fired upon and Captain Eakin was struck and killed by enemy ground fire."[2]

Captain Eakin was one of the first advisors to die in the Delta.

I stood there, concentrating on the "An Xuyên Province" part of the dedication plaque. That was where Chuck was headed.

"Hey, *Trung Úy* (1st Lieutenant)!" It was Chuck's voice, snapping me out of my trance. "It's oh-seven-twenty, let's go! We don't want to miss those pancakes and eggs. Jeez, it's getting hot already!"

"Pancakes and eggs?" I laughed, as we hurried past the make-shift buildings in search of the mess hall, "You're going to have shit on a shingle and love it." Just then, I caught sight of a major rounding the corner of a building, but Chuck hadn't seen him yet.

"Bull*SHIT!*" Chuck yelled out, emphasizing the latter part, just as the major got within earshot. I could see a scowl forming on the officer's face as we both rendered a smart salute.

"Good morning, sir!" I blurted out, to cover Chuck's profanity.

"Mrng," he barely mumbled, thinking this is just what MACV needs, a few more young, green, stupid lieutenants.

The briefings that day gave us a good overall picture of the challenges to advisors in the Delta. There were heavy communist strongholds in the U-Minh forest that overlapped Kiến

Giáng and An Xuyên, our provinces. The only U.S. Army unit, U.S. 9th infantry Division, was much further east at Đồng Tâm, along with Navy PBRs (river patrol boats) at that location. They were much too far away to be of help. "We'll be pretty much on our own out there," I thought to myself.

Chuck and I headed for the REMF bar that evening for one more good time.

### FEBRUARY 11, 1969
Diary Entry:

*Up at 0600. Caught a ride out to Eakin Compound outside of Cần Thơ. Processed through finance. Went out to the flight line, said goodbye to Chuck, and caught a flight to Kiến Giáng Province at 1300 - landed at Rạch Giá on west coast. Processed in and went to the BOQ which happens to be in a Chinese funeral parlor. The inside of this place is unbelievable. Everything is hand carved. Heard gunshots on the outside of town. Not very close though.*

Chuck Emery and I parted company the way everyone did in Vietnam, with an unceremonious, "Take care man, good luck." No one knew if or when their paths might cross again. Very few guys exchanged home addresses or phone numbers, it just wasn't practical. You didn't even know where you'd be living after the war. Young soldiers focused on going into combat, not who they would see after the war. I shook my head as I looked at Chuck on the runway and Chuck reached for my handshake. "Good luck Bob," he said.

"You too Chuck, take care of yourself."

I felt very alone on the flight to Rạch Giá. I realized I missed him badly. During the coming year I was not to establish a friendship with anyone as close as the one I had with Chuck. I learned a lot from him and he taught me enough to help me avoid stupid situations. He, too, believed in what we were doing, that we could make a difference, that we could help the Vietnamese win. I carried that attitude, his attitude, with me throughout my tour.

I'd have to start over making new friends again. Or maybe not. If I was going to be a MAT leader, I'd have to lead the team, not be friends with them.

"Well," I thought, "I can make friends with other team leaders." After a while my thoughts turned to where I was going and what I might be doing. No one can read the future, though. How could I have known, by coincidence, that I would see Chuck again before the whole crazy year would unfold?

The plane touched down at Rạch Giá. An olive-drab M151 jeep with a white star on the hood was waiting for me. I threw my duffle bag into the back and the driver sped off through four gears to the Rạch Giá BOQ, a former Chinese funeral parlor converted for use as billets.

Kiến Giáng Advisory Team 55 had arranged to rent the funeral parlor-turned BOQ from the Chinese owners. It was on a side street in Rạch Giá, and I remember a stone wall with a high, wrought-iron fence on it which ran along the front, immediately next to the street. Nasty-looking concertina barbed wire topped off the fence. A decorative iron gate swung open and an ARVN soldier motioned us inside the small compound.

The driver told me the place was a little unusual, but I really could not believe what I saw inside. Every interior square foot of wall space had been ornately carved by hand to form images of dragons and other Chinese works of art! There were large, round columns made of hardwood, reaching from floor to ceiling. Each had been painstakingly chiseled and gouged with hand tools by skilled craftsmen, then hand painted in bright colors with small artists' brushes.

The funeral parlor now housed American "permanent party" as well as transient officers like myself, heading to and from their MAT teams in the field. I was told to put my gear in a cubicle to the left of the front doorway. My cubicle contained two mosquito-netted bunks, large enough for two men and their duffle bags. Even the wooden cubicle dividers were covered with hand-carved, hand-painted Chinese figures. The entire ceiling had ornamentation on it, the doorway was framed in ornamentation. That Chinese funeral parlor was just unbelievable!

I put my gear into my cubicle which had once displayed decaying remains of countless deceased Chinese national citizens. When I laid my head back in my bunk that night and looked up at the ornamented ceiling in the dim light, I thought about how many people had been laid out in that same spot. Then I heard automatic weapons fire in the distance, somewhere on the outskirts of Rạch Giá, and I considered myself fortunate to be sleeping where I was.

I remembered that I hadn't written this stuff down in my diary yet. I was reminded of the year ahead, possibly the most unbelievable year of my life.

"This is really getting to be some kind of adventure," I thought. "I've got to make sure I record everything so I don't forget." I got back out of bed and dug out my diary in the dim light.

FEBRUARY 12, 1969
Diary Entry:

*Up at 0600. Went into Province Headquarters for breakfast at the mess hall. Went back to BOQ at the Chinese funeral parlor - took a nap and waited to get a call. Went into Headquarters again and met LTC Stanberry and Major Dowd. Also, a civilian Advisor, Mr. Somebody or other. They assigned me to MAT 88 (Mobile Advisory Team 88), and informed me we don't have a jeep or a sampan. At present they are living in a grass hut.*

At breakfast I met another new replacement, Lt. Gordon. He had also just arrived, and together we reported to the Province Senior Advisor's office. The colonel occupied the top floor of an open-air, two story building in a section of town cordoned off as the Rạch Giá Team 55 advisory compound. The building had large windows encased by wooden shutters which could be closed during the monsoon season. On this bright, scorching afternoon, they were all open, allowing a scant breeze to flow through the building.

Lieutenant Colonel Bill M. Stanberry was a tall, energetic man who welcomed us to Kiến Giáng Province with a smart return salute and a firm handshake. I immediately noticed his fatigue shirt. It displayed his airborne jump wings and CIB as well as a Special Forces combat patch on his right shoulder. I only had jump wings on my uniform, but they at least made me feel somewhat accepted in the presence of this combat-experienced career officer. But it was the colonel's warm, engaging leadership style accompanied by his soft Texas accent that made me feel most comfortable. Major Dowd and Mr. Sloan (Mr. "Somebody" in my diary) joined us.

Mr. Sloan was a civilian, a CORDS employee working closely with LTC Stanberry to monitor pacification of the rural areas of Kiến Giáng Province. Although military objectives and pacification might seem incompatible and even contradictory, to an advisor in Vietnam, they were inseparable.

LTC Stanberry's command presence and sincere desire to help the Vietnamese maintain their freedom was immediately evident and gained my respect instantly, but I did not know his background until many years later.

LTC Bill Stanberry, Senior Military Advisor, Kien Giang Province.

Bill Stanberry joined the Army as a private in 1952 and quickly rose in rank, becoming an officer, volunteering for Airborne/Ranger Schools and eventually Special Forces. It was during his second tour in Vietnam with the legendary Green Berets that he was contacted by then commander of all U.S. forces in Vietnam, General William Westmoreland, for an urgent assignment in Kiến Giáng Province. The VC had managed to regain control there after the Tet offensive, particularly in their VC-infested U-Minh Forest stronghold. Stanberry had been selected by Westmoreland because of his combat experience in-country and because he was the only officer in Vietnam at the time who was rated fluent in the Vietnamese language.

Stanberry's Vietnamese counterpart, Colonel Nguyên Van Tài, had been a history professor at the University of Saigon when President Nguyễn Văn Thiệu's subordinate, General Khiêm, appointed Tài province chief of Kiến Giáng Province. Colonel Tài was not present at my briefing by the colonel, but Stanberry assured me he was a very capable commander who had good soldiers under him.

During the briefing, Colonel Stanberry informed me that I'd be going to one of his eleven MAT teams in the province. Although my team would be many miles from Rạch Giá and near the U-Minh Forest, the senior advisory compound had a powerful radio operating 24 hours a day from a sandbagged command and control bunker located a block from the colonel's office. Rạch Giá had some heavy 155mm artillery pieces, but my MAT team would be out of range of these.

Requests for medical evacuation helicopters (medivacs) had to be called in and cleared through province, who would then call Cần Thơ on another frequency to put in the request. Water would be impossible to supply to my MAT team since there were no roads. A "Swing Ship" would be visiting our location once every two days on a "swing" around to all the MAT teams, delivering mail, food, and other routine requests previously called in on the radio. The Swing Ship was not to be used for medivacs or ammunition resupply.

## 'Rice Roots'

After the colonel's briefing, Major Dowd took Gordon and me for a walk around the compound. As we walked past the radio bunker, the crackle of radio communications could be heard through the entrance way.

"Would you like to take a look inside?" the major asked.

The inside of the sandbagged bunker seemed air conditioned, the multiple layers of sandbags insulating the room. A sergeant E-6 sat at a desk made of plywood, and messages scribbled on pieces of paper littered his work area.

"Hey, I like it in here," I said, as the cigar-smoking Sergeant Hank Setkusky looked up with a grin.

"This is alright, 'eh sir?"

The radio crackled again, "Red Dog One, this is Swampy Fox One-Zero, over."

"Swampy Fox One-Zero, this is Red Dog One, over," Setkusky responded.

"This is One-Zero, what time is that echo-tango-alpha (ETA) you said for the sierra-sierra (Swing Ship) to be at my location, over?"

"This is Red Dog One, you're looking at another three-zero minutes, over," Setkusky replied.

"This is Swampy Fox One-Zero, roger, but this little girl is looking pretty bad now and I'd really like to get her up to your location to have the *Bác-sí* (doctor) take a look-see. She's the daughter of one of the hamlet chiefs, and we could score some points in the village if you know what I mean, over."

"This is Red Dog One, roger, be advised your location will be next and we'll get her here ASAP, out."

"What's that all about?" Major Dowd queried.

"Well, sir, MAT 45 has a little girl that's pretty sick, could be something serious, and if they bring her in by sampan, they're afraid they're going to lose her. She's running a real high fever," Sergeant Setkusky replied.

"Okay, but make sure someone comes with her - don't put her on the chopper alone," Dowd said.

"Yes, sir," Setkusky acknowledged.

I liked the major. He was bending the rules on this one. The colonel had just told us Swing Ships weren't to be used as medivacs, and the little girl was a Vietnamese civilian, so technically, Major Dowd was allowing Sgt. Setkusky to break two of Stanberry's rules by condoning the medivac. I instantly admired him for that.

I parked the incident in the back of my mind. I told myself there might come a day when I'd have to break a few rules if common sense dictated. I imagined times when I'd have to make a choice between obeying the Army's rules and doing what I thought was right.

Now I couldn't wait to get out to my team and get involved. I wanted to see for myself what was going on out there. "Vietnam is going to be an adventure-and-a-half!" I thought to myself.

CHAPTER THREE

# The 168 Company

FEBRUARY 14, 1969
Diary Entry:
*Up at 6:15. Took my last hot shower (it was also my first one in Vietnam) and ate at the mess hall at Province HQ. Lt. Gordon and I got a ride to the chopper pad and waited for our flight out to our assignments.*

*10:00 a.m.: Chopper took off and landed in Kiến Binh District Headquarters. Not a very big compound, but it seems secure. Met Major Bonner who appeared in the movie Green Beret. Won't move out to Team 88 for a little while. Tet Offensive might start any day now.*

*5:00 p.m.: Was invited to "Tet" party by Dai Úy Hioív. Drank and ate various foods.*

FEBRUARY 14, 1969
Letter Home:

*Dear Folks,*
*I'm having a ball relaxing here in sunny, tropical Kiến Giáng Province, Mekong Delta. The province is located along the west coast of Vietnam.*

*Just southwest of here is a place called the U-Minh Forest. In military circles it's known as the R&R center for the Viet Công. This is where a Green Beret Major was held for 5 years after being captured. The closest American unit, the U.S. 9th Infantry Division, is quite a bit east of here.*

*A chopper comes out here every two days, so I will be going out to my MAT team (Mobile Advisory Team) pretty soon. Dad, if you get a chance, I am taking lots of pictures with my new camera, so could you send me some 35mm slide film? Thanks!*

*Love, Bob*

When Lieutenant Gordon and myself flew into Kiến Bình District we were greeted by Lt. Gannon, one of the district advisors. He helped us load our duffle bags into his jeep. We drove the short distance from the helipad to the advisory teamhouse. There I met Major Bonner, the district senior advisor in charge of the MAT teams in Kiến Bình District.

I immediately liked Major Bonner. He was a field soldier's kind of officer: spunky, direct to the point, and a great leader. Bonner had been an enlisted man, a sergeant, and had received a battlefield commission to the rank of second lieutenant in Korea. Now, sixteen years later, it had taken him that many years to achieve the rank of major. He seemed content to finish out his time in the only career he had ever known and loved, the United States Army, even though he had probably been passed over a few times for promotion. More than likely he would continue to be passed over in the future. West Pointers weren't likely to promote his type of officer, at least not much beyond the rank of major.

But Bonner carried about him a presence that conveyed to the world that he knew this, understood and accepted this fate, and that he really didn't give a rat's ass. Major Bonner loved the Army, enjoyed what he was doing, and was exactly where he wanted to be: "in the field" in a combat zone during wartime. No emphasis on spit and polish, not too many reports to fill out, no inspections to worry about and no "brass" around to have to kiss up to.

"Fellas, we got ourselves a little war out here," he said, "let's just do our job and help these little bastards find those Vietcông sons-of-bitches and kick the shit out of them."

"Spend much time at Ft. Benning, Lieutenant Amon?" Bonner said, eyeing the jump wings on my chest.

# The 168 Company

"Just Jump School, sir," I said, "then I went to Ft. Bragg and was jumping with the 82$^{nd}$ Airborne."

"Oh, okay. So how many jumps you do with them, huh?" he continued. I told him thirteen.

"Thirteen!" he pondered, as he reached for a bottle of Four Roses whiskey on the shelf made of ammo crates behind him.

"Thirteen's not a very lucky number, ya know?"

"No, sir." I said. "I know about the superstition. So, I guess I've got fourteen for the record, the way they count them there. And we never jumped at Bragg on Friday the 13$^{th}$ either."

"That's right, lieutenant!" Bonner responded. He poured himself a drink and began to relate how, when they filmed the John Wayne movie "Green Beret" at Benning, he had been used in some of the scenes as a stand-in. I had heard that they had used real soldiers, but until that moment I had never met another paratrooper who had actually appeared in the background scenes.

Major Bonner then quickly changed the subject. Our conversation was getting too cozy.

"In a couple of days, it'll be Tet," he continued.

"Tonight, you and Gordon are gonna meet Dai Úy Hioív and we're all invited to his place in the village for a party. We won't stay too much past dark, though. This'll be your first chance to see what it's like to work with these people. You gotta eat and drink everything they hand you, otherwise you don't get on the good side of 'em. Don't refuse anything they put in front of you, right? I hope you can hold your booze, lieutenant." he questioned.

"Yes, sir," I replied. Gordon was sitting on his bunk, rummaging through his duffle bag for something, and I was sitting at the kitchen table with Bonner.

"Good," he continued. "You're new here, so the Vietnamese are gonna wanna toast you with the *bá xi dé*. Just drink it even if it tastes like shit and whatever you do, don't show 'em they can out-drink you, got it?"

"Yes, sir," I responded.

"I want you to go out on at least one operation with Gannon and the Dai Úy so you can get your feet wet while you're here, so I'm gonna keep you guys here for a while before I send you to your MAT teams. Last week the Dai Úy ran into half a platoon or so of VC and got four of them. We only had one of our guys get wounded. But you'll get the hang of it."

"So, you think you're ready for an operation, lieutenant?" he questioned.

I was feeling pretty cocky by now. Hell, the major and I were practically buddies, what with us both being Airborne and all.

"Yes, sir, looking forward to it," was my reply. The major poured himself another shot of whiskey and this time, he slid the bottle down the table in my direction, his eyes narrowing as they caught mine.

"So, you're looking forward to it, huh?" he said. "I mean, going out on operations?"

And then louder, over his left shoulder he reiterated "Hey Gannon, Amon says he's looking forward to going on the next operation."

Gannon emerged from behind the ammo-crate bookshelves that separated the kitchen area from the rest of the teamhouse, almost on cue. It was like some sort of signal had been given, and he was being summoned to witness what comes next. He knew his commander well.

"I'll tell you what lieutenant... you ever take a human being in your sights before?" Major Bonner's question totally took me by surprise. Take another human being in my gun sights before? What kind of question was that? Of course I had never taken anybody in my gun sights before. I was in college before OCS! I hadn't even really thought about it that much either. Target practice was one thing - shooting at paper bullseyes. But shooting somebody in self-defense?

Well, maybe. Well, no, not maybe. If I had to, I would. But had I ever taken another person in my sights before? I realized how naive I had been, how I thought I could impress this

# The 168 Company

combat veteran. I was in trouble now. I didn't know squat. Good question. Score one for you, Bonner.

"No, sir." I responded, taking the bait now because I had no other choice. Gordon's eyes glanced up and quickly lowered back down into the duffle bag.

"No?" Bonner continued, knowing damned well what my answer would be. And now he had me.

"I'll tell you something Amon, man to man. When you have another person in the sights of your weapon, and you squeeze the trigger, and you watch him drop, there's no other feeling like that in the world... no other feeling. And maybe you'll get to do just that. And when you do, Lieutenant Amon, then you'll Fuckin'-A well know you're in Vietnam. Until then, pay attention and pick up on what me and Gannon tell you. I don't want you and Gordon goin' out and steppin' in shit. You got that?"

"Yes, sir!" I snapped. The major had spoken. He meant well. He didn't want any eager-beavers, and my life was his responsibility. I felt like one naive, stupid son-of-a-bitch.

That night the major was the life of the party. In the tin-roofed house of the incumbent district chief, he introduced Gordon and me to everybody who was somebody in the district. We met all the Vietnamese commanders in charge of the Regional Force units we would be advising. We were also introduced to the Vietnamese politicians who were the overlords of the villages within Kiến Bình District, including Hóa Quản, the village I would be going to. I heard nothing but praise for MAT Team 88 and the military unit they were currently advising, the 168 (one-six-eight) Regional Forces Company.

In Kiến Giáng Province, all advisors referred to their units' numerical designation as, for example, "The One-Six-Eight Company," not "the One Hundred and Sixty-Eighth Company." Hence, throughout this book, you'll read "The 168 Company" ... (the One Six Eight), not the 168th.

Later, laying in a metal bunk under the mosquito netting I had erected earlier, I could still see the major's face as he talked about taking a man in his gun sights and watching him drop as he pulled the trigger.

I knew I didn't want to do that. I would do it only if I had to, but I was going to try to avoid it if possible. I didn't want to be part of the killing. I really didn't want to be around the killing either. I was here for the "adventure." To prove something to myself, I suppose.

But now Major Bonner was for real, and I realized I was really in Vietnam. Major Bonner was reality. The situation was reality. And I was on my way to the real village of Hóa Quản, where there would be real killing going on and real people dying.

"You've gone and done it this time!" I told myself. "You wanted an adventure and now look what you've gotten yourself into! What the hell are you going to do now?"

### FEBRUARY 15, 1969
#### Diary Entry:

*0700: Up and had farina and coffee for breakfast. Everyone got loaded last night. The major looks like he's in bad shape. Lt. Gordon slept till 11:00. Tomorrow we will go on an operation.*

*Went to bed about 11:00 p.m. Got awakened about 0300 hours - gunfire on perimeter - 105 artillery firing from our position. An ex-VC Kit Carson scout came in and said his father had been kidnapped by the VC.*

At 3 a.m. I was awakened by voices, Vietnamese and American. Lt. Gannon was at the door, joined by Major Bonner. As Bonner flipped on the lights, I sat up to see what was going on. One of the "Kit Carson" scouts was in the kitchen begging for help.

Kit Carson scouts were Vietcông enemy defectors who were now working on our side. Having once been a Vietcông soldier, Kit Carsons knew all about the local VC - all their names, all their hideouts and all of their patterns.

On that night some Vietcông soldiers had entered Kiến Binh and kidnapped the scout's father as "payback." That was the first, but not the last time I witnessed that. The Vietcông were notorious for exacting ruthless punishment against those who had defected their ranks. In their eyes he was a turncoat and traitor.

And now the teary-eyed scout was standing before us, knowing what the VC would do to his father. He wanted our help to go after them right away. My emotions told me we should do it, maybe we could catch up with them if we left immediately. But I held my silence as the major handled it and promised to organize a search at dawn.

"Gannon, go tell the Dai Úy we leave at first light." Gannon was a crazy Cajun from Louisiana with a wild streak in him. He left the hootch to go find the Vietnamese captain.

FEBRUARY 16, 1969
Diary Entry:

*Up at 0500 hours. Got ready for my first operation with Dai Úy Hioív. I am bringing 10 magazines of M16 ammo - 200 rounds - plus a canteen.*

*Moved out at 0600. Walked along canal. No VC contact. We learned the VC had collected rice taxes and threatened the villagers last night. Lt. Gannon moved up to lead Kit Carson scouts further up the canal. Later we got invited to another party. Had pig ears and rice. They made us drink very fast and I got sick. Midnight - the whole company opened up on the perimeter. It turned out to be celebration of Tet. The soldiers expended 50% of their ammo.*

At five a.m. we were up and making good on Bonner's word. The major explained why he hadn't left at three, but I already figured out the reason, and it would serve as my first valuable lesson.

"Shit, that's all we need to do is go runnin' off half-cocked in the middle of the night and run smack into a God-damned ambush," he said. "And don't forget, these Kit Carsons already crossed the line once..."

The Kit Carson scouts led the way out of the wire surrounding the district chief's compound. Gordon and I moved with the main body of troops along the canal. We stopped at a point perhaps two miles from Kiên Binh, as the search was fruitless. It would be a long time before I learned whether or not the scout's father had been recovered. It was my first "operation" of many to come, and it was frustrating. The father was gone and the VC had him.

But I was impressed by some of the Vietnamese to whom I had been introduced. Gannon's interpreter, Vĩnh, for example, spoke excellent English and was a great help to the district team. He earnestly tried to solve the problem of the kidnapped man. During my tour of duty, I saw Vĩnh again from time to time, and each time he remembered my name.

But nine months from this date I saw Vĩnh for the last time, and under terrible circumstances. I couldn't have known what the future would hold for him, nor could he. Maybe it's better that way. The ironic thing about relationships in war is that no one expects anyone they know to be a casualty of war. Least of all, themselves.

By now I was really looking forward to going out to my outpost. Dai Úy Hioív and several of his junior officers had all spoken highly of the 168 (one-six-eight) Company. From the sounds of it, I was going to be in good hands and would accomplish a lot of very positive things with them. I was impressed by the South Vietnamese soldiers I had met so far. I discounted some of the things I'd heard about them before coming to Vietnam, like their cowardice and unwillingness to cooperate. Those I met seemed very determined to work hard at seeing democracy and capitalism prevail in their country. I felt a sense of long-term resolve on their part to see their freedom through to the end.

I hoped that by helping the South Vietnamese people win that war, I'd be of help to countless numbers of future Vietnamese civilians who would be able to enjoy all of the liberties and freedoms we enjoy in the United States. It was my best shot at helping people of another country enjoy that which we Americans so often took for granted.

# The 168 Company

FEBRUARY 17, 1969
Diary Entry:
## TET HOLIDAY BEGINS

All night long the South Vietnamese fired their automatic weapons. They must have used up thousands of rounds.

0800: Dai Úy Hioív brought about 20 village dignitaries to the compound. They were all dressed up in civilian clothes and they all wanted a drink. Major Bonner gave them each a shot of Four Roses whiskey. This is just like our New Year celebration but lasts for days.

1100: Chopper picked me up. Flew me to Hóa Quản Village outpost[A] MAT (Team 88) and met Lt. Darden, my team leader. Also, SFC Ponce, light weapons man; SFC Guerrero, heavy weapons man; and SSGT Parson, the team medic. Good men. There will be five of us in all. Live in a grass hut inside the outpost with a tiny bunker attached to the side. Also met two counterparts, Trung Úy (1st LT) Quoys, and Thiéu Úy (2nd LT) Hungl of the 168.

From the open door of the Huey, my first look at the outpost at Hóa Quản[A] was not what Chuck and I had imagined. It was in terrible shape. The mud "berm" walls were significantly eroded from the previous monsoon season. The single strand of concertina wire along the moat which surrounded the outpost had gaps in it. I wasn't prepared for the number of women and children in the outpost either, explaining the holes in the barbed wire. They had cut out sections as a convenience to relieve themselves on the other side of the berm. The firing ports in the berm were sagging, gaping holes. From the air the whole thing resembled a miniature medieval fort made of chocolate that had been left out in the sun too long. Now the chocolate was melting in the heat and the people inside the fort were a swarm of multicolored ants, bustling around in the goo.

The outpost outside of Hoa Quan Village – February, 1969.

FEBRUARY 18, 1969
Diary Entry:

*TET HOLIDAY*

*0630 Awake. Our interpreter Binh says we are going on an operation with Dai Úy Thanl, the Battalion Commander. We left by sampan and headed south about 12 miles - no VC contact - troops secured the area and we were invited in to eat pork and rice. These people down here are well fed. Brought in beer and poured it over ice. Their beer isn't too bad. The Dai Úy is a quiet man, but he seems to be a fairly good leader. Trung Úy Quoys didn't come along.*

With the Tet holiday still in full swing, Dai Úy Thanl's "operation" was really the equivalent of a Fourth of July cookout. By Vietnamese standards, someone went to considerable expense to serve the pork and rice dinner. But it was the trip *to* the party that bothered me.

We had been told about riding around in sampans. The Dai Úy insisted we use this way, suggesting there was nothing to worry about, and I acquiesced. We putt-putted along in the narrow boat. The small canal we were in was only ten feet wide.

# The 168 Company

Most of the way was clear where the canal cut through open rice paddy area. But as we approached the hamlet where the party was, both sides of the embankment were concealed with nipa palm and thick brush.

"Good area for an ambush," I thought, remembering Advisor School, and the lectures Chuck and I listened to about riding in sampans: "Every effort should be made to persuade your counterpart to move his troops on foot."

"Maybe they know what they are doing," I thought. "Maybe the Dai Úy sent his men ahead to secure the route." When we arrived, sure enough, the Dai Úy had done just that.

Well, I thought, so much for me telling the Dai Úy "he full of shit" like the hilarious Trung Úy De suggested. I realized, at least in this case, that the application of what we'd been taught was easily compromised and difficult to implement.

FEBRUARY 19, 1969
Diary Entry:

*TET HOLIDAY ENDS*

*Up at 0630. Major Bonner is expected to visit us today. 1000 hours - approaching chopper in sight. I popped smoke and they came in on it. The major sent me up for a visual reconnaissance. Trung Úy Quoys was with me. Chopper went up north about 1 to 2 miles - flew over free fire zone with empty houses - fired into area with both door guns, right into roof tops. This is suspected VC country. The Trung Úy told me where to shoot and I directed the door gunners. Chopper banked almost to a 90-degree angle and flew at tree top level very fast. I was a little scared.*

FEBRUARY 20, 1969
Diary Entry:

*Woke up at 0700. Went on operation through the village of Hóa Quản and to the north, about 1 mile. The Dai Úy and Lt. Darden stayed back and my counterpart, Trung Úy Quoys and I went ahead another 2 miles with the rest of the 168 Com-*

pany. I carried my radio in case we made contact with any VC. We pushed up near the edge of the free fire zone over which we had flown yesterday in the chopper. No contact, but I don't doubt that someone was watching. Those empty houses weren't really empty.

*Walked across canal up to my hips - dirty water. Stopped at someone's house and had Vietnamese soda.*

I was now thoroughly embedded with the 168 Company with Trung Úy (1st Lieutenant) Quoys and Thiếu Úy (2nd Lieutenant) Hungl as my two very first counterparts.

Hóa Quản Village was populated mostly by ethnic Cambodians whose families had migrated into Vietnam and settled in the Hóa Quản area. The 168 Company was recruited from the area and were therefore mostly Cambodians. The soldiers watched over their fellow Cambodian Khmer immigrants and settlers in the village like a mother hen tends to her brood. And the 168 had a reputation for not taking any crap from the local Vietcông. This was to be the best company that my Mobile Advisory Team 88 would advise during my entire one-year tour as an advisor. The 168 was a good "fit," a good marriage at Hóa Quản. Unfortunately, the marriage was not to last.

FEBRUARY 21, 1969
Diary Entry:
*The canal where the team usually gets its drinking water from is becoming backed up with salt water from the ocean and is no longer usable. We have begun skimming our water from a stagnant water hole quite a distance from here - very smelly water - and a lot of work - but when you settle it with alum and then put in a little Clorox bleach, it is drinkable. The alum and the bleach make a bad cup of coffee though.*

*9:00 p.m.: We got a message in code from Kiến Bình intelligence sources to expect an increase in VC activity. We gave the message to the Dai Úy. He knows what to do.*

Many U.S. advisors in the Delta were not furnished potable drinking water because there are not many roads, so bringing

# The 168 Company

it out by truck was impossible. Since we had to have water to drink in the intense heat, MAT 88 was using the same source the Vietnamese were using: the water in the muddy canal. We divided the chore of carrying it back to our grass teamhouse in buckets. At the teamhouse, the water was dumped into 55-gallon drums which the team had tarred with roofing tar to prevent rust. While dipping the buckets into the filthy canal, it was not uncommon to see a Vietnamese upstream urinating, defecating, bathing, or doing laundry.

SFC Ponce taught me how to break off a crystal of alum about the size of a quarter, put it into an aluminum pot and boil the alum to dissolve it. This solution was then poured into the drum to flocculate the solid particles. After several hours the solids separated from the water, forming cloudy globs, and a thick film of scum either floated to the top or settled to the bottom. The scum was skimmed off the top using a mess-kit pan, while the bottom sludge had to remain. This process only clarified the water. To make it potable, we had to add five capfuls of straight Clorox bleach. We then had to carefully scoop out the water without disturbing the bottom and boil it before drinking.

Purifying filthy canal water with alum and bleach.

This procedure worked until the water in the canal started to turn brackish from a backup of seawater from the ocean at high tide, contributing a salty taste to the water already tainted with the taste of the alum and bleach. It got so bad we could no longer use the canal water because the salt content was enough to make one vomit. On this day we began carrying our water from a stagnant, mosquito larvae-infested watering hole an eighth of a mile away, making water procurement more arduous in the oppressive heat. The villagers availed themselves of it too, but they didn't relieve themselves at this watering hole. They were usually only washing their dirty laundry or bathing in it.

FEBRUARY 22, 1969
Diary Entry:

*Up at 0730. Got washed up. Heard gunfire about a half mile away, near the pagoda.<sup>C</sup> Mostly M16 fire. The Dai Úy told us that the 168 Company was under attack and had already killed 3 VC.<sup>D</sup> Guerrero and I rode up by sampan. They had the dead VC lying on the ground and all three had at least one bullet in the head. One was a known Vietcông platoon leader. His stomach was blown open and bleeding profusely. People took pictures. The 168 Company also wounded 8 Vietcông, captured two Chicom carbines, one U.S. hand grenade, 1 Chicom grenade and 1 U.S. carbine.*

Welcome to Vietnam! Today was the start of my fifth day in the field. I had been in the Army for just about 2 years, but all of the training and all of the war stories I had heard could not possibly prepare me to see my first freshly shot dead bodies.

SFC Guerrero grabbed his camera and weapon and took along the naive new Lieutenant Amon. I found myself warily disembarking the sampan with Guerrero near the pagoda.<sup>C</sup> To my right, I noticed a felled coconut tree, blown in two. Part of the tree lay in the water.

The story later unfolded: At approximately 3 a.m., fifteen Vietcông had entered Hóa Quản from the north end, where I had been the day before. They set up an ambush along the heavily traveled trail running along the canal in the center of Hóa Quản. Using a coconut tree as the focal point of the ambush, they strapped to it a large unexploded artillery round, and waited in the jungle with a detonating device.[D]

Our 168 Company soldiers had awakened and were preparing for another operation. As was their habit, some of them wandered up the trail in a group toward the pagoda for their morning *"caphe"* and pastries at a little grass hut-turned coffee shop in the village. When they reached the coconut tree, the VC detonated the explosive with the intent of killing some and incapacitating the rest, so they could finish them off with small-arms fire and quickly leave. The force of the explosion went the wrong way, however, and did nothing more than cut down the coconut tree. The 168 scrambled for cover uninjured, and used their M16 rifles to pour a heavy volume of fire at the waiting VC, who began taking casualties.

Thiéu Úy Hungl ran to the scene with the remainder of his platoon and joined in, pouring more firepower at the VC, who were by now on the defensive, dragging off wounded comrades from the firefight. The tables continued turning as the rest of the 168 arrived. Three of the most defiant of the VC, led by a local Vietcông platoon leader, continued the firefight while climbing into a sampan to escape. While two of them returned fire from the sampan, the third stood up in the back of the boat, yanking on the motor, trying to get it started.

Hungl bravely advanced his men toward the bank of the canal for a clearer shot and managed to pick off the Vietcông who was standing up, pulling on the starter cord. Then, in a hail of bullets and with no mercy, the whole platoon riddled the other two inhabitants, capsizing the boat.

As Guerrero and I climbed onto the bank of the canal, people from all over the village were moving cautiously toward the crowd in front of the pagoda. Trung Úy Quoys greeted us in his underwear.

I could see three bodies sprawled out in the center of the crowd. Some of our soldiers had already disrespectfully placed lit cigarettes in the mouths of the dead. The Vietcông platoon leader had been fished out of the water alive and conscious, but not for long. One of my 168 soldiers was so pissed at having almost been killed that he walked over to him and exacted revenge for having the hell scared out of him. He fired his entire magazine of 20 rounds into his stomach while he was still alive.

The bullets ricocheted off the concrete slab, came back up through his mid-section and caused his body to dance and twitch as the gunfire once again sent civilians and soldiers scurrying for cover. When it was over, one of the monks threw a blue dish towel over the mess that was once his midsection, partially to discourage the dozens of flies that had already converged and also to cover the contents of what was once his stomach.

Each of the Vietcông were then systematically shot in the head. Years later, I read accounts of ground actions in other wars, and this behavior is not atypical, an act simultaneously born of fear and mercy. On some, parts of their brains were visible from the exit wound. I remember how odd their faces appeared. The final bullet to the head of the platoon leader distorted his facial features, causing an asymmetrical shifting of his cheek bone. I could tell he had probably been a good-looking young man just minutes before. He was the oldest, approximately 21 years of age. One of our soldiers went over and kicked the head of the one in the middle and the back of his head was gone.

I had seen bodies in funeral parlors before. They never particularly affected me too much. Funeral parlor bodies are always cleaned up, dressed up, arms folded, nice and neat. No muddy wet hair, uncombed and disheveled. No cigarettes dangling from their mouths. Funeral parlor corpses are refined, dignified. These were warm, fresh-killed bodies - no chance to get cleaned up or change out of their wet clothes to get their picture taken. Warm, freshly-killed, muddy bodies drying off in the sun.

I remember two things vividly: the smell of the Vietnamese cigarettes and the flies. The flies were the first on the scene. The delicious, wet, blood-soaked bodies were irresistible to them. They landed in embarrassing places searching for a meal.

# The 168 Company

A fly landed on the young man's lips, then walked to the opening in his nose, inspecting the hole as if pondering whether or not to enter. No, it decided to move toward the bloody side of his head, to wander through the blood-soaked, jet-black hair. Everyone was very quiet. Only the sound of the flies pervaded, arriving in swarms, buzzing in short bursts to get as much as they could. I felt like shooing them, they didn't belong here, they didn't have the right to make it even more dehumanizing.

Vietnamese cigarette smoke has a smell unlike any tobacco grown in the United States. Their cigarettes have a distinctively sweet smell, a pungently curious aroma which, once smelled, is difficult to forget. Our senses have a memory for such things, just as our minds have a memory to store facts and sights we see. The sight of the fly-ridden bodies combined with the redolence of the cigarettes formed a double hit on my consciousness. For the rest of the year the smell of those cigarettes was synonymous with death. For the rest of my life I'll not forget the smell of sweet, overpowering, pungent death.

Guerrero began taking photographs of the dead VC and I did the same, watching him and imitating his cocky composure. I lit up a cigarette also. Hey, got to appear nonchalant now and look unaffected. Take a few more pictures, don't be scared. It ain't no big thing.

In the midst of this ruse, I glanced over toward the pagoda. Some young monks were standing in a group at the entrance to the pagoda and they didn't look at all amused. They looked sad, concerned, the circus was getting out of hand. Suddenly I was ashamed. I put the camera away and stopped the pretense. *What the hell am I doing?*

That evening I wrote in my diary the words "people took pictures." I couldn't bring myself to write "I took pictures," because I was ashamed. I knew it was wrong, even back on the evening of the 22nd when I wrote it in the diary. Taking pictures of dead bodies was a cowardly and insensitive thing to do. Later, I almost felt that, by having done it, I became part of the act - certainly part of the circus.

That was to be the first and last time I took part in that behavior. That night I couldn't sleep, thinking about the bodies I had taken pictures of. Who were they, really? Did they have any loved ones? What sort of children had they been? Surely, they must have family members. What will the families think when they are notified that their loved one was killed? Worse, what grief will they experience when they learn that the bodies were so publicly and irreverently ridiculed?

How strong their political beliefs must have been to propel them to that river to kill us. Moments before the snap of my shutter they had been healthy, functioning human beings. Then they were laid out in front of the pagoda, the entire village glaring at the spectacle.

However grotesque, the 168 Company had sent an unmistakable message to the Vietcông: stay the hell out of Hóa Quản Village. That day was my fifth day in the field in Vietnam, an early introduction to the killing and brutality. Vietnam hadn't wasted any time punching me in the face.

I wanted an adventure and I wanted to see for myself. Now I still had a whole year to go. I'd better watch it, or I might wind up like Mayo Parks, getting shot. Or maybe worse: I could wind up wet and muddy with a bullet in my head and a cigarette dangling from my lips.

FEBRUARY 25, 1969
Diary Entry:

*Guerrero and I left early on operation with Trung Úy Quoys to the north to form a blocking position. The rest of the VC that attacked the 168 Company near the pagoda were supposed to be up there. We formed a blocking position for 770 Company on a big combined sweep to contact the VC, but no contact. Tonight, we took 3 mortar rounds directly into compound and received small arms fire. 4.2" mortar fired at fleeing VC. If they hit any, the VC must have dragged them away. Also got a prefab house today.*

This night was my first time experiencing "incoming"

## The 168 Company

and I remember being in a very deep sleep. Besides the loud, jarring explosions, there was a lot of yelling. As the second round exploded into the outpost, I got out of bed and couldn't find my glasses. I was the last one into the bunker by the time the third mortar round came in.

The team had previously built our bunker immediately next to our nipa-grass teamhouse. From my bed to the side door of the team house was only fifteen feet, with another four feet of open sky before you got to the bunker.

As I dashed inside the bunker, Guerrero was already firing the M-60 machine gun. I remember other explosions going off as our own 4.2-inch mortar crew got into action, sending up parachute flares that cast an eerie, flickering light through the firing ports of the bunker. The smoke and bitter smell of the gunpowder filled the bunker as Guerrero raked the woodline without interruption. The red-hot brass shell casings coming out of the receiver danced and ricocheted inside the smoke-filled cave and struck the side of my face. I was still thinking of the dead bodies from the other day, and I didn't want to wind up like them. Go ahead, Guerrero. Screw it. Nail anything that moves!

FEBRUARY 26, 1969
Diary Entry:

*Up at 0630. Started working on the prefab with the four other team members. Hard work! We humped lumber all day and completed it by 5:30 p.m. At 5:30 p.m. a chopper spotted some VC near the pagoda in our village, the same place where the 168 killed the last three. SSGT Parson and myself went out as a reaction force with the 168 to cut them off, but the VC had already gone down south toward the outpost at Thời An.[B] Heard gunfire coming from that direction.*

FEBRUARY 27, 1969
Diary Entry:

*Went out on my first night ambush with Sgt. Guerrero and 12 soldiers from 168 Company... the same place where the*

Vietcông had entered the village the other day.

    *9:00 p.m.:* Set up the ambush along woodline facing open field. Trung Sí, sergeant-in-charge, says that the VC come into the pagoda like this at night. We waited until midnight and Trung Sí said, "They will not come tonight because the moon is too bright." Went back to outpost. They carried rifles on shoulders.

### FEBRUARY 28, 1969
#### Diary Entry:

*Up at 6:30. Called in Trung Sí and gave him a critique on what I thought of the ambush. Told him ambush was good but too much noise. Also, one man shined a flashlight on the radio. Told him I didn't like the rifles on the shoulders and some were smoking on the way back - a good way to get ambushed yourself! Worked carrying water and filling sandbags.*

### MARCH 1, 1969
#### Diary Entry:

*Sgt. Binh, our interpreter, came back from leave today. He visited his brother in Saigon who just had both legs amputated. He moped around and we gave him some time off.*

*Binh came in and informed me 168 has operation at 0700.*

### MARCH 2, 1969
#### Diary Entry:

*Hóa Quản ELECTION DAY!*

*Up at 0630. No activity in camp. 168 Company finally moved out at 0800. We swept country north of here and linked up with 770 Company from Thời An and 338. No VC contact. Trung Úy Quoys and myself, plus about four bodyguards, went back to elections. They had little ballots and I.D. cards and took fingerprints. Very impressed. Trung Úy and I sat talking. I opened peanut butter and crackers from my C rations - kids gathered around and I gave it out. Former village chief lost election.*

    The election in the village was an amazing thing to witness. I remember thinking how routinely I had taken election

## The 168 Company

days for granted back home. The amazing thing was, the Vietnamese did not! Voter turnout in the village was estimated by officials to be 80-90%, an incredible statistic if true!

The VC terrorized election days throughout Vietnam by exploding hand grenades and other acts of violence to disrupt the casting of ballots. My attendance along with Trung Úy Quoys lent credibility and security to the election. For our protection in that crowd of people, the Trung Úy brought along four bodyguards carrying M16s, who constantly eyed the crowd around us.

### MARCH 3, 1969
#### Diary Entry:

*Up at 0700. Went to Thời An by sampan to pick up Maj. Dowd (Asst. PSA) and Mr. Sloan (civilian). Spent day showing them around. That night we went on ambush. Left 8:00 p.m. with Thiếu Úy Hungl and 20 men from the 1st Platoon. Went north and crossed two deep canals, over one more canal to the west, and came back down south near pagoda. Drums in pagoda started beating - maybe it was a signal to the VC that our ambush patrol was in the area. Set up along canal and waited. No VC - but heard a dog barking over near pagoda about 1:00 a.m. Came back at 3:30 a.m. after crossing another canal. Major Dowd stayed up rest of night. Another operation in the morning.*

All advisors in the field were required to go out on a minimum of three night ambushes per week. So were many of the officers and NCO's at district and province levels. But the ambush requirement for them was a minimum of one per month. Still, realizing the danger involved, many of those from the "rear" areas were reluctant to fulfill the requirement. Most falsified reports indicating they'd participated or they visited a more secure outpost like a district compound. If they brought enough cold beer along, it was possible they didn't have to go out at all!

The fact that Major Dowd was visiting with the legitimate intention of going out on a night ambush was surprising. After all, he was the XO (executive officer) in Kiến Giáng Province, second in command to Colonel Stanberry. I respected him for wanting to come out to visit with us and accompany us on one of our required night ambushes. It told me he wasn't a typical REMF either. He brought along Mr. Sloan, the civilian CORDS official I met on Feb 12.

I got hold of Thiếu Úy Hungl and told him about Major Dowd and the civilian coming along, but I asked him to not tell his men. I didn't need one of them inadvertently mentioning it in the village. We didn't need to be advertising to the Vietcông that an American major would be with us. When we assembled with Hungl at 7:45 p.m. to depart, I noticed he had twenty men with him instead of the usual seven or eight in order to safeguard Major Dowd and Mr. Sloan.

The "roving" ambush Hungl devised was quite clever because he disguised our departure from the outpost as if we would be ambushing at a location away from Hóa Quản. He had us head north, straight through the village past the pagoda in plain view of everyone. A dog barked at us as we walked by. We continued north out of the village until we disappeared from view. Then we cut west into a woodline, slogged through a couple of waist-deep canals and circled south again, picking up the trail leading east, which took us right back toward the pagoda in Hóa Quản.

By now we had crossed three canals, a mud pit and a water buffalo hole in which I smelled feces. Mr. Sloan was wearing a decent pair of slacks and had no doubt ruined them. Thiếu Úy Hungl had us line up in a straight-line ambush on the left side of the trail. Hungl kept the major, myself and Sloan in the middle of the ambush formation as was usually the case. I told Major Dowd this was the avenue of approach taken by the Vietcông when they entered the village in the early morning hours of February 22.

Suddenly, one of the monks started beating the drum at the pagoda and I heard the dog barking again. I didn't know why they were doing that and couldn't explain it to Dowd. Could it be that the monks were warning the VC? Buddhist monks in Vietnam abhorred violence on either side. Perhaps the monks learned of where we had ultimately set up and realized we were on a collision course with the Vietcông that night. To avert disaster for both sides and not wanting a repeat of the violence of the other day, that could explain why they were beating the drum.

Of even more concern to me was the barking dog. Dogs don't bark at night unless they see a stranger, hear strange noises, or sense something unusual. Why was the dog barking at 1:00 a.m.? No one should have been up and around at that hour. If the VC attempted to visit the pagoda that night, perhaps they caused the dog to bark as they hurried out of the village to the north, scared off by the drum signal from the monks. In any event, they didn't find us nor we them that night, which was okay with me.

We decided to pack it in at 3:30 a.m. To get back to the outpost, we had to head back through the village again and straight past the pagoda. In the pitch blackness we moved in single-file along the same trail the Vietcông had used, past the concrete slab where the bodies had been and past all the rows of houses. Not one person was up, not a light on and not a sound could be heard, except for the sound of the twenty-three of us moving along the trail, and that damned dog barking again, this time at us instead of Charlie (the VC). They had been there alright.

Back at the teamhouse, "safe" inside the outpost, Major Dowd and Mr. Sloan sat shivering in their muddy wet clothes on canvas Army cots I had set up for them. I gave them poncho liners to use as a blanket. It was now 4:30 a.m., and the major couldn't sleep. I explained that I had an operation to go on in two hours, and he told me to get some rest. Lt. Darden was away on R&R and I felt obligated to go out on all the operations in case something happened. At 4:45 a.m. I took off my muddy wet fatigues, pulled several juicy leaches from my ankles and climbed into my nice dry sleeping bag.

When I awoke at 6 a.m. to go on the company operation, the two of them were still sitting on the same cots. They couldn't wait for the chopper to pick them up and take them back to the headquarters compound where they'd have hot showers, flushing toilets and a good breakfast. I remember thinking, "I guess it'll be a cold day in hell before they decide to come visit *us* again!"

MARCH 7, 1969
Diary Entry:

*Up around 0800. Did chores during day. Went on another night ambush with SFC Guerrero and with the same Trung Sĩ as my first time. Left in direction of Thời An and doubled back across rice paddy (open area) and walked into woodline along canal. If there was ever a time when I thought the VC could pull off a good ambush on us it would have been right there. Kind of gives you the jitters. Too much noise again. Set up near some hootches. We saw men going and coming but without weapons! I would bet they were Vietcông. If they had had their weapons our boys would have done a job on them.*

MARCH 9, 1969
Diary Entry:

*Took some pictures today. This night Thiếu Úy Hungl invited me to "his house" for dinner. He lives near our teamhouse in a tiny grass hut next to the berm. We ate carrots and rice and fish. The carrots were Thiếu Úy Hungl's favorite dish, they were sweet and at the same time spicy hot - very different from our carrots - almost raw.*

I loaded up my camera and decided to take some pictures today. My diary entries screamed for visual company. Photos would help my recollection and help tie together the diary entries. I wanted to record this place and some of the people I was working with. One of them was my new friend and counterpart, Thiếu Úy Hungl.

Wearing a brand new, yet-to-be laundered, olive green T-shirt, I had one of the guys take my picture standing next to Hungl in the early morning sun. Moments later, nine of Hungl's men badgered me into posing with them for a picture of us all. Those two photos of the 168 Company remain among my most cherished Vietnam photos, the latter appearing on the cover of this book.

After the operation that day, Thiếu Úy Hungl invited me to his "house" for dinner. It had been 2nd Lieutenant Hungl's platoon that repelled the Vietcông attack in the village, killing the three of them on February 22. And it would be Hungl and his men again, two days from now, who would repel a sniper attack on myself at Thời An outpost.

On the afternoon of March 9, Hungl already knew that he and I would be separating. We talked, and although I ate only some of the "hot" carrots, steamed fish and rice, I pretended to love everything he made.

Our busy combat roles involved hour-to-hour and minute-by-minute conversations and rarely consisted of any topic other than immediate military needs. I hadn't known of his personal life, we never seemed to have time for that. I hadn't even known that he was married, not having seen him around the outpost in the company of a woman.

On March 9, Hungl told me at dinner that his wife had a baby! His son was almost a year old in 1969, and the baby was safe along with his wife who lived with her parents up near Rạch Giá. Smart, I thought, not having his wife and child living in our unsecure, overcrowded outpost. I only wish it was possible to reach back to the evening of March 9, 1969 and grasp the future while sitting on the mud floor of his lean-to, eating carrots, and be warned of what was to come.

MARCH 11, 1969
Diary Entry:

*We went to Thời An to meet with MAT 45. While I was there, we got hit from the southeast by a squad of Vietcông in broad daylight. Binh and I ran out to the edge of the berm. Airborne E-6 was there with me peeking over berm. Saw nothing - could hear the bullets whistle as they went overhead. I called up Guerrero and he got Pháo Binh to fire about seven mortar rounds into the area - air bursts. Darden was P.O.'d because the air bursts blew above the village. No one was wounded, fortunately.*

*Thiếu Úy Hungl's 1st Platoon accompanied us on the trip to Thời An. The Dai Úy particularly wanted to inspect the discipline and morale of the 770 Company, one of the rifle companies* under the control of his Liên-Dôi Battalion. There was considerable VC activity at Thời An. He wanted to find out for himself what the 770 and neighboring 338 Companies were doing about it.

The outpost at Thời An was the furthest thing from the examples Chuck and I had seen at Advisor School. Firing positions needed repair, there were gaps in the wire, trash and filth were everywhere and the outpost stunk of garbage and human waste. The demoralized attitude of the 770 had even rubbed off on the American advisors there. They hadn't even improvised a shower or water purification barrel.

We all walked to the center of the outpost. Interpreter Binh and I stood outside the company commander's nipa-palm hut while the Dai Úy went inside to look for his subordinate. It was approximately 3 p.m. and the sun was blasting. I removed the heavy PRC-25 radio from my shoulders and placed it at the base of the thatched hut.

The silence of the afternoon disappeared abruptly as a very loud gunshot rang out from my right. And I thought I heard a slapping noise against the thatched nipa wall next to my left ear just before the gunshot. I wasn't alarmed at first, because I had already observed our Vietnamese soldiers promiscuously discharging their weapons at birds or snakes, etc. My reaction was to turn my head to the right toward the direction of the gunshot, because it seemed louder than a typical outgoing gunshot. My frown caught Binh's attention. I noticed the same curious whapping noise into the thatching again, simultaneous with another loud gunshot. As a third shot rang out, Binh yelled, "*Trung Úy, Lai dế!*" (come here). My six-foot frame had attracted a sniper!

We both had to run *in the direction of the gunshots* to get behind a healthy section of mud wall at the berm. The shots intensified and I heard a whining noise as we threw ourselves at the base of the berm. "Great," I thought, "Now I'm thirty feet from my freaking radio," which was still on the ground by the hut. Binh, who was not required to carry a weapon, was next to me, our backs to the wall.

## The 168 Company

Binh's philosophy about not carrying a weapon was simple: If the Vietcông ever captured him, he would have a better chance of bullshitting his way out of being skinned alive if he was not "a combatant" carrying a weapon. He was "merely" an interpreter. By not carrying a weapon, so he reasoned, he would not be exposed to enemy fire. Well, so much for that idea! He was terror-stricken beyond belief of the VC, which explained why he finagled his way into becoming an interpreter in the first place.

Anyone with a weapon was now firing on fully automatic from behind the berm. I turned on my right knee from my position against the wall and attempted to get my head and M16 up and over the mud berm to fire back, but I just couldn't do it! Every time I tried, fear seized control of my body.

"Get up, come on, return fire!" someone was yelling. But I was frozen! It was as if someone were standing on my shoulders saying, "You know you're his target. He had a bead on you and blew it. He saw you run to this exact spot and he knows you're still here. Go ahead, you want to die? Put your head up, and this time he'll put a freaking bullet right in the middle of your forehead." Maybe it was Mayo Parks' voice coming through the din of rifle fire, "I'm not shittin' ya Bob, keep your ass down," he was saying laughingly.

"Return Fire," the sergeant yelled again. To my left was a member of the U.S. Advisory Team (MAT 45) at Thời An. I had noticed him earlier, a lanky fellow paratrooper, with white jump wings on his fatigue shirt. The E-6 was screaming directly at me, "Return Fire!"

I could not. I couldn't bring myself to expose my face over the berm. He yelled at me once more. I just couldn't do it. Only after the firing stopped was I finally able to peek over the top. I looked over at the airborne sergeant, who had a complete look of disdain for me on his face. I had to turn my eyes away. I knew I had been in the sniper's crosshairs, but I wasn't about to offer that excuse to him. I never had occasion to run into that man after that, which was a good thing, because I felt like such a coward that day. Seeing him would have been more than embarrassing to me, a fellow paratrooper who didn't even have the balls to expose himself to enemy fire.

"*Trung Úy,*" it was Binh, "VC try to shoot you." He started grinning, and then laughing. Holding up his hand in the air with his palm facing the ground, he added, "They see you are tall lieutenant with radio, they know to shoot you." He couldn't control the laughter.

"Yeah, real funny, Binh," I said, "just fucking hilarious!"

I ran back to the center of the outpost to get my radio. On my map, I pinpointed the exact coordinates of a corridor of trees running southwest of the outpost. With open rice paddy to either side, the VC were probably running back down toward the U-Minh Forest, using that corridor for cover and concealment from the air.

Okay, this is my chance, I thought. My very first fire mission! I knew Trung Úy Kanh and his *Phảo Binh* (mortar crew) back at Hóa Quản could reach this area with their 4.2-inch mortar. I double-checked the map coordinates in relation to the village and the outpost. "I don't want to bring this stuff in on us," I thought. I quickly called Guerrero and gave him the coordinates, and he ran over to Kanh's men in the mortar pit.

Binh had an excited look on his face. His eyes widened as he realized I was about to bring mortars in on top of the VC. "Okay, Binh," I told him, "let's see how they like *this* shit!"

I had been told by Kanh that they had previously "sighted in" numerous coordinates. In an American unit, a "marker" round would be first, and then the fire would be adjusted before the lethal "fire for effect" barrage was sent off. But under the circumstances and because they had supposedly marked positions, Kanh was going to "fire for effect," let them all go at once. We waited. Soon I could hear the first round leaving the tube at Hóa Quản, followed by others in rapid order.

All of a sudden, between the village and the outpost, shells started exploding in mid-air. They were "air bursts," shells designed with timers to go off at treetop level and shower steel fragments down onto the enemy from above. But they were off the mark, almost on top of us! "Cease fire, cease fire," I screamed into the radio. It took a while for the explosions to stop as Guerrero had to run back next door to shut them down.

"Great," I thought, "I can't do anything right today, and now I've probably hurt some innocent village people." Later I checked the coordinates that Guerrero relayed to Kanh's men, and they were spot on. Further investigation by the Trung Úy revealed that one of his men put the wrong distance charges at the bases of the rounds. If they had been a little shorter, we would all have been wearing steel shards out of the tops of our shoulders!

Fortunately, I had injured no one in the village. As for the sniper, it was common knowledge that the Vietcông had a reward system in place for the killing of U.S. advisors, particularly an officer. I had a bounty on my head. It was the equivalent of about $100 U.S. dollars. Not a lot in the States, but a small fortune to be had if you were a poor rice farmer.

MARCH 12, 1969
Diary Entry:
*Up at 0700. Today Sgt. Guerrero has to go to Rạch Giá and then Cần Thơ on legal business. Spent the morning writing to Kathy and John. 168 Company leaving tomorrow.*

On the evening of March 12, the 168 Regional Forces Company readied itself to move out of Hóa Quản. Thiếu Úy Hungl and the 168 had distinguished themselves at Hóa Quản. Their record was such that the district chief of Kiến Binh decided to summon them for use as a "reaction force" within the district, to be airlifted into major engagements at a moment's notice against large VC forces. During the short period we had advised them, they had not sustained a single casualty themselves, but had inflicted considerable damage to the VC, including their most recent accomplishment on the 22nd of February.

But all that good luck was about to change for them now. For the next nine months, I periodically heard stories about the 168. Vietnamese and others who knew I had once advised them would tell me about the casualties. Even Binh mentioned names of soldiers to me, but I mostly remembered faces: "Trung Úy, remember Ha Sí Quan from 168?" I did not. "He die last week. And remember company first sergeant?" I did. He was one of my bodyguards on election day. "He get foot blown off near U-Minh ... step on land mine."

Over the next nine months I ran into members of the 168 Company once in a while. But as the months wore on, I was to never again see my favorite counterpart, Thiếu Úy Hungl.

The 398 Regional Forces Company we were receiving the following day was a different story than the 168 Company. The first strike against them was their Hoa Hảo religion. The Hoa Hảo (pronounced Wa How) were deemed a radical militant sect by most Vietnamese.

Founded in 1939, they strongly opposed French and Japanese colonialism. They later aligned themselves with the communist Viet Minh against the U.S.-backed government of Ngô Đình Diệm. By 1956, Diệm crushed the Hoa Hảo with several ARVN battalions now being paid by the Americans.[3] But after Diệm was deposed and killed in 1963, the Hòa Hảo changed their emphasis from anti-Diệm to anti-Communist[4] and re-aligned with the government of South Vietnam.

The new 398 Company and its two Hoa Hảo sister companies, the 338 and 770, were, for the time being, fighting on our side, and I was going to be their advisor. But it remained unclear to many whether they were totally in support of the South Vietnamese government. It was doubtful to some of the villagers that the new company would be supportive of all of the "free election/free market" business.

Worse, the new 398 personnel were "pure" Vietnamese. They had milky white skin. The Hoa Hảo were nationalistic to the point of being racists. The mocha-colored Cambodian civilians of Hóa Quản had no business integrating into their pure-Vietnamese society. The Hoa Hảo's looked down upon Cambodians as lower class. They weren't fair-skinned enough to suit them.

Because the Hoa Hảo once had Vietcông ties and then defected, they were despised by the VC as traitors. This explained

## The 168 Company

why the 770 was constantly being harassed down at Thời An. And also because of their former Vietcông ties, the South Vietnamese government put them last on their list to receive the new M16 rifle. The Hoa Hảos were disliked and distrusted on both sides, an outfit caught in the middle.

I didn't want to "lose" Hóa Quản Village. MAT 88 had worked too hard to secure it and keep it safe. Would the villagers connect and cooperate with the 398 as they had the 168 Company, or secretly work against them? Could the 398 defend themselves and the village without the M16 rifle? More importantly, was it safe for the men on my team to be with them? On the 12th of March, I was more than a little concerned about seeing the 168 depart and being replaced by the 398.

## CHAPTER FOUR

# 'Trời Ơi!... Trời Ơi!'

MARCH 13, 1969
Diary Entry:
*Up at 0630. The 168 Company left the outpost this morning and moved out for Kiến Bình. 398 Company moved in. I met the company commander, a Chuẩn Uý (a 3rd lieutenant or aspirant), and the battalion commander, Dai Úy Hoa. He offered us warm beer, "Bierre LaRue."*

MARCH 17, 1969
Diary Entry:
*Up at 0700. Sgt. Guerrero and I went on our first operation with the 398 Company. Sgt. Guerrero's face is broken out in some kind of rash. We went way out to the west, almost to the big canal, I thought we'd make contact, but we didn't.*

*Soldiers take a break and burn haystacks to get rats to eat. We returned at 1500 hours.*

*The Liên-Dôi battalion Commander, Dai Úy Hoa, left for Cần Thơ with a swollen ankle.*

Guerrero and I left the outpost around 8 a.m. and accompanied the 398 on a long hot walk in the sun. It was still the "dry season" in Vietnam, with very little rain. We made good time patrolling across the rice paddies, trudging on the hard, cracked, parched dirt that would before long become submerged mud. Guerrero's face had gotten worse. I knew it would only be a matter of time before he would need medical attention.

# 'Trời Ơi!... Trời Ơi!'

We encountered no enemy and took a break with the company at the edge of one of the rice paddies. Guerrero and I took swigs out of our canteens and lit up a couple of Salem cigarettes. I noticed the soldiers setting fire to haystacked piles of straw-like stalks, the residue of the rice harvest from the preceding season. The stacks were piles of dry tinder, requiring a mere touch of a flame to set them ablaze. Then I noticed our soldiers running around the burning stacks, diving on the ground.

No longer able to control my curiosity, I queried Trung Sí Binh: "Binh, what in God's name are they doing?"

"They hunt *cộn chuát,* Trung Úy. You know... how you say? Rats?"

"What? I'm sorry Binh, did you say rats?" I questioned.

"Yes," he replied, "rats to eat. Come, I show you." We walked over to the piles being ignited and watched the soldiers pouncing on the small rats as they scurried to get away from the flames. They were actually smaller rodents, more like field mice. Once the rodents were in their hands with only their faces protruding, with a skillful flick of the thumb, they broke their necks.

The dead creatures would then be deposited into their knapsacks. I stared at this in disbelief as one of the soldiers walked up to me with one in his hand to demonstrate the precision with which he could snap its little neck. Then, laughing hysterically, he ran off to set more fires.

I explained to Binh that back in the States, rats are considered to be the carriers of disease, a health hazard. "They can get pretty sick eating these things," I told Binh.

"No, Trung Úy!" he corrected me. "Rats from the countryside *Numba One*, no have disease. Rats from the city, like Saigon, you right, *Numba Ten, xàu lám*" (very bad). I looked over in Guerrero's direction and he grinned back at me.

"Now you know why I don't eat with the Vietnamese, lieutenant."

Capturing Con Chuat for dinner.

MARCH 22, 1969
Diary Entry:

*Up at 0715. Explosion about 100 feet away gets me out of bed. Sgt. Guerrero points to the smoke on the other side of perimeter. Grenade or grenade launcher. Go out in front of house. Someone is carrying stretcher. Interpreter Binh says man is dead - accidentally tripped booby trap. I go over there with Chuãn Úy, man is still alive, no left hand, face all blown up. Wife is on knees screaming. I call chopper. Ran all the way out to LZ with smoke grenade, loaded him on.*

*Did nothing rest of day. Chopper took one hour, fifteen minutes. Doc gave him morphine.*

ARVN units, especially the ones in the Delta, had the lowest priority imaginable in Vietnam. It didn't matter whether they needed a material item, support, or a service, they were last on the list. I was beginning to realize the magnitude of helping them under these conditions.

MAT 88 had been trying to get Claymore mines and barbed wire since before I arrived on the team. Claymore mines were safe, effective, easy-to-set-up anti-personnel mines. They were good for night defensive positions and ambushes.

Lacking adequate barbed wire and unable to requisition Claymores, our company was resorting to all kinds of homemade devices as shown to Chuck and I at Advisor School. One such night defensive technique involved the jury-rigging of U.S. baseball hand grenades. By tying the grenade to a small tree, pulling the pin, and attaching a trip wire to the handle, it served the same purpose as the reliable and effective Claymore. Except for one thing: it was quite dangerous. The more one fondles the detonating mechanism, the more likely a mishap.

In OCS we had a class on hand grenades. They passed around an inert grenade which had been cut in half. The "new generation" of hand grenades contained a much more powerful explosive than its WWII predecessor. Wrapped around the explosive was a "slinky," a coil of flat wire with notches cut halfway through at intervals. The resulting explosion caused the slinky to disintegrate into thousands of particles. This wasn't your grandfather's "pineapple" hand grenade.

The loud explosion had me out of bed in a flash and out the door of the teamhouse. Guerrero was already outside the doorway, hand shielding the morning sun, looking over at the smoke rising from the other side of the compound.

The outpost was quickly filled with Vietnamese voices yelling to one another, accompanied by a lot of activity. I saw a Vietnamese medic run toward the scene with a stretcher. Meanwhile, Binh, who had no stomach for that sort of thing, had walked halfway there, talked to a couple of soldiers, and was returning to where Guerrero and I stood.

"Trung Úy," he rendered his simplistic report. "One of the men set off hand grenade and he is dead." None of the other guys particularly wanted to join the crowd of onlookers, but when I saw my new counterpart, Chuẫn Úy Khome, heading to the scene, I knew my place as his advisor was next to him. In the event someone was still alive, it was going to be my job to have to visually inspect the casualty before calling for a medivac. This was my required protocol.

I caught up with Khome and together we worked our way through the sizeable crowd that had already gathered. We got to the center, and looking down, I couldn't believe my eyes.

Over the next several minutes we were able to piece together what had taken place. Private Quang returned from a night ambush and was in the process of re-inserting the pin back into a hand grenade when it exploded. The blast literally tore the clothing off of his chest.

Standing over Private Quang, I could see his eyes had been knocked out. He was on his back, flailing back and forth from side to side. His face (barely recognizable as a face) and chest were both covered with hundreds of perforations. His left hand was missing and pieces of his right hand were dangling from his wrist by tendons. Blood was squirting out of both stumps into the air due to his rocking motion, and myself and the Chuẩn Úy had to step back. There was very little blood coming from all of the perforations, but he looked like he was trying to put his hands over what used to be his eyes to cover them, not realizing that he no longer had hands (or eyes). In an effort to bring his hands to his face, he was showering himself and everyone else with blood.

Then Quang's wife ran into the middle of the crowd, dropped to her knees, and emitted the loudest wailing noise I have ever heard from a human being. The screaming, the Vietnamese equivalent of "Oh my God!" could be heard throughout the camp: "*Trời ói!... Trời ói!*"

Now I was running for all I was worth. Running toward the teamhouse in my flip flops for the only relief I could think of. I ran past Hungl's lean-to, losing one of my flip flops as I rounded the corner past Binh's hootch. The wailing continued. As I grabbed my morphine out of my gear, one of the other guys yelled, "What's going on?"

"Hand grenade," I said, as I ran out the door and back to

## 'Trời Ơi!... Trời Ơi!'

the crowd. I wanted the suffering to stop *right now!*

Quang's wife was being torn from her husband, tears and blood all down her front, and the Vietnamese 398 Company *Bác-sí* (medic) was kneeling over Quang. A voice spoke to me from behind my right shoulder as I handed the *Bác-sí* my morphine. It was Parson, our team medic.

"Give him half, lieutenant, make sure you tell him half, and see if that's enough. The whole thing all at once might kill him."

"Binh, where are you, Binh?" I yelled.

"Right here, Trung Úy," he said, moving next to me, as the *Bác-sí* started to inject the needle.

"Binh, tell the medic half, only half the tube of morphine," I said. Binh said something in Vietnamese, to which the *Bác-sí* mumbled a reply.

"Binh, did you tell him, did you tell him, Binh?" I yelled again.

"Yes, I told him, Trung Úy. *I told him!*" he retorted.

I watched as the medic quickly squeezed the entire tube of morphine into Quang, every last drop, not half as instructed. Quang's flailing began to stop, and the medic started wrapping his stumps in gauze. I looked at Binh, and he shrugged his shoulders at me.

This would be my first lesson in communication with the Vietnamese. Bridging the communication gap required more than just a translation from one language to another. The translation is only the first step, an exchange of mere words and no assurance of an exchange of ideas or understanding. Or maybe he understood and knew exactly what the full tube of morphine would do to Quang. I will admit that the thought had crossed my mind to put a .45 caliber bullet in Quang's head. But the presence of his wife quickly put an end to that idea.

I ran back to the teamhouse and called Rạch Giá for the medivac. The call went fine until I heard the question I dreaded: "Roger, is this Uniform Sierra (U.S.) or Victor November (Vietnamese) personnel, over?"

I acknowledged that Quang was a Vietnamese, but tried to push my case to the limit, "We're going to lose this one. If we don't get him out real soon, he's going to die, over." The reply was the end of my appeal: "We'll do the best we can, out."

We waited out on the helicopter pad while I chain-smoked cigarettes. The hour and a half seemed like a week. I pulled the pin on a smoke grenade and tossed it out in front of me as the chopper approached.

All was curiously quiet to me now, even the din of the chopper blades. Gone was the wailing and shrieking. The pretty yellow smoke billowed skyward, mixing with the bright blue Vietnamese morning. Arms up, I guided the ship in and watched the blades mix the yellow with the blue in a beautiful hue. Quang looked like a mummy wrapped in gauze.

The skids hit the ground as I turned to help load him on. A couple of Quang's buddies already had him and gently loaded him in the chopper. I symbolically touched the stretcher and looked up at the crew chief who was looking back at me. He knows. We all know.

South Vietnamese soldiers were expendable pawns in this war, a much misunderstood and unappreciated participant, especially by U.S. forces and those back in the States. They were under-equipped and underpaid. I know this was "their war," but this incident wouldn't have happened if I had been able to get them Claymore mines to use for night defense, instead of dangerously-rigged hand grenades.

The helicopter pilot opened up his side window. "Hey," he yelled, "is this one dead?"

"No," I said, not really knowing.

"Well, just be advised, I don't have to take dead ARVNs," he yelled back.

MARCH 24, 1969<br>Letter Home:

*Hi Dad,*
*Everything is going quite fine here. The GI's and South*

## 'Trời Ơi!... Trời Ơi!'

*Vietnamese here would like to have some prints of these dead VC and also some other pictures of themselves. If you could make me some copies that would be great. I didn't want to send them to my wife because she would only worry.*

*The other day one of our South Vietnamese troops accidentally set off a hand grenade while he was holding it. It was pretty bad because his wife was there with the little kids and of course, she was hysterical.*

*As you might have guessed, I am starting to get a little tired of the bloodshed and death. And I just found out the other day that U.S. advisors have a price on their heads... wonderful. I don't know what I'm worth in piasters but I think it's only about $100 in U.S. currency. Anyway, I don't intend to give anyone a chance to collect on me!*

*We don't leave the security of our outpost unless it is with the company on an operation or ambush.*

*Love, Bob*

It's interesting that on February 22nd I was mortified by the day's killing and of my picture-taking of the aftermath. Yet, here I was on March 31st, sending the photos home to my dad, of all people, to make copies for me to give to the soldiers – but just don't send them to my wife, because it might upset her. Really? Ya think?

And curiously, I start the letter by telling my dad everything was "fine here."

Post-Traumatic Stress Disorder begins with the occurrence of the traumatic event. The severity of the PTSD depends on the degree of trauma and the duration or time one is exposed to it and/or other traumatic events. In Vietnam, this is how it developed. In a little more than a month I had learned to "stuff it" to the back of my mind. There was an expression in the field among infantrymen: "It don't mean nothin'."

Get over it. Even the death of your best friend. It ain't nothin'. Harden yourself. This is war. Put it out of your mind.

I was already learning to stuff it quite efficiently.

MARCH 31, 1969
Diary Entry:

*Up at 0630. Went on operation with 398 to find the Vietcông seen yesterday, 40 VC near coordinates 1886.$^E$ 770 Company from Thời An came up and took a different route. We had negative contact, negative results. The 770 captured 2 VC men, 1 VC girl, and 2 weapons.*

*Chopper came in and gave us shots and I got paid.*

Today was "shot" day. The Province Senior Medical Advisor, Dr. Davis, was on board the helicopter with several other medical personnel. "Got your shot record?" Captain Davis called out from the noisy chopper, the blades still spinning.

We all pulled out our little wallet-sized cards indicating dates of previous inoculations. I held it tightly in my fingers, not wanting the wind from the whirring blades to carry it off. The medic in the chopper was on the ground now, using the floor of the helicopter as a worktable for needles and other paraphernalia. He looked at my shot record and turned around to grab some needles.

"Bend over!" he yelled.

"Right here?" I questioned, standing in the open rice paddy.

"Well, where else would you like to do it, *Sir?*" he answered sarcastically. "Come on, bend over, I don't have all day."

Vietnamese from Hóa Quản Village, particularly the women and children, were always intrigued by the arrival of any flying machine. It made their day, breaking the boredom of what was for them an uneventful rural existence. Anyone from the village who happened to be walking past the outpost when a helicopter touched down would stop to gawk at the noisy green machines. It was a magnet for the children, who loved to get close to the contraptions to feel the wind on their bodies and to play in the backwash. We were constantly yelling at them and shooing them away, concerned one might accidentally run into the tail rotor. There were plenty of spectators this day, and little did they know the show that was in store for them.

Not wanting them to see my front, I faced the chopper, undid my fatigue pants, and "mooned" the entire crowd! The medic stepped around behind me and plugged a couple of needles into my bare buttocks. One by one we all repeated this procedure, embarrassed to be standing in the middle of the open rice paddy with our pants pulled down.

The Vietnamese pointed and laughed hysterically at the antics of the crazy Americans. And of course, the children went wild. Later, over a few beers, we all had a good laugh over that one.

APRIL 1, 1969
Diary Entry:

*Dai Úy Hoa returned today from Rạch Giá. His ankle looks a lot better; it had been very badly swollen.*

*Went on night ambush at 7:30 to the south.[F] Noise and light discipline fair. Point man was smoking. Got all set up and waited. About 10:00 p.m. right flank man started shooting at VC suspect. Lucky we didn't kill him because he turned out to be a card-carrying civilian. Had to go to his house to get his ID. We let him go about 10:30 p.m.*

Anytime something unexpected happened on a night ambush, it was extremely frightening. We had been ambushing without success up near the pagoda because we knew the Vietcông were coming there occasionally at night. On this night, we decided to ambush to the south of Hóa Quản, along a strip of jungle dotted by only a few homes. It presented a very likely avenue of approach from the U-Minh Forest and it broke up our usual pattern. And this was a good spot because we didn't have to worry about anyone approaching from behind. Our Vietnamese sergeant set us up in a "straight-line ambush" along the trail.[F]

Given the intelligence reports of March 30 (eyewitness sightings of 40 VC), and coupled with the capture the previous day of three VC by the 770 Company, we knew we had movement in the area.

The trail had a slight bend to it. I was in the middle of

a line of about nine soldiers spread out along the trail, approximately four meters apart from one another. To get better concealment, I had to move back about five meters from the trail. Normally, from the middle of the ambush line, it was possible to see down the trail in both directions, but because of the bend, my vision to the right was somewhat obscured.

Everyone in the surrounding area was well aware that no one was to be traversing at night. Not on foot or by sampan. Those were the least detected ways the Vietcông moved supplies and ammunition, as well as conducted their proselytizing by entering the village and threatening those who cooperated with the Americans.

But on that night, at about 10:00 p.m., one of our soldiers on the right flank saw a figure moving up the trail from the south, heading toward the village. The soldier was supposed to let the "target" walk into the center of the kill zone, which was directly to my front in the middle of the line. We would have undoubtedly killed him at that point. Instead, surprised and jumpy, our flank guy opened up prematurely. The young man dove off the trail to the opposite side while being shot at. Soon the entire line began firing and tracer bullets followed the diving target.

I turned to my right while flicking the selector lever on my M16 to "fully automatic." Staring into the darkness, I saw no target, so I held my fire. Others to my left were promiscuously firing directly past me and to my right, shooting at nothing. Tracers whined past my left shoulder only several feet to my front. It was a good thing I had backed up a little. Their tracer bullets were grazing the ground where I'd been sitting!

When the shooting stopped, I heard loud Vietnamese commands. Soon, the same figure that had come up the trail emerged with his hands on top of his head. With all those bullets flying in his direction, he had managed to dive off the trail and get low enough to avoid being hit!

We discovered our target was a teenager from Hóa Quản who was returning home from a date. He had been visiting his girlfriend in a neighboring hamlet to the south. After escorting him to where he lived, his terrified parents vouched for him and produced his civilian ID card. It was all we had to go by, so we let him go.

The ambush was now "blown," and it was dangerous for us to be walking around the area in the dark, having announced to the world our presence. We said goodbye to the young man's grateful parents and carefully moved single file back up the trail toward the outpost.

I remember how soft-spoken and humble his parents were and how they couldn't thank us enough for not killing their son. Shaking my hand with both of his, the father repeatedly bowed in front of me saying over and over again, "*Cám ơn* (Thank you), *Cám ơn ông, Trung Úy, Cám ơn.*" He didn't know I had nothing to do with the fact that his son was still alive. Nothing whatsoever.

It was becoming apparent to me in that crazy place that skill had little to do with one's fate and perhaps luck had a lot to do with it. I was relieved that I didn't have to shoot him.

I felt lucky. He certainly was.

APRIL 2, 1969
Diary Entry:
*LTC Stanberry visited with Mr. Wilson, a civilian from Cần Thơ. Wilson told LTC to get us barbed wire. An outpost in An Xuyên Province to the south was overrun and two team members were killed - two were taken prisoner.*

I was still the assistant team leader under 1LT Darden, but he had gone to Rạch Giá to get his paperwork in order before leaving Vietnam. That made me the only officer in charge to shoulder all the responsibilities, including giving briefings to high-ranking officers and civilians. This was my first official briefing in front of LTC Stanberry and if I wanted to be promoted to team leader, I didn't want to screw it up.

I had no idea at the time, but "Mr. Wilson" had been quite a legend in the Army and was now a civilian working in Vietnam with CORDS (Civil Operations and Revolutionary Support). A former Army colonel and paratrooper, the notoriously cantankerous "Coal Bin Willie" had a "rough side," a frankness to the point of brutality, reserved for his equals and even some superiors.[5]

While questioning me during my briefing, he asked me if we needed anything. Not wanting to pass up an opportunity to get necessary items, I told him about Quang's unnecessary death and that it would be better if we could get some Claymores for night defense instead of forcing our soldiers to use booby-trapped hand grenades. I also told him of recent intelligence reports of increased enemy activity and that more barbed wire would really be appreciated. We only had one single strand of concertina barbed wire around our moat.

"Have you paralleled your counterpart's requisition for the barbed wire you need, lieutenant?" asked Wilson.

"Yes, sir," I replied. Wilson looked at Col. Stanberry, who nodded his head while writing it down.

"Make sure we get some wire out here," Wilson told Stanberry.

He followed up his order by announcing that a nearby outpost in An Xuyên Province had recently been overrun. His passive demeanor belied the chilling content of his words: "The Vietcông got inside the outpost because they hadn't put up enough wire," he said. "We don't want that happening here."

The warning shocked us. We had all been aware of outposts being overrun. Chuck Emery and I had been told about some of them at Advisor School, but until this date I'd never actually known of a specific incident. This one had just happened. "They killed two advisors," he said, "and took two prisoners."

Mr. Wilson was rightfully concerned about all the MAT teams, especially outposts like ours that didn't look well fortified.

APRIL 5, 1969<br>Diary Entry:

*Up at 0400. Still dark. Went north and ran into a hysterical woman who was coming down the canal in a sampan, looking for help. She said some soldiers took her son this morning. I told* her no one from this company would take her son, and then I figured out the soldiers she spoke of had to be VC. We searched a likely VC house and then I moved out with PF platoon leader to the head of column. Went looking for boy. Didn't find him.<sup>G</sup>

A particularly frustrating day. The 398 Company received intelligence that some Vietcông had been spotted in the free fire zone to the north. To catch them by surprise, we headed along the bank of the canal to the northernmost edge of the village. As we got there, a woman came toward us in a sampan. She hastily pulled over at the sight of us, waving her arms frantically, and came straight for me, chattering away in Vietnamese.<sup>G</sup>

She had seen me in the village practicing my Vietnamese language skills and assumed I was able to understand her rapid-fire chatter. She kept repeating that soldiers had taken her son, kidnapped him. I assured her our soldiers wouldn't do that. The recruitment of locals for the PF and RF militia didn't include kidnapping. I finally ascertained it wasn't our soldiers she was referring to at all, but rather Vietcông soldiers who had "drafted" her son within the last hour, taking him against his will!

The PF platoon leader offered to search further north into the free fire zone and wanted to know if I was coming along.

"Let's go!" I told him.

We joined the lead element of the PFs, moving quickly but cautiously along the canal. In the back of my mind I remembered Major Bonner's decision to "not go off half-cocked." We had to be careful in the event this was some kind of trap, a prearranged ambush. But I was caught up in the moment, determined to find the boy.

We came upon an abandoned house, uninhabitable because of the frequent, unannounced strafing and bombings in this free-fire zone. We searched inside the house and found nothing. I looked around to find myself with the point man, leading a handful of men along with my counterpart in the dense five-o'clock fog. It was a very dangerous place to be at any hour. The PF leader and myself and a handful of PFs pushed on, looking fruitlessly for any signs of anything, anyone. There was nothing. The boy was gone and the VC had him.

### APRIL 6, 1969
### Diary Entry:

*Went on operation with 770 and 398 to map coordinates WR180827.[H] Negative contact. On the way back, 770 picked up another female Vietcông suspect. Threw her in the canal and gave her a "shower" - she sang like a bird.*

Today was Sgt. Hogan's third day on the team, having arrived as Ponce's replacement on April 3. He was eager for action right from the start and wanted go on as many operations as he could. He and I thought alike. Going out on operations was better than hanging around the stifling, sweltering outpost. And besides, it made the time go faster.

Today Hogan witnessed his first water boarding, the torture of a female VC suspect. I realized this was an interrogation technique our South Vietnamese counterparts did regularly.

In those early days at Hóa Quản, I told him of the things I had already seen and been through to bring him up to speed. With my impending promotion to team leader, Hogan was my first "new guy," and I didn't want anything to happen to him or any of my men.

### APRIL 12, 1969
### Diary Entry:

*Morning operation to coordinates WR210785. Negative contact. Returned early.*

*One of the corporals from Phảo Binh bought a dog and brought it back to the compound. I took about 40 pictures of that dog being cut up and prepared. First, they killed it with a knife, then skinned it and cleaned it. The Vietnamese cut up everything they eat into little tiny pieces. They stuffed the intestines, made sausages out of it, the works.*

Every day in the field was a new experience. On this particular morning, Trung Úy Kanh waited for me to return from our patrol and flagged me down as I was entering the outpost. He invited me and the other advisors to a party he was having later. I told him I would come.

I then looked for someone else on the team to accompany me. Darden's reaction was predictable. "No way, man."

"What about it, Sarge?" I questioned Hogan, who put his head down while starting to laugh and shake his head. He suspected something funky on the menu. Now I was the "Old Maid," and the rest of the guys knew I was stuck.

Later, Ha Sí Chi returned from the village with something kicking around inside of a burlap sack he had over his shoulder. Hogan and I watched as he presented his purchase to Trung Úy Kanh for approval. My hopes for a chicken vanished as I saw them pull out a dog.

"A dog!" yelled Hogan back at the teamhouse. "Christ, they're going to eat a dog."

Making things more pitiful, the poor shaking creature had a bad case of mange; some of its hair had fallen out.

I remember Kanh telling me that his family had originally emigrated to the South from the Hanoi area. I had heard that North Vietnamese eat dog as a delicacy. It should have come as no surprise to me his choice of entrée. I couldn't believe what I was seeing and ran inside the teamhouse for my camera.

They wasted no time hanging the poor condemned mongrel upside down by the legs and slitting its throat. They used a container to catch the raw blood pouring from the poor canine and took turns passing around a canteen cup to sip the warm blood. Suyen yelled over to me as he held up the cup in my direction. They knew I was watching.

"Trung Úy," Suyen hollered over, "make you brave like VC if you drink the blood." Shaking my head, I yelled back, "*Không, cám ơn* (No, thank you)." Accepting my initial rejection, Chi still made it clear he expected to see me later: "*Latnua,*" he said, pointing to the now limp mongrel, "*Ngon lam* (very delicious)."

I attended the banquet much to the ribbing of the other guys on the team. "*Ngon lam, ngon lam,*" Hogan ribbed.

"You're really going over there?" Darden questioned.

"Yeah," I gave it back to him, "I'm hungry. Hey, I'll save you some leftovers."

"No fucking way," he fired back. I got cleaned up, put on fresh clothes, and walked over to the banquet.

I arrived with warm beer and a bottle of Four Roses. I washed everything down with beer and shots of Four Roses, picking through the steamed rice and vegetables and trying to leave the dog meat behind. I photographed everything from the gourmet preparation to the four-star presentation.

In bed that night, I pondered if I was living among barbarians. Was I becoming one?

APRIL 26, 1969
Diary Entry:

*Lt. Darden departed today for the U.S. That leaves me as Senior Advisor of the team. I feel like I just had a ton of weight dumped on my shoulders and nobody to help.*

Letter Home:

*Hi Everyone,*

*I haven't written in a long time. Been kind of busy. My team leader rotated back to the states and they've given me the job. It's an infantry Captain's job, but I welcome the managerial experience and responsibility. Besides, the busier I am the faster the time goes.*

*Enclosed is a polaroid shot of me with the PSDF, the Peoples' Self Defense Force from Hóa Quản. The village to date has 1327 people as compared to about 500 when it was classified 100% VC last November. When we pushed the VC out, people started moving back in.*

*From left to right, Our interpreter Binh, Đại Úy (Captain) Hoa, Trung Úy Amon, our Village Chief, the RD Cadre Leader and our 3 hamlet chiefs. We have about 60 of the PSDF trained now. I know some of them are probably VC but what are you gonna do? Got to go.*

*Bob*

Left to right: Lt. Amon, the village chief, RD Cadre Leader and three hamlet chiefs. The men in the background are the PSDF recruits.

MAY 1, 1969
Diary Entry:

*This night the RD Cadre team (Team 17) in the village was attacked by estimated 100 VC. The VC fired a B-40 rocket at the RD Headquarters and it detonated on a coconut tree across the canal at WR210849 and completely severed the tree at the stump. The VC also fired two 60 mm mortars and AK-47s from across canal. RD Cadre held them to the other side of the canal. No KIAs or WIAs. The RD Cadre here do an excellent job.*[1]

Letter Home (Several Days Later):

*Dear Family,*

*I have really been enjoying these Care Packages, Dad. Thanks! A couple of nights ago 100 VC hit the village about 400 meters north. But the tracers flew into the berm in our outpost so we thought we were under attack. The thing that really scared us was that we had intelligence of 2 VC Battalions (about 800) close by. We only have about 80 in our outpost. Let me tell you about this attack.*

*I got in the bunker first and had to run out to get the*

radio. Sgt. Hogan was running in and knocked me flat on my back. By this time tracers are flying all over the place. I finally got the radio and jammed my M16 in the firing port and started spraying. But Sgt. Guerrero grabs the M-60 machine gun and jams it into the port and opened up with it. Hot brass was flying everywhere.

I got on the radio and called in the attack and we must have had every American in the Delta clearing the net so we could get through. When I finished calling, Guerrero was out on the perimeter with the M-60, blasting away at the woodline, so I went out there with him and threw 4 illumination flares out there. My college ring flew off my hand when I was throwing the hand flares and now, I have a 2-inch gash on my foot. How it got there I have no idea.

I found my college ring the next morning about 20' on the other side of the berm!

Thanks again for the Care Packages. Kind of expensive, no? But I won't complain if you send more.

Love, Bob

MAY 2, 1969
Diary Entry:

Had combined operation north to WR 205865 with 398 Company and PFs. The battalion got intelligence of 5 VC still there. Company moved out with Guerrero and myself by sampan. PFs led the way and rounded up 5 VC suspects: 2 men, 1 boy and 2 women.[J]

The company First Sergeant beat the boy and then threw him and his brother in the water and held them under. The boy said his brother had a VC rifle so he gave them a "shower" again. Took them back and tied them up outside on the ground with a guard.

The operation was a quickly-assembled "raid operation" to map coordinates WR205865, north of the village again, and into the free-fire zone.[J] It was the same area we were in the other day, looking for the kidnapped boy. It was a twisted landscape punctuated with bomb craters and strafed-out hootches and bunkers. It was the approved dump in our area for any B-52s returning from the U-Minh Forest that needed to drop leftover bombs from a bombing run.

It was a dangerous place to be in again. This was the location mentioned in the intelligence reports of 1000 Vietcông. Worse, it was dangerous because at any time, without approval or prior warning, bombs or napalm could be dropped there. Gunships looking for target practice could work the area too, never expecting friendlies to be on the ground. If we had been spotted from the air, we would have been mistaken for the enemy and shot by "friendly fire." Free-fire zones were off-limits to everyone at any hour, and for that reason, the VC never expected us to go in there after them. And that's why we did.

The raid on that day was also effective because we were immediately reacting to fresh information only hours old. Someone from the village informed the Trung Úy that the VC who attacked the RD Cadre last night were still up there. The boldness of the company to move into the free-fire zone after them, coupled with our late afternoon surprise arrival by sampan, allowed us to catch the Vietcông off-guard.

We disembarked the sampans a reasonable distance away from the Vietcong sightings and sent in a handful of PFs who were not wearing their uniforms. Dressed in their normal everyday peasant attire, they were able to walk right up to the VC in their camp and take them by surprise at gunpoint! The rest of us quickly moved into the encampment and rounded up all five of them without firing a shot!

The company immediately led them to a bomb crater filled with water. The crater, approximately fifty to sixty feet in diameter, was created as a result of the explosion of either a five-hundred or one-thousand-pound bomb. The size of the bomb craters in the muddy Delta varied, depending on the size of the bomb and the season in which the bomb was dropped. The watery pond of the crater was perfect for what the company first sergeant had in mind - one of his "showers."

I'll never forget one of the prisoners. He was a young man in his early twenties with a "withered" left arm and a slight touch of the same deformity in his left leg: polio, I guessed. But as small as his left arm was, his right arm was twice as big as it should be. Almost lobster-like, his entire right shoulder and right bicep were muscular and overdeveloped from single-handedly working in a rice paddy all his life. He looked menacing with that physique, like someone hard to size up. And he was unafraid. The boy with him was his brother. The boy was no older than ten or eleven, and I felt sorry for him, as he was obviously very frightened.

The company first sergeant immediately went to work and had them all bound at the elbows. Tying them at the elbows rather than the wrists, the way an American would do, was done for a specific reason. By lifting up on the rope attached to the elbows, he forced his victims to bend forward. Then, bringing his foot around in front, he could trip them face-first into the muddy water. He used the elbow ropes to pull them out of the water. If he didn't hear the answer he was looking for, he'd push them under again, kneeling into the small of the back while lifting on the rope. This process, gone far enough, causes shoulder separation and excruciating pain. An expert such as the first sergeant could bring it to the threshold, then back off, causing them to experience the pain of a shoulder separation over and over again.

I couldn't understand what the first sergeant was saying but I knew he meant business by the tone of his voice. He left the women alone, choosing instead to work on the man. When this didn't succeed, he went for the boy, dragging him into the mud of the bomb crater. He slapped, punched, and shoved the young boy under. Open handed slaps turned into crashing blows to the side of his left cheek bone with a closed fist.

"*Nói gì, mau, nói gì, mau* (talk)," he yelled. The size difference and the brutal way he tortured the boy made me dislike the first sergeant immensely.

After several minutes of that, I couldn't take it anymore and knew I had to intervene. I had no way of knowing if any of them were Vietcông or not, but I didn't want the brutality on the little boy to continue.

Besides, I was carrying a Geneva Convention Card for a reason. As an officer, I was expected to adhere to a Code of Conduct which specifically prohibited torturing prisoners. I remembered I could get in a lot of trouble for just being there and condoning it.

"Okay Binh, this has to stop," I quietly said with eyebrows raised, glaring at my trusted interpreter. But Binh immediately cut me short. He insisted that the sergeant knew what he was doing.

"Trung Úy, I think they VC!" Binh said. It was his opinion, his language, his knowledge, his experience, and his country. What did I know?

I'm sure the first sergeant didn't know of or care about the Geneva Convention. Besides, the company which is roughest on the VC is usually the one that takes the least casualties. And everyone wants to survive. So, the VC got a shower, including the boy.

After several more minutes, the badly beaten young boy admitted that his older brother owned a rifle and worked for the Vietcông. And the elder brother with the withered arm, the unwilling spectator, wanted it to end too, so he confirmed it.

I wasn't surprised. I had been waterboarded at Fort Sherman in the Panama Canal Zone during Jungle Training School in the Fall of 1968, so I personally knew how effective that form of torture could be.

Back at the outpost, my soldiers still had the prisoners tied at the elbows. They were squatting in a row in the dust on the other side of the mud berm. We went back to the teamhouse to wait for a chopper to take them to Rạch Giá for more questioning.

Before the helicopter arrived, I needed something that was stored in our 8'x8' steel Conex container out by the berm. That required passing our prisoners to get there. I remember psyching myself up to walk past the Vietcông to get to the container out by the helipad. I walked past the machine gun emplacement, out the front gate, and past the five of them. The squatting figures looked like little muddy ducks, the film of muck now drying and caking on their clothes, skin and in their hair.

I glanced up at the row of them, and sure enough all were watching me. All but one took their eyes off mine as I looked into theirs, including the boy who had welts and red marks all over him. One solitary pair of eyes stared into my eyes and held the stare.

It was the older brother, the one with the withered arm. My gaze went to the overdeveloped right arm again and returned to find his eyes still riveted to mine, glaring into my soul. The look of intense hatred on his battered face is something I will never forget. His beloved younger brother was at his side, and his stare blamed me for the condition of the boy. "We're torturing kids to get information now," I thought. "What a great way to win hearts and minds."

What would he do to me if the situation was reversed? What would he do if he managed to return to Hóa Quản to even the score? My eyes left his stare and I had to look down.

As I walked away, his laser-like stare singed a hole through the back of my skull and a chill went down my spine. That night, thinking of the day's events, there would be no sleep for me again in Hóa Quản Village.

MAY 4, 1969
Intelligence Report

The following page shows the intelligence report we received as a follow-up to Friday afternoon's capturing of the Vietcông POWs. One of the captured women was Mrs. Huynh Thi Dat, 47, head of the Vietcông Communist Party of Thoi An Village. The man with the withered arm was Hai Thep, Secretary of the Party. Both admitted consorting with the local Vietcông "C.4 Company" (about 70 men), which was part of the notorious U-Minh 10 Battalion (about 300-400 VC) from the infamous U-Minh Forest to our south.

'Trời Ơi!... Trời Ơi!'

Both individuals were actively planning to overrun and annihilate the 770 Company outpost ("OP" in the report) in Thoi An and probably us as well, or at least "pin us down." It appears the U-Minh 10 Battalion had it in for Thoi An and Hóa Quản because we caused them "trouble" in reorganizing the "VCI" (Vietcông Infrastructure) in their area. The following report got our undivided attention.

```
                         CONFIDENTIAL
                       INTELLIGENCE REPORT

FM:  US S-2

Date of Information:  031000H May 1969

Date of Report:  04 May 1969

Exploiting the statement of POW Mrs. Huynh Thi Dat, 47 years old, Chief of Thoi
An Village Executive Committee, Kien Binh, Kien Giang notified that she has
attended a village Party Chapter meeting at Thoi An on 2 May 1969. Mr. Hai
Thep, Thoi An Village Party Chapter Secretary Disclosed that:

    1.  Chau Thanh B LF Co has a responsibility to stay close to the Hoa Quan
        OP, WR 214 841 to observe behavior of OP and to pin down the occupation
        forces.

    2.  The entire Thoi An Village Party Chapter coordinated with C.4 company
        of the U/Minh 10 BN to attack and annihilate Thoi An OP, WR 203 810.
        She added that this plan will be applied within June 1969 but no dates
        or time were known.

Sector intelligent S-2 comments: Many reports indicate the enemy is studying
and surveying the two OPs concerned because these two OPs are in the corridor
which cause trouble in reorganizing VCI as well as controlling the population in
this area.

DISTRIBUTION:
OSA----------1
PRU----------1
PSA----------1
JTAD---------1                GROUP 4
RDC/O--------1                DOWNGRADE AT 3 YEAR INTERVALS;
NPFF---------1                DECLASSIFIED AFTER 12 YEARS
NILO---------1                DOD DIR 5200.10
PHOENIX------1
FILE---------2

                         CONFIDENTIAL
```

MAY 5, 1969
Diary Entry:
*Had another sector operation to WRI93833 with 398 and 770 Companies. No contact or results.*

On that morning, Hogan and I set out for WR193833 with my Vietnamese counterpart and the 398 Company. Having made no contact with the VC, we headed back to Hóa Quản and took a shaded break at the "lemonade stand" in the heart of the village.

I watched the Cambodian woman who ran the stand prepare the drinks and hand them to her smiling daughter, who carried the drinks to our table. Chuẫn Úy Khome pointed to the family and said, "*Cambot,*" the Vietnamese word for "Cambodian."

I nodded, "*Hóa Quản có nhiéu Cambot*" (Hóa Quản has many Cambodians). In fact, Hóa Quản Village was comprised mostly of Cambodian (Khmer) descendants, people who had migrated south to the fertile lands in the Delta. There was no love lost between the Cambodians and the Vietnamese. Khmers referred to the Vietnamese as "*yuon,*" a derogatory term meaning "barbarians," while the Vietnamese looked down on the Cambodians as being lazy for not farming every available patch of rice paddy, a necessity in the more densely populated Vietnam.[6]

"*Cambot,*" Khome continued, "*xàu lám* (very bad)." I didn't like what I was hearing, and had to ask, "*Tai sao?*" I wanted to know why he felt that way. With his right index finger, he stroked the back of his left hand, "*Cambot xàu lám,*" he repeated, an obvious reference to the darker, mocha color of their skin.

Sitting next to me, Staff Sergeant Hogan, an African-American, looked down at the Chuẫn Úy's hand and understood full well what he was saying. And as if what the arrogant Khome said wasn't bad enough, he had the hubris to make his racist remark in front of Hogan.

Embarrassed, I instantly despised Khome and couldn't believe his audacity. Did Khome expect no reaction from either one of us, as if this kind of intolerance was a fact of life among American advisors as it was within his own, narrow-minded society?

"Hogan," I said, "I'm sorry, I don't know what to say."

Hogan looked down at the table with a smirk on his face, shaking his head, "Shit, if he doesn't like them because of their skin color, I can just imagine what he thinks of me!"

"Screw him," I said, "it doesn't matter what he thinks, he's an ignorant little jerk."

"It's okay, sir," Hogan smiled, "it ain't nothin' new to us brothers. I'm used to it."

"Hogan…" I reiterated, shaking my head.

"It's okay," he said, cutting me off. "It's not your fault, LT."

"Come on," I said, "let's go back to the outpost. This conversation is over and I'm not sitting here anymore with this little asshole." We picked up our gear and walked back to the outpost, leaving Chuẫn Úy Khome sitting at the table by himself.

Walking back, I realized the depth of Khome's dislike for the Cambodian civilians in Hóa Quản because of their Khmer heritage and skin color. And what did he think of his commander, Colonel Stanberry's counterpart, Colonel Tài, who was half Cambodian? And his disrespect for the very advisors who were here to help him!

How good would relations be between the village and the soldiers with this much racism getting in the way? Hogan and I talked about it on the way back.

"The Cambodian 168 Company was probably a better company for this village, LT," Hogan said.

"I'll tell you what, Sarge," I replied. "The 168 was a better company, period."

On patrol with counterpart Chuan Uy Khome and the 398 Company.

Taking a break at the lemonade stand
with the racist Chuan Uy Khome.

MAY 15, 1969
Diary Entry:
*It is starting to rain more frequently and heavily now. Hogan and I rigged up some tin and hooked it to the eve of our house to catch the rain water.*

MAY 15, 1969
Letter Home:
*Dear Family,*
*Well, we're really in the rainy season now. There's water inside the outpost and it's like a lake all around our teamhouse. Even the bunker has water in it. We're using sandbags to elevate the floor above water level.*

*Just got intelligence of a VC Battalion about 4 kilometers to the north. Our ARVNs fired 5 rounds of 4.2" mortars at them but one got hung up in the tube and they had to wait until it cooled off. This mortar is best for firing parachute flares at night. They light up the perimeter like daylight.*

*Love, Bob*

The rain on this day started early and became quite heavy. Hogan helped me cut a strip of roofing tin to fashion a gutter, which we attached along the edge of our roof. We put a slight pitch to it so it would deposit the precious rain into a 55-gallon drum. This was going to take the place of carrying water buckets from the watering hole and eliminate the use of the alum and bleach. By the time we were done we were soaking wet anyway, so we took off everything but our shorts.

As we passed a bar of soap back and forth, the cool breeze and the sparkling, clear rain seemed to rinse away the past four months, rinse away my own stench from weeks on end without a real shower, and rinse away all those stifling operations under the relentless sun. We were having fun.

Showering in the rain helped melt away, at least for now, some of the memories of the things I had already witnessed, the stench of what I had condoned and so far, participated in.

We were the only ones standing in the downpour. The

soldiers' families squatted in their huts, peering out of their open doorways, pointing and laughing at the two crazy Americans bathing in the thunder and lightning. But I haven't had a shower since that was quite as refreshing.

MAY 23, 1969<br>Diary Entry:

*Today I went with SSgt Parson and Dai Úy Hoa to inspect two outposts of the 338 Company in Co' Khiá and Duóng Xuông hamlets. Later in the morning we had a visit from Major General Ekhardt and I gave him a briefing.*

*2315 hours - grenade incident in village, it was the father of the newly elected assistant hamlet chief.*

Another long, trying day. Parson and I were out at the crack of dawn on a sampan trip with Dai Úy Hoa to the two new outposts to the north and west. Upon returning, we no sooner entered the teamhouse when a call came in that LTC Stanberry was in route with "Fuzzy Empire 68" for another briefing. But who the heck was "Fuzzy Empire?"

We all scurried to give our messy teamhouse a quick cleanup. Within minutes, a chopper was circling, and I ran out to the helipad to pop smoke. I guided the helicopter in, and out jumped LTC Stanberry with a two-star general and a rather large entourage.

"Lead the way, lieutenant," screamed Stanberry, pointing to the outpost. So off I went, like the Pied Piper, the entire entourage in pursuit.

"Fuzzy Empire 68" was Major General Ekhardt, the commanding general of the entire IV Corps Theatre in the Mekong Delta! This unannounced visit was only my second briefing. I wondered why he was here. What was so important about visiting our little outpost?

I remember the general frequently interrupting, firing questions before I could even finish sentences. He wanted specifics about what we were doing and what my plans were. I gave him the best answers I could and then told him about the 3 VC

'Trời Ơi!... Trời Ơi!'

we killed, about the 5 captured prisoners, about the free elections and the numbers of civilians moving back in. We were "winning hearts and minds!" Hóa Quản was a success story, and I wanted him to know it!

He stood up before I had a chance to finish and I barely had time for a salute before they were out the door. As they walked to the helipad, General Ekhardt was side-by-side with Stanberry, gesturing in the air and pointing here and there. The briefing was more demanding than briefing "Coal Bin Willie" Wilson. I still wondered why all the interest in Hóa Quản, but it was a relief to see the party take off.

Late that afternoon we all kicked off our boots, opened up some warm Carling Black Label and played cards. We turned in about 10 p.m., hoping for a good night's sleep. We had a big operation in the morning, and we were going to have another busy day.

No sooner had we dozed off than the sound of an explosion woke everyone in the outpost. It came from the north, in the center of the village. Out of bed and pulling on my fatigues, I was out the door in a flash and headed for the Dai Úy's hootch. Dai Úy Hoa had already dispatched two squads of infantry up through Hóa Quản on the dangerous mission of determining the cause of the explosion.

A few days before the March 2 elections in Hóa Quản Village, one of the young men running for the office of hamlet chief in Co' Khiá was given a message by the Vietcông: withdraw your name from the ballot or harm will come to your family! They didn't like the fact that he was helping us build another outpost in Co' Khiá Hamlet.

Undeterred, he defiantly ran for office anyway, and I celebrated with him in the village on March 2 after he had won! He completed the outpost, and Co' Khiá began to flourish again with returning refugees.

Their marketplace grew as a spin-off of our successful, entrepreneurial market in the center of Hóa Quản. And because of the threat of harm from the Vietcông, he had moved his family to the center of Hóa Quản and had them sleeping in the nipa-palm home of a friend.

But enraged by the hamlet chief's progress and after waiting nearly three months to exact revenge, the Vietcông managed to sneak into the heart of the village on this night to carry out their threat. Along the wall of the house in which the family slept, an enemy soldier stealthily reached through the nipa-leaf exterior and placed a hand grenade under the bed of the sleeping hamlet chief's father. The explosion blew the poor old man out of bed. The force of the explosion broke one of his arms and showered his back with metal shrapnel.

It was midnight at the edge of the village. I crouched with Dai Úy Hoa and "Doc" Parson in the dark, watching our soldiers clumsily moving toward us carrying a lantern to guide the stretcher.

Parson worked on the poor old man while I pleaded for a medivac on the radio. Again, everything in Vietnam had priorities. Medivacs for ARVN soldiers were slow in coming, medivacs for Vietnamese civilians were nonexistent.

But tonight, I was lucky. It was Sgt. Setkusky's voice on the radio again, and I convinced him to bend the rules one more time. And as before, he dispatched a medivac for me!

By 2 a.m., Parson and I were huddled in a group at the helipad, staying low in the dark with the lantern out so as not to attract unwanted attention. Remnants of the VC band that had planted the grenade might still be around looking for more fun.

When the chopper finally approached, the pilot had me wave a flashlight at him. And then, as I stood up, he turned on a bright headlight located under the belly of the ship, completely illuminating me!

With my arms outstretched and looking up, completely night-blinded and shirtless, I guided the ship in, aware of what an unbelievable target I now presented. I felt naked, helpless, almost suicidal. I was living proof to anyone watching that the Vietcông had left for the evening because if they hadn't, this was their opportunity to shoot me.

When it was over, the hamlet chief couldn't thank us enough. I even let him jump on board to accompany his 65-year-old dad.

When Parson and I finally turned in for the night, we felt good. We thought we had saved his life. Days later we received word of the old man's death. He succumbed to the shrapnel wounds in his back.

## CHAPTER FIVE

# To Hell in a Handbasket

MAY 26, 1969
Diary Entry:
*SFC Guerrero departed for the U.S.*

Guerrero's departure marked the end of my opportunity to learn from the experienced guys. The seasoned guys on the team were all gone now. I couldn't believe that we had lost all the experienced ones so quickly. First Ponce, then Darden, now Guerrero.

In their place would come the new guys like Hogan, Lloyd and Winters. They'd be looking to me to teach them, relying on my experience and guidance. What experience? I was still new here myself, the new guy only a couple of months ago.

Do the best you can, lieutenant. Their lives depend on your decisions. Rely on what you already know and be confident you'll make the right choices.

It was at that point in my tour of duty that I decided to go out on almost all of the daytime operations and night ambushes. At least until the new guys learned.

Those ops usually required only two of the five of us and it was customary to rotate. Share the danger and rotate. But I felt I still needed more experience. And besides, it was better for me to be exposed to the danger than one of my new guys. A way to learn more while keeping the newer ones under my wing, just as Major Bonner had done for me. Just as Guerrero had done when I first arrived on the team.

MAY 30, 1969
Diary Entry:

*Temporary cease fire. Received SFC McFadden. Also received "grease guns" from Lt. Cousin for the PSDF (Peoples Self Defense Force).*

We knew the temporary cease fire had something to do with the Paris peace talks, but in the field, we had no idea of the politics involved. For us, it was a temporary reprieve from daytime patrols and night ambushes. To the enemy, an unbelievable gift: a time for uninterrupted re-supply, a time to transport wounded, a time for plan-making and rejuvenation. The idea seemed asinine to us, but we welcomed it.

The M3 "grease guns" brought in by Lt. Cousin to arm the 90-man PSDF (People's Self-Defense Force) we had trained from the village were outdated WWII submachine guns formerly carried by paratroopers and tankers in that war. It was aptly named for its resemblance to an automobile mechanic's lubrication gun. It had a long, straight ammunition clip protruding from the bottom, which doubled as a hand grip, and it fired standard .45 caliber ball ammunition.

Hogan and I loaded one up and tried it out and decided that Annie Oakley herself couldn't have hit the broad side of a barn with it even from inside the barn! If we had to dispense weapons to the men in the village, we decided that weapon was perfect for the PSDF. Beyond a range of 25 meters it was useless, which meant that it would serve the purpose for close-in defense of the village and nothing more.

JUNE 3, 1969
Diary Entry:

*Today we held a big MEDCAP in village. 400 people turned out. Lt. Winters arrived by chopper as my new assistant team leader.*

The 5-man team was back up to full strength with the arrival of my new assistant team leader: 2LT Bob Winters. For the next six months, Bob proved to be a loyal and valuable asset to me in the leadership of MAT 88. I got lucky with Winters and with the addition of SSGT McFadden (Mac), who had arrived on May 30. The team was now complete again, consisting of myself, LT Winters, and Sergeants Hogan (heavy weapons NCO), McFadden (light weapons NCO) and Parson (medic).

Parson and I headed out to the first MEDCAP we had organized in Hóa Quản. MEDCAP was an acronym for Medical "Combined Action" Program, a combined action of American and Vietnamese medical personnel to provide free medical care to the village. Priority for the funding of medical supplies to the Vietnamese was extremely low in Vietnam. But our competent medic, "Doc" Parson, had been requisitioning, hoarding, and "scrounging" extra medical supplies "for team use" for months in preparation. And what a pile he had! We even had candy for the children, thanks to one of the "care packages" my dad had sent me!

The MEDCAP wasn't only for our village; we welcomed anyone from anywhere. No questions were asked, no ID Cards required, just good will.

That made good sense to me. Were some of these people communist Vietcong or VC sympathizers? Perhaps, but part of our mission was to win the "hearts and minds," just like Chuck Emery and I had discussed in Advisor School. And now I was actually implementing it.

The word had been out for weeks about the upcoming free medicine and the presence of a *bác-sĩ* (doctor) at the pagoda.

Dai Úy Hoa was concerned about security. He felt the Vietcông would try something to disrupt our act of good will, and he ordered our prejudiced little friend, Chuẩn Úy Khome, to sweep the pagoda area early that morning. He also assigned "bodyguards" to us during the event to watch our backs. With the help of the monks, we set up tables outside the pagoda. People were already amassed before we arrived.

Sergeant Parson directed a line to be formed, parading first past our Vietnamese company medic, then Binh, who could interpret the symptoms, and finally Parson. It was Parson's show

Outside the pagoda at the MEDCAP with bodyguards – June, 1969.

Civilians on line waiting for medical evaluation by our Vietnamese medic.

and I stayed out of his way, content to observe overall and be aware of the surroundings.

An estimated 400 Vietnamese, the largest turnout ever, made the journey to Hóa Quản that day for free medical examinations and treatment. The word had spread so far that people came from remote hamlets as far away as a half-day's journey by foot. Families arriving by sampan found parking to be a problem out in front of the pagoda and had to settle for a parking spot further downstream.

Many young mothers stood on the long line and patiently waited to stand in front of Binh with infants planted at their hips. The worm-infested, bloated bellies of their *em* (children) explained why they had come, but they also sought help with everything from toothaches to infections that wouldn't heal.

Hóa Quản itself was considered remote, but Binh noted that farmers were arriving from hamlets so far removed from civilization that they had no schools. He estimated their vocabulary to consist of approximately 300-400 words. They referred to helicopters, for example, as *"mai bai whop-whop,"* a translation so simplified by lack of vocabulary that it literally means "a flying machine that makes the sound *whop-whop*." They didn't know the Vietnamese word for helicopter. Some had never even seen a Caucasian, African-American, or anyone other than Cambodian and Vietnamese descent; hence the stares we advisors were receiving. Parson was probably the first black man most of them had ever seen.

Many elderly people had been transported to Hóa Quản as well. Unlike the "worm pills" Parson was able to dispense to the little ones, there wasn't much he could do for the arthritis, osteoporosis, and psoriasis cases we encountered. Growing old in such poverty in Vietnam was unpleasant at best. Parson handed out free samples of Bayer aspirin, bars of soap, shampoo and various skin cremes. Most of the mothers asked specifically for soap for their *em*, and candy: "*Xàbông* (soap), *Bác-Sí, xin xàbông?*" and, "*Xin, keo* (please, candy)?"

Looking down the line, I spotted a figure wrapped in

cloth being escorted by family members. The person immediately caught my attention in the pushy morning heat. Why would anyone want to be wrapped up in this manner, knowing that by noon it would be stiflingly hot? As the person moved closer to Binh, and the family began unwrapping the rags, I could see that it was a woman. Her face had been wrapped in rags.

"Sarge," I said, trying inconspicuously to get Parson's attention, "you're not gonna believe the poor woman coming up next."

Parson casually glanced at her and then, looking down, replied, "I think it's leprosy, Lieutenant." Binh looked up at the woman and looked back at me, his eyes wide, "See, Trung Úy? I told you! People coming from everywhere!"

Lepers date back to antiquity, and still, by 1969, not much was known about the hideous disease. The worst leprosy cases in 1969 were ostracized in Southeast Asia to leper colonies, or forced to leave the village for a life of solitude in remote, unfarmable, mosquito-infested mangrove swamps far from habitable areas.

The village turned eerily quiet as the poor woman stood directly in front of us. Her family continued unwrapping the filthy rags around her face. They took care to unwrap and display as little as possible to the rest of the village population, who were keeping their distance and staring, mumbling quietly among themselves. Her family stood on both sides of her to help block the view, and slowly, silently, they revealed to us the wretched horror that poor woman endured.

Her face was lumpy and covered with open sores. I will never forget how painful she was to look at. Raised, inflamed lesions with red outlines covered her face, neck and arms. The leper was no more than three feet in front of our table. I selfishly thought about our safety.

"How contagious is this, Sarge?" I asked.

"Certain types are highly contagious," Parson explained. "I don't know for sure if this is one of them." No one but us and family members dared even get close to the poor woman.

Parson gave her dapsone tablets and told the family to come to the outpost if she ran out. Dapsone, a sulfone drug, can produce undesirable side effects, and by 1980 health officials observed a world-wide resistance to dapsone. But in 1969 it was all we had to help her. We kept a supply of dapsone on hand at all times, referenced again in our requisition for more of the same in my diary entry of November 14th.

The woman's family couldn't seem to thank Parson enough, bowing over and over as they rendered their appreciation: "*Cám ón, Bác-Sí* (doctor), *Cám ón* (Thank you)."

Wrapped once again in the stifling rags, she turned to leave in the oppressive morning heat. The crowd parted and kept their distance as the pitiful woman was escorted back to the family's sampan.

Further on down the line was a middle-aged woman whose lower face was also wrapped in rags. As she drew near, I noticed her lower jaw was three times the size it should normally be. Friends helped her remove the rags as she approached our front. She had herbs packed underneath her immense jaw, held in place by the filthy gauze looped over the top of her head.

Elephantiasis is a condition associated with the infectious disease known in Southeast Asia as *Brugia malayi*. It is transmitted to humans and animals by mosquitoes which breed along streams and canals. In its worst human forms in Asia, it causes painful swelling brought about by nodules underneath the skin, characteristically in the head region. The lymph nodes are grossly enlarged which produces the "elephant man" look. Adult worms can sometimes be seen beneath the skin, and if left untreated will cause blindness and death.[7] As was common in Vietnam, she had been using herbs and locally grown natural remedies, hoping it was just an infection.

"What can you treat this with, Doc?" I questioned.

"I can't. She's got to go to Rạch Giá, probably Cần Thơ." Binh explained to the woman that the elephantiasis could be treated, or at least brought under control, but she had to go to either of those cities. She agreed to go, and we gave her extra soap and personal health-care items such as shampoo, band-aids, Merthiolate, Q-Tips, and a clean roll of gauze.

We worked through the noon hour, never stopping for a C-rations break, and the crowd began to diminish toward mid-afternoon. At about 3 p.m., a man appeared with a cute little boy at his side, both emerging barefooted from the rice paddy. The youngster's arm was bandaged and supported by a sling. I estimated the boy to be only ten years old. His father was obviously a very poor rice farmer, and he explained shyly that they had walked to Hóa Quản from a long distance, not owning a sampan. The man appeared to be apprehensive and untrusting, alternately staring at both myself and Parson. He said his son had a bad "infection" in his arm.

The little boy was in considerable pain as our Vietnamese medic helped un-dress the wound. Upon examination, the boy's arm was infected to the point of gangrene. The infected arm was swollen and discolored, and foul-smelling. Parson explained to Binh that we had antibiotics to give him now, but that he must take the boy to the hospital at Cần Thơ, perhaps Saigon.

"Sarge," I said to Parson, "he can die from this, right?"

"Absolutely, LT. I think the arm has to be amputated. I'm not sure, but it looks pretty far gone to be saved. The surgeons in Cần Thơ will be able to determine that. But if we don't get him there it will eventually kill him."

By now, the father was nervous and appeared even more apprehensive, listening to Parson and I, obviously two people of differing ethnicities he had never seen before, speaking in a language he'd never heard before.

To my disbelief, the man explained to Binh that a trip to Cần Thơ or Saigon would be impossible. He had no sampan and could not afford the time because he had to support the rest of his family at home.

"Binh," I said, "tell him the boy can get very sick if he doesn't go." Binh explained this to him, and his only reply was to thank Binh for the antibiotics, at which point he turned to leave.

"Wait a minute," I said. "Binh, tell him I will try to get a helicopter to take him and his son to Rạch Giá." Binh translated.

"*Không* (no)," the father replied, "*Không mai bai whop-whop.*" I couldn't believe my ears.

"No helicopter, Trung Úy," Binh translated. "Not a good idea."

"Okay, Binh," I said, "you tell him his son has a good chance of dying. Tell him the boy will probably die when the infection travels up his arm. Tell him I will get permission for him to get on the chopper too. This way it won't take long, and he can go back to his family very soon." Binh told him.

"*Không, không mai bai whop-whop,*" was his answer, as he looked down and shook his head.

"Why, why not, Binh?" I said, by now completely frustrated.

"Because he afraid of helicopter. Very unsafe, cannot do." Parson and I stared at one another in disbelief and shook our heads.

"I know, Trung Úy," Binh said, "I agree with you, but I told you before, some of these people very primitive, very superstitious."

"Okay," I said to myself, "calm down, there has to be a solution. I'm not quitting on this."

I decided the boy had to be saved even if I had to put myself out on a limb. I could offer to take him myself, without the father having to divert his time away from the support of his family. I had no idea how I'd get permission to do that, but I imagined calling Major Dowd on the radio, who might let me.

On my first day in the province I watched Major Dowd break the rules for the little girl at Thời An Village. He authorized Sergeant Setkusky to go ahead and call in the medivac. And what about the old man we just medivaced? He was a civilian too!

Maybe I could make it happen. Or, if I couldn't get permission, I could just get on the radio and call in for a medivac anyway and take him with me to the hospital in Cần Thơ, then worry about getting my ass chewed out and possibly demoted later on.

"Binh, tell him I'll get on the helicopter with the boy and I will personally escort his son to the hospital. The father doesn't have to go. He can return to the rice paddy and leave the boy with me. I'll take good care of him, I'll make sure he gets good medical treatment, and I'll bring him home when he gets better. Tell him what I said, Binh." Parson stared at me in disbelief.

Again, Binh translated. More banter back and forth in Vietnamese. Binh tried desperately to convince the boy's father as I waited in silence, hoping he would reconsider. My heart sank as I heard the father say to Binh once more, "*Không duoc* (can't do, not possible)."

The farmer finished by telling Binh he would have the little boy take his medicine. And then he said goodbye.

Parson and I stood in silent disbelief as we watched the father and his ten-year-old son walk away from the pagoda. They headed toward a trail heading west, away from Hóa Quản, and off into the jungle. We never saw them again.

Another heartbreaking lesson in Vietnam and another painful memory that will stay with me forever. Combat deaths are one thing, but the damned "adventure" I'd once anticipated had long-since turned into a nightmare – a life-long nightmare. Every now and then I still see the little one, his arm in a sling, walking away holding his father's hand.

JUNE 4, 1969
Diary Entry:

*Visit from LTC Stanberry, Mr. Sylvester, and other civilian officials from Saigon.*

Stanberry's visit was to officially inform us that we would be moving from Hóa Quản outpost to a place called Vĩnh Thanh Village. He said he needed a reliable, experienced team of advisors to go into Vĩnh Thanh, a village not yet pacified, and that it would be a "challenge." We would be working with some newly-formed Vietnamese Hoa Hảo companies, and additionally, possibly the 770 Company from Thời An.

I immediately had some concerns, particularly about the

use of Hoa Hảo companies and the especially-sloppy 770 rifle company. But I kept my opinions to myself. It wasn't for me to decide anyway.

The Vietnamese infantry units we had worked with up until that point had been fairly capable soldiers. I would have felt more comfortable going into an unpacified village with a rifle company like the 168. We didn't know much about the place called Vĩnh Thanh, but I knew someone would show up with more information about the mission. Stanberry left off by telling me, once again, that Vĩnh Thanh "might be a little more active." I filled the team in on our conversation.

JUNE 8, 1969
Diary Entry:

*Operation to WR183832. We discovered and detonated one VC land mine.*[K]

We accompanied the 379 on another operation searching for Vietcông. While on patrol, our lead element discovered a land mine in the ground. Our guys were able to put some explosives on it and set it off from a distance. The rest of the patrol was uneventful.[K]

JUNE 9, 1969
Diary Entry:

*Operation to WR179853.*[L] *Negative contact, except with one VC who was running away. But three civilians were killed and three wounded by our own U.S. gunships. Very bad day.*

June 9th was a very bad day indeed. I left the outpost early with Binh and Sgt. McFadden (Mac). Hogan, Parson, and Winters were back at the teamhouse monitoring the radio and packing things for our move to Vĩnh Thanh. Someone ordered the use of five helicopters, including a pair of U.S. Army Cobra gunships. I had not been apprised of that decision, and the arrival of the heavy-duty gunships surprised me: I didn't think we needed them.

The helicopters came in low and buzzed right over the top of us, raking fire into the woodline to our front.[L] They looked menacing, obviously trying to elicit sniper fire. I was concerned about some Popular Forces we were using as point men and I didn't want my black pajama-clad PFs being mistaken for VC and being shot by the now aggressive-maneuvering choppers. I searched for their frequency on my radio and finally found a major in charge. I told him of my concern and received a somewhat dismissive reply. He reminded me that he was in charge of the operation.

I decided it was safer for me to monitor the helicopters' frequency as opposed to staying on my own frequency with my men back at the teamhouse. By doing so, I had the option of switching back to our advisor frequency to reach Winters, who was monitoring our radio.

At about 9:30 a.m., a solitary Vietcông in a distant woodline to my right began firing single shots at one of the UH-1D helicopters. The 398 Company opened up on him but couldn't hit him because of the distance. We could see him running away for all he was worth; we tried to pick him off, but he jumped back into the thick jungle further up the woodline. The enemy soldier accomplished what he set out to do. He managed to shatter the Plexiglas on the front of the helicopter, which necessitated it's return to Cần Thơ.

I was still listening to the conversations among all five helicopters. The ship flying back toward Cần Thơ reported to the commander that they had a "Whiskey India Alpha" on board (Wounded In Action). It later turned out that a speck of the Plexiglas was flying around in the wind on the inside of the helicopter and became lodged in the eye of the co-pilot. He was the "Whiskey" on board, the WIA.

Four choppers still remained on station at that point. They began pouring intense fire into that woodline. We knelt down in the middle of the open rice paddy and were afraid to go any closer. We were concerned for our own safety as the choppers buzzed and swarmed like angry bees overhead. I got back on my regular frequency to give Lt. Winters a "SITREP," a SITuation REPort.

During that brief period of time, I lost track of the choppers, who were buzzing everywhere. The men flying them didn't know the extent of their fellow pilot's injuries; none of us did. They imagined all sorts of things, I'm certain. I finished up my conversation with Winters and started flipping channels to get back onto the frequency being used by the helicopter pilots.

While accomplishing that, I heard explosions and automatic weapons fire over toward Hóa Quản Village. I looked back over my right shoulder to see smoke rising from the open paddy west of the pagoda, and the same angry bees swarming over that area now. On the radio, I heard conversations amongst the pilots about "nailing" some Vietcông.

I checked back with Winters, who told me there weren't any VC near the outpost, but that he was aware of a lot of helicopters shooting and exploding ordnance in the vicinity of the pagoda.

Winters and myself were wondering the same thing, given that our patrol had passed the pagoda while leaving Hóa Quản just a while ago. And we hadn't encountered any enemy. What the hell was going on at the pagoda?

I got back on the helicopter frequency and got the major on the air, who was now obviously annoyed at my calling him for a second time on his own frequency, where I didn't belong. I told him I had just combed the pagoda area on foot a short time ago and had not encountered any Vietcông. The only solitary sniper we already knew about was at our present location, which was considerably west of Hóa Quản Village. He gave me no reply.

I again keyed the handset and blurted, "What are you firing at by the pagoda, over?"

"Roger, we've got Victor Charlie in the open here, over," he replied, the noise of the whining engine in the background, accompanied by the whirp, whirp, whirp.

"That's impossible," I said. "We were just there a short while ago, and you're too close to the village. Are you sure they are Victor Charlie, over?" I said.

"That's a Rodge," he replied (slang for Roger, meaning affirmative, or yes).

Binh was excitedly shaking my shoulder now. As I looked up, one of our PF platoon leaders was out of breath, telling Binh of something tragic, something gone terribly wrong, and he was pointing over toward Hóa Quản. The soldier had just come from there, running to us at a full clip across the open rice paddy.

Fear and disgust struck me as I heard Binh's announcement: "Trung Úy, stop the shooting! Helicopters are shooting down civilian farmers at Hóa Quản! Must stop *now!*"

Now I had to have that major. By the time he answered his call-sign, the shooting had already stopped, probably because he himself had taken a closer look, maybe had some doubts, and decided to back off.

"Cease fire! Cease fire!" I screamed, over his own frequency. "I have a problem with your targets. Do you copy, over?" With the rest of his pilots listening on the radio, he had no choice but to defend his position.

"They were Victor Charlie, over," he said again.

"I have an eyewitness right here who says they are civilian farmers from Hóa Quản," I told him.

By now, he was pissed that a lieutenant on the ground, a know-nothing "ground-pounder," would have the audacity to speak to a major this way on his own frequency, which was undoubtedly being monitored by his own pilots!

"Listen, you don't know what you're talking about," he accused. "And you're not in charge! *I am!* And you don't belong on my frequency!"

"Just don't fire anymore, *CEASE FIRE!* I want to find out more about this," I replied.

"Listen son, you don't tell me Jack Shit! Got it? *I'm* in charge of this operation. Am I making myself clear, *Lima Tango* (LT)?" he screamed.

By now, others were arriving, pointing and telling Binh six men had been shot by the helicopters' rocket and machine gun fire. Some were members of our own People's Self Defense Force, the ones we had worked so hard to train!

I completely lost it, and not giving two shits about how

much the man outranked me, I blasted back into the mouthpiece:

"Listen, you fucking asshole," I shot into the handset, "I want to know your name. I'm going over there right now, and I want to see your fucking Victor Charlie for myself. And if they're not, you're in deep shit. You better hold your fire. I've got a lot of friendlies on the ground down here, and we're going over there right now!"

"Fine," he retaliated, "go see for yourself, dud.[8] You'll see they were VC. They even had rifles and ammo containers with them. But we're oughta here anyway, and I intend to go back and fill out paperwork to have your God-damned ass court-martialed! ... OUT."

I looked at Mac and he just replied with uplifted eyebrows. "Shit," I said to myself, "I'd better be right." We beelined back over to the scene of the shooting with the Dai Úy.

The villagers were out at the edge of the rice paddy and thankfully, the helicopters were gone. Some of the men and women from the village related with tears streaming down their faces how the six farmers were out working in the open paddy when the helicopters went berserk. Three were dead, three were wounded.

I found the "weapons" the major had seen from the air. They were hoes. Hoes used to till the soil. They must have slightly resembled rifles from the air. I found the "ammunition containers" he referred to as well. They were fire-blackened cooking pots containing rice and crab meat which their wives had prepared for them that morning. The pots were still lined up in a row on the rice paddy dike to keep them warm in the early afternoon sun.

I stared at the "ammunition containers." I walked around, dumbfounded. Mac couldn't believe it either, shaking his head and mumbling. There were blood trails everywhere on the ground and blood-soaked rags laying in the water. Words cannot describe the sick feeling in my stomach. Suddenly, I was ashamed to be an American.

"*Trung Úy*," Dai Úy Hoa was saying, "*Chúng tôi phi di,*

*bây giờ.*" I knew what he said, but Binh reiterated that the Dai Úy said we must go back to the outpost now.

I asked the Dai Úy about a medivac. I offered to call and ask for special permission in lieu of what happened. He told me the wounded were being taken to Rạch Giá by sampan, and the families had the three dead men at the pagoda. He insisted through Binh that we leave now, go back to the outpost by circling back along the open rice paddy area instead of the most direct route: cutting through the village past the pagoda where the bodies were. I offered once more to call for a medivac. The answer was still no.

"Trung Úy," Binh said, "Dai Úy say we must go back now. Not safe here anymore for you. They no want anymore helicopters, want to be left alone. People in village very angry, Trung Úy. They think we do this. Dai Úy and I know you try to stop it. But people in village don't know and right now you numba ten in village. Not safe here now, we must go. Not safe for you in village. Tell the other advisors."

Mack and I followed Dai Úy Hoa as he skirted around the village on our way home. I remembered those M3 grease guns we had handed out in the village and the Dai Úy was thinking the same thing: armed villagers with a vengeance to assassinate us with those .45 caliber weapons could do it in seconds if we cut through the village.

It was a horrendous day for me. All of our efforts to date: the MEDCAP, the elections, helping the hamlet chief's father, building the school, protecting the village from the bad guys - all of it. It had all gone to hell in less than ten minutes.

JUNE 10, 1969
Diary Entry:
*Night ambush with the company. Village off limits to the whole team.*
Letter Home:
*Dear Folks,*
*Yesterday I went on an operation and it turned out to be*

the most discouraging day for me so far in Vietnam. Mac and I left the village with the 398 Company and 770 Company from Thời An. It was a big sweep with about 7 Vietnamese Companies involved plus the U.S. Navy river boats and Air Force Jets on call.

We left Hóa Quản and saw the air power pounding the area ahead. Then 2 helicopter gunships started chopping up the area right in front of us with rockets and machine guns. Our lead scouts were up there entering the woodline, so I called the helicopters. As I'm talking to him to tell him about our scouts, our PF platoon leader runs up and tells me the choppers wounded some civilians from our village.

The guy in the chopper said "the people had rifles and ran away suspiciously, so I shot them." When I got back to the village there were 3 guys dead and they had no weapons.

An old woman came up to me and asked, "Why do the American helicopters shoot at a farmer who goes to the field to make rice?" I just said, "Khome biet," (don't know). Then she offered me a glass of water.

The thing that gets me is, I called up (the major and he) got on the radio and says, "Those people had rifles." I know damned well they didn't. When we walked back past the village none of the children followed us and yelled "Okay, number one" like they always do. I don't think I'll be going back into the village anymore because Doc and I will probably be the ones going into our new location 5 days from now.

Last Saturday we had another big joint operation and our old 168 rifle company killed 45 VC in an all-day firefight. The major up there didn't believe one Vietnamese soldier when he told him he personally killed 1 VC, so the guy went back and loped off the Vietcong's head, brought it back and dropped it on the front steps of the advisor's headquarters. The 168 is still kicking tail.

Love, Bob

The memory of the elderly woman who offered me the glass of water after asking me to explain why the helicopters shot innocent farmers stays with me to this day. She must have been a very courageous and forgiving person. I suspect she saw the horrified look on my face and perhaps believed Dai Úy Hoa when he told her I was not able to stop them.

JUNE 11, 1969
Diary Entry:
*Village still off limits to the whole team.*

For the next five days, Dai Úy Hoa went into the village and made numerous visits to the pagoda. He talked with the village chief and the hamlet chiefs. He talked with the monks and with some of the family members who would listen to his version of what happened.

I still felt terrible about what happened and that I was blamed for it. Surely the rapport that took me so long to build would count for something. The Dai Úy was on my side. He knew and understood my anguish, and he gave me daily reports on his progress in getting the word out about how it happened and how I actually stopped it.

Dai Úy Hoa told me that although he was making progress convincing people, there was still a chance that some wanted revenge. We talked about all those grease guns and cases of .45 caliber ammo we passed out to the entire 90-man People's Self Defense Force, about half the male population of the village. With all those weapons in the hands of the village people, the Dai Úy wanted to make sure that none of us went "downtown."

Meanwhile, I composed a detailed five-page report to LTC Stanberry. In the report, I let it all hang out. If they wanted me court-martialed, fine, but I knew I was right. I requested from the colonel that an investigation be conducted about what happened. I included the date and time in the report and told him the reason for my profane outburst: in five minutes the major undid what had taken months to accomplish. In completing the report, I asked the colonel to review what happened with Mr. Sloan as well. I knew that Sloan, a civilian with CORDS, and the man in the province in charge of pacification, would be just as appalled about the incident as I was. Moreover, he might want to do something to prevent it in the future.

I also formally requested that payment be made to the families by the U.S. government. I had heard that if a citizen was a victim of "friendly fire," the family was entitled to a payment equivalent to $100. By American standards a small stipend, but I still wanted it paid.

I put the report on the next Swing Ship as the team continued to stay away from the village.

JUNE 13, 1969
Diary Entry:
*Inspected the weapons of the PSDF with Dai Úy Hoa.*
On this morning the Dai Úy ordered all the civilian PSDF from Hóa Quản Village to report to the outpost to inspect their grease guns. It was a brilliant move. The real reason he did this was to tell them what happened with the helicopters. He lined them up and flatly told them that neither I nor any of my advisors were responsible for the incident. He told them I did everything possible to prevent it, and I would probably be demoted because of my argument with the major in the air. He told them I was the reason the shooting stopped and that it would have been much worse had I not immediately intervened.

We continued packing and disassembling the teamhouse for our trip into Vĩnh Thanh Village. I didn't want to leave Hóa Quản without first getting the shooting incident straightened out. I knew it was going to be hard enough to live with, that I'd carry with me a certain level of guilt for the rest of my days for not being able to predict or prevent it from happening. I was sick over it.

All the positive things we had accomplished in Hóa Quản Village to "win the hearts and minds" had been destroyed.

JUNE 14, 1969
Diary Entry:
*I finally visited the pagoda with Dai Úy Hoa today after*

*things had cooled down. Paid respects to the Cambodian families who had men killed and wounded the other day.*

Finally, Dai Úy Hoa got word from the monks that MAT 88 could come into the village. Even though the Dai Úy was still a little apprehensive, he knew I needed to go into the village with my head held high. I wasn't going to get on the chopper for Vĩnh Thanh without expressing my deepest regrets to those poor families. On that day Captain Hoa thought it might be safe enough. There was to be a funeral service at the pagoda and he asked me if I wanted to attend. He already knew what my answer would be, however risky.

Dai Uy Hoa and I examine our topographical map while on operation.

With the monks outside the pagoda in Hoa Quan Village.

    I was quite nervous when I arrived at the pagoda. I went alone, the sole representative of my advisory team. I remember sweating profusely, a combination of nerves and the humidity caused by the frequent rain showers in recent days. Many male members of the village PSDF were waiting outside, smoking. I approached them wearing only my .45 pistol as a side-arm. I didn't want to be walking into the pagoda with my M16, looking for all the world like I needed protection because I was guilty, which I wasn't, or afraid for my life, which I was. I could smell the burning incense and the sickeningly-sweet smell of Vietnamese cigarettes, the smell of violent death. We approached the entrance to the pagoda. I stood on the spot where, back in February, Guerrero and I had taken the pictures of the three dead Vietcông. The memories mixed with the smoke and humidity and the apprehension of the moment wracked my nerves. The tension began to upset my stomach.

    The pagoda was packed with people. The funeral service was about to begin, but the monks had waited for our arrival before starting. To my astonishment, Dai Úy Hoa and I were escorted to an area at the front, as if we were dignitaries. The service was an amazing thing to witness, and I was careful to follow everything that Dai Úy Hoa did. I felt uncomfortable with my back to that many people, but reassured myself that I was in their pagoda, their place of worship, and that monks abhor violence.

Afterward, in a large crowd of peasants outside, the Dai Úy introduced me to all of the family members who had suffered a loss because of the incident. Sons, daughters, aunts, uncles, brothers, sisters, mothers and fathers, waited on line to shake my hand as if I were some kind of important person, some kind of dignitary. They shook my hand with both of theirs and bowed their heads respectfully as the Vietnamese often do. I couldn't believe it.

I told them in my "pidgin Vietnamese" how sorry I was about what had happened. They all said kind words to me, some even smiled at me. They told me they knew it wasn't my fault. I was so overcome with emotion, I had tears streaming down my cheeks, which evoked even more handshakes and sympathetic smiles from them.

I never expected those families to forgive the helicopter door-gunners, but I guess in their hearts they found a way to forgive me.

JUNE 17, 1969
Diary Entry:

*Captain Henderson visited and discussed last minute plans for the move.*

Captain Henderson was the operations officer for the province. He visited to fill in the details and the situation in Vĩnh Thanh.

There was no outpost at Vĩnh Thanh Village. There weren't any other outposts or U.S. or Vietnamese government forces in the area either. The only exposure Vĩnh Thanh had to the outside world was an occasional incursion by the 168 Company from Kiến Binh and other ARVN forces on random search and destroy missions to eliminate Vietcông units.

Initially, we would be advising two new regional force

companies, both Hoa Hảo. I would not be meeting any of my new counterparts until the morning of the insertion. We would all then be picked up by helicopter, flown to a rice paddy just outside Vĩnh Thanh, and myself and one other team member would accompany the rifle companies into Vĩnh Thanh on foot. The plans then called for the two of us to stay in Vĩnh Thanh, wherever we could establish a command post, and eventually be joined by the rest of the team.

And from that foothold, which would only be an encampment in the middle of the village, we'd supervise the construction of a government outpost just outside the village. The ultimate mission was to "pacify" Vĩnh Thanh by eliminating the Vietcông and implementing all of the successful military tactics and civilian programs we used in Hóa Quản.

But there was one other thing: "Bob, make sure you don't say anything to your new counterpart about staying in Vĩnh Thanh on the morning of the insertion," he told me. I was a bit confused.

"The morning of the insertion? I'm not quite following," I told Henderson. "We'll be with the new companies the morning of the insertion, surely they'll already know what the mission is," I said.

"No, they won't." he went on. "The province chief, Colonel Tài, doesn't want them to know. They're not going to be told they have to stay there until they are on the ground in the village. Then he'll tell them on the radio."

"What the hell?" I said to myself, dumbfounded. How can two rifle companies be sent into Vĩnh Thanh to clear out the VC, build an outpost and pacify the village without knowing it beforehand? And why would Colonel Tài want to do it that way? I asked Captain Henderson to fill in the blanks. I owed it to my team to find out the truth and let them know what we were getting into.

"Okay," he continued with a grin. "The Hoa Hảo companies you will be going in with aren't… well… they're not exactly the colonel's best, and they think they're going on an operation that will just last until the afternoon. If they know ahead of time that this is going to be a permanent assignment and that they won't be extracted by helicopter, they might go AWOL or refuse to go. Also, the colonel doesn't trust them to know ahead of time because, being Hoa Hảo's, it could leak, and then you guys will have a big surprise party waiting for you, if you get my drift."

"Great," I said to myself, "you wanted a fucking adventure, now you've got one." I had to explain this to my team, too. I tried to think of ways to make it all sound logical, and I couldn't. By now they understood the Vietnamese mind as well as I did, so I simply reiterated what Henderson told me. We were going in one way or another, so my guys might as well know the truth about the circumstances.

I'd been told by Stanberry that Vĩnh Thanh "might be a little more active." What I didn't know was that the Vĩnh Thanh area was controlled by the Vietcông and by the communist Viet Minh before them, and had been since 1954. It had a notorious reputation. Incursions into the area always met with resistance. For the past 15 years it had been under strong communist dominance and had not been seriously challenged by government forces in Kiến Giáng Province. Until now.

JUNE 18, 1969
Diary Entry:
*Disassembled the teamhouse, piled it on top of the Conex container. Attached straps so it can be lifted by Chinook.*

The plywood prefab hut that we had recently received came apart fairly easily. Winters, Hogan and Mac would stay behind, finish things up, and join us when a Chinook was available.

I selected Sergeant Parson to go in with me. He was our medic, and from the sounds of it, there was a chance I'd need him tomorrow in Vĩnh Thanh. Parson and I spent the rest of the evening getting all our gear and weapons ready. I went over the operations map one more time and noticed that Vĩnh Thanh was at the very eastern edge of Kiến Giáng Province at the border of Chương Thiện Province.

My mind went back to the briefing Chuck and I attended at Eakin Compound back in early February. I remember Chương Thiện referred to as a Vietcông stronghold, another "active" province. And I thought about Chuck Emery and how he was doing in An Xuyên.

CHAPTER SIX

# 'Nasty'

JUNE 19, 1969
Diary Entry:
*Myself, Binh, and SSgt Parson were picked up by chopper and inserted into Vĩnh Thanh with two rifle companies.*

"Doc" Parson, Binh and I were up at the crack of dawn, waiting at the landing pad. LTC Stanberry arrived by helicopter, accompanied by his counterpart, COL Tài, and CPT Henderson. We flew to the square in Kiến Binh, the district capital, where I had first met Gannon and Major Bonner many months prior.

Two Vietnamese rifle companies were milling around in loose formation in an open area near the district headquarters compound. Binh, myself and Parson were introduced to our new Vietnamese counterparts. The 780 and 781 RF (Regional Force) Companies were Hoa Hảo by religion. They looked somewhat disheveled and disorganized to me. I found out later that they were new recruits, right out of basic training near Saigon.

I didn't like the idea of going into a hot area with Hoa Hảo soldiers who had already crossed the line too many times. In 1947 the Hoa Hảos turned against the communist Viet Minh when their leader, Huynh Pho So, was murdered by the communists for disallowing his Hoa Hảo religious sect to join them.[9] But by the late '50s, they sided with the communists against their mutual enemy, the Catholic Diem regime.[10] After Diem's assassination in 1963, they once again flip-flopped to our side. I didn't trust them. Worse, the communist Vietcông, the offshoot of the

Viet Minh, hated them with a passion and particularly enjoyed ambushing and killing them for their traitorous, turncoat ways.

Parson and I hardly looked like we were there for a brief afternoon stroll. I was afraid the equipment we were wearing would give away our long-term intentions. Wearing my steel pot and flak jacket, I had the radio on my back, a fully loaded butt-pack, pistol belt around my waist attached to which was my entrenching tool and .45 pistol, smoke canisters, first aid pouch with extra morphine, 6" Buck hunting knife, rolled up poncho and bedroll, and two canteens-full of fresh Hóa Quản rain water. Parson didn't have the radio to carry, but he was loaded down with his combat medic's bag full of compresses, tourniquets, splints, morphine, etc. Besides our M16's, we each carried two bandoliers of magazines (400 rounds) and three hand grenades.

Soon, five UH-1D troop transport helicopters arrived. Without wasting time, the three of us loaded onto the lead helicopter. One of the Vietnamese officers jumped in too, along with as many of his men as could squeeze in. We flew directly to Vĩnh Thanh Village and the chopper set us down in an open paddy just west of the village.

We disembarked into a completely "cold" LZ (landing zone), crouching in the rice paddy water and not receiving any fire. Four other helicopters landed behind us, and all the Vietnamese disembarked. The American door gunners sat nervously behind their M60 machine guns, staring into the woodline at the edge of the village. There was no one around, not even anyone working in the fields. We now had the element of surprise and the majority of one of the companies on the ground.

The UH-1Ds lifted off and returned to Kiến Binh to pick up the second round as I fanned the troops out from left to right in a single line about 50 meters across. We all entered the woodline together. So far, so good.

Upon establishing radio contact, my SIT-REP (situation report) was uneventful: "We have negative contact, over." We immediately encountered some startled village people who directed us to the center of the village, where we found the pagoda and set up a perimeter. The Vietnamese soldiers made small fires and cooked rice for lunch. Parson and I shared some C-rations with Binh. It felt good to have all that junk off my back.

By now, a Vietnamese captain showed up, having come in on one of the later choppers. I wondered why he hadn't led his men in on the first load. He didn't want to have much to do with Parson and me and looked annoyed, already trying to radio Kiến Bình to find out what time he'd be extracted, which, of course, wasn't going to happen.

Binh was off somewhere, which was not unusual for him. He was a very social and intelligent young man, having learned English in Saigon, and he had an eye for the young ladies. Binh's good looks and ability to make friends often proved useful. He usually returned from such jaunts with good information, particularly if it concerned his own hide. Other advisors might have been annoyed with an interpreter like Binh for wandering off sometimes, but it never bothered me very much. My Vietnamese language skills were coming along pretty well and I could function fairly well without him.

Parson and I watched as the Dai Úy tried to get someone of authority on the radio to get an extraction. "The shit's gonna hit the fan pretty soon, Sarge," I said to Parson, as I lit up a Salem.

"Yeah," he said with a grin. "This oughta be good."

"Wait 'till he finds out he's not getting out of here today and he's gotta stay here," I said, grinning back. Parson was laughing. We looked over at the Dai Úy, who noticed that both of us were laughing in his direction. He had a strange look on his face, trying to figure out why we were so amused. I should have been more discreet.

A couple of soldiers bummed some cigarettes from me as we sat at the entrance to the pagoda and watched the Dai Úy beseeching the radio operator on the other end. His men had traveled light and weren't prepared to spend even one night, much less months. Finally, it became apparent that our Dai Úy was told to remain in Vĩnh Thanh tonight. It was also apparent that he didn't like the idea very much.

Binh showed up and I asked him to find out where we were going to set up for the night. It was already pushing 2 p.m., and Parson and I wanted to get a start on a foxhole for ourselves. Binh asked the captain, who became even more irate. He came over and wanted to know what our superiors had told us.

"Tell him we were told we may be here for quite some time. Ask him if we are staying right here tonight," I said, pointing to the ground. Binh conveyed the message, and then replied, "He say he no stay here tonight. Too many VC."

The Dai Úy was back on the radio, this time raising Colonel Tài himself. Parson and I looked at one another in astonishment as the colonel screamed into the radio. Vietnamese rarely allow themselves to become emotionally irate, at least not publicly. We listened in amazement to the colonel's high-pitched shrill at the Dai Úy. The Dai Úy tried feebly to object and was having his ears pinned back by the colonel, who was now threatening him with demotion of rank for insubordination. Binh kept us abreast of the conversation. It went back and forth. I looked at my watch. It was 3 p.m.

"Enough of this!" I told Binh. "Find out where we're sleeping tonight. If there are VC around here, we need to get a plan going for a night defensive position or we're going to get our asses kicked. We don't have time to bullshit around all afternoon!"

This time Binh was successful in getting a commitment from the Dai Úy. "We stay right here, Trung Úy." I had speculated that all along. The Vietcông will rarely attack a pagoda or pagoda area. It is sacred ground, and they don't want to take the chance of harming any monks with mortars or small arms fire. That explained why the company had initially bee-lined for the pagoda in the first place.

Parson and I picked out a depression about twenty feet from the entrance to the pagoda and dug a two-man foxhole. None of the Vietnamese were digging in but seemed content to watch us dig ours. I guessed they thought it was a waste of time.

Fortunately, the night passed without incident.

JUNE 20, 1969
Diary Entry:
*Received word that Captain York paid the families of the injured and dead in Hóa Quản Village.*

This morning I got on the radio to let the rest of our team back in Hóa Quản know Parson and I were okay. "By the way," Lt. Winters added at the end of the transmission, "Captain York was here yesterday and paid the families of the people who were shot by the gunships. They paid them at a big meeting at the pagoda."

Bob knew how much that meant to me, to all of us. The timing of our transfer out of Hóa Quản couldn't have been worse, but at least my report on the gunship incident got LTC Stanberry's attention and he put into motion the paperwork for the compensation for the families. Stanberry deeply cared for the advisory effort.

When I got off the radio, Binh showed up. He'd been off on another fact-finding mission and getting to know some of the village people. But this time he had a worried look on his face. He appeared shaken and concerned and stared at me as he approached.

"Trung Úy," he began, "last night fifty North Vietnamese regulars (NVA) moved through Vĩnh Thanh along that trail right over there. Look," he pointed, "you can see from here." At a distance of 300 meters or so I could see a trail peeking out along a woodline.

The information given to Binh was supplied by a villager from over there who had seen the enemy patrol and confided in Binh. The disturbing news became even more bizarre as Binh relayed the rest of what the informant told him: the NVA had several other Orientals with them, and they were not Vietnamese. The others wore tan uniforms with red epaulets and spoke another language.

"What? Spoke another language?" I frowned.

"Yes," he replied.

I was dumbfounded. "Binh, what 'other Orientals' are you talking about, and what 'other' language?"

"We think they Chinese," he went on. "Chinese Co Ván (advisors), same-same like you, Trung Úy, but from China!"

He went on to tell Parson and me the NVA were "heavily armed" with AK-47's, mortars, machine guns, and B-40 rockets (RPG's, Rocket Propelled Grenades). They were moving east toward Cần Thơ. I got on the radio at once and passed the information on to Kiến Binh. That kind of troop movement had to be passed on immediately.

"Chinese communists 'advising' NVA regulars?" I puzzled. If the information given to Binh was true, it had far-reaching implications. I hadn't heard anything at Advisor School about Chinese troops in Vietnam. Could it be that the Chinese were sending military advisors like us to aid the communist NVA? And if the story had been made up to scare us off, how would the man Binh interviewed, a villager with very little contact with the outside world, know such detail about the color of Chinese uniforms or the epaulets on their shoulders?

At the time I dismissed Binh's story: it would have been unusual for the NVA to have troops that far south. I later discovered Binh's information was correct. At least four North Vietnamese Regiments were inserted into the Mekong Delta by the summer of 1969, which substantiated the information given to us on June 20.[11]

The NVA were probably moving east toward the larger military installation at Cần Thơ. They had to know our two small RF Companies were at the pagoda that night but probably preferred not compromising their more important mission by wasting time on the likes of us. Vĩnh Thanh had been a convenient resting place for them, a sanctuary, until we showed up. Our unexpected arrival the day before denied them the use of Vĩnh Thanh as a stopover. For whatever reason, they spared our lives that night. Had they wanted to, they could have chewed us up and sent us all scurrying for our lives.

JUNE 23, 1969
Diary Entry:
*Received word that three VC armed with M16s ambushed RD Cadre back in Hóa Quản Village. One RD Cadreman was wounded. VC also captured one sampan.*

JUNE 24, 1969
Diary Entry:
*Rest of team moved to Vĩnh Thanh Village.*
With the rest of the team arriving by Chinook, we were finally all reunited. It felt good to have everyone together again. There were plenty of wisecracks over our little foxhole and living "accommodations." We moved into the pagoda and set up our bunks in one corner as the Dai Úy moved his headquarters into the other half of the room. The team would sleep in the pagoda for the next thirty days, the time it would take to complete the outpost. During that time we were most vulnerable to enemy attack. The pagoda was nestled in a small clearing, but patches of jungle were far too close. Without even the most basic defenses of a mud-walled berm, a moat, some barbed wire, booby-trapped hand grenades, and a clear field of fire, we missed the "security" of the outpost at Hóa Quản.

JUNE 25, 1969
Diary Entry:
*The 770 Company from Thời An was inserted today by helicopter into Nha Sĩ Hamlet to our south.*
By now we were learning that Nha Sĩ Hamlet, a sub-sector of Vĩnh Thanh Village, was at least as heavily controlled by the communists as the main village. Colonel Tài ordered the insertion of the sloppy Seven-Seven-Oh (770 Company) to expand our physical presence.
That meant my MAT team's mission had been expanded as well. Besides being responsible for the new 780 and 781 Rifle Companies in Vĩnh Thanh proper, I was also responsible for the 770 Company and Nha Sĩ Hamlet. That meant overseeing the

construction of an outpost there (while building ours), and the construction of at least two others, one each at Cái Nhum and Xẻo Sáu Hamlets to the north. All of that would require frequent incursions by us to those locations to check on progress. Colonels Stanberry and Tài had assigned us an ambitious mission designed to establish sizable government presence in Vĩnh Thanh. I appreciated the vote of confidence, but my mind again turned toward my team.

I had good, dedicated men under me, and my concerns heightened about making sure nothing happened to any of them.

June 25 would be our last day of peace there. The 26th marked the birth of the battle for Vĩnh Thanh. We had been right about the village. The VC were not about to give it over to government control without a serious fight, especially to the turncoat Hoa Hảo traitors.

JUNE 26, 1969
Diary Entry:
*One squad of VC ambushed 770. Four men wounded.*

The 770 was ambushed by the VC in Nha Sĩ only one day after their arrival. Nha Sĩ was still considered too "hot" to risk insertion of a MAT team living there, so MAT 45, formerly of Thời An and led by Captain Delgado, wasn't inserted with their 770 Company when the company went into Nha Sĩ.

The 770 at Nha Sĩ instead became my advisory responsibility. Of the five hamlets that made up Vĩnh Thanh Village – Vĩnh Lộc, Cái Nhum, Vĩnh Loi, Xẻo Sáu and Nha Sĩ – the latter would prove to be the untamable one.

Without any advisors there, the 770 had great difficulty getting medivacs for the wounded. All four had gunshot wounds. My counterpart was kept busy relaying requests to Kiến Bình well into the night.

JUNE 27, 1969
Diary Entry:
*One squad of VC ambushed 770 Company. Had one WIA.*

The Hoa Hảo 770 Company had never been my favorite back at Hóa Quản because of their undisciplined habits at Thời An. But they were experienced at fighting the VC there and had helped disrupt the "corridor" out of the U-Minh Forest, the one mentioned in the Intelligence Report. And I suppose, for that reason, the colonel chose them for Nha Sĩ. Now, on their second day, they took another hit, and I felt bad for them.

I had Binh tell the commander to bring me the wounded man. They brought him by sampan, and I inspected his wounds as I always had to do, first-hand, before calling for the medivac. That policy eliminated the unnecessary summoning of brave U.S. pilots to some remote location to medivac an ARVN with only superficial wounds. Rather than making him take the painful and dangerous trip to Rạch Giá by sampan, I was able to get him a direct medivac to the hospital.

While our South Vietnamese casualties in little Vĩnh Thanh Village were escalating, American casualties throughout Vietnam were out of control. 1968 had produced frightening statistics of Americans killed, and 1969 was running a close second. National archives would eventually record that the combined total of those two years alone accounted for 28,679 Americans killed, nearly half of the 58,220 total Americans killed during the entire fifteen-year length of the Vietnam War.[12] History would record 1968 and 1969 as the two "hot" years, the years of the highest casualties.

Back home on June 27, 1969, and as far from Vĩnh Thanh as one could be, Life Magazine's weekly publication hit the news stands. The cover announced its feature article, *The Faces of the American Dead in Vietnam: One Week's Toll: May 28 - June 3, 1969*.[13] It featured a photographic collage of all 242 American boys killed that week. American KIA statistics were clipping along at approximately 1,000 per month.

Vietnam was obviously a dangerous place to be. But it was especially dangerous at that time, in the field, in an infantry slot and serving as a 1st lieutenant, the one rank with the dubious distinction of having the highest total number of fatalities of any officer pay grade during the entire Vietnam War.[14]

JUNE 28, 1969
Diary Entry:
*Operation into Chương Thiện Province. Flushed out some VC. 781 and 780 sent one platoon each as a reaction force.*

Vĩnh Thanh Village was situated on the far eastern border of Kiến Giáng Province bordering Chương Thiện Province, about 1200 meters to our east. We really had no "jurisdiction" in Chương Thiện. We had no authority even to be in a neighboring province. And the local Vietcông knew how to work the borders and work the system in a game of cat and mouse. They knew that our Mobile Advisory Team wasn't on the same radio frequency as the Chương Thiện teams were and that information was not commonly shared between provinces. That might explain why Nha Sĩ was so brazenly active. We were determined not to allow the border to be a safe haven for them.

So, on this date, we had our first of many incursions into Chương Thiện Province, where we didn't belong. We headed due east across the open paddy area and straight for our objective, the first hamlet at the border. Through my field glasses, I could see some activity there as the villagers saw two platoons approaching. Not having experienced such a sight in the past, people in the hamlet began scurrying around.

As we got within 400 meters, we spotted two men with rifles running out of the hamlet to the east, away from us. We sprinted across the remaining area. Some of our soldiers fired off rounds in an attempt to hit them, but the distance was too great. By the time we got to where they had disappeared into the woodline, we couldn't find them.

We doubled back to the hamlet from which they'd emerged. None of the people there acknowledged knowing the men. They claimed they were VC alright, and that we just happened to interrupt their "passing-through." And of course, they would be sure to inform us if ever they returned.

"What do you think, Binh?" I queried.

"I think they lie, Trung Úy, I think they VC from here. You notice, not too many men in village? That because they see us come. This is bad place."

JUNE 29, 1969
Letter Home:

*Dear Folks,*

*Well, I've been here in our new village (Vĩnh Thanh) about 10 days now. We're in a choice spot because we have one company to the west, about 3 kilometers, and the 770 Company to the south, about 3 kilometers. The 770 is the one that used to be in Thời An and they got hit all the time there. Now in the past 2 days they've lost 5 men WIA due to small, 6-man VC ambushes. They say 3 of the VC are carrying M16s!*

*I don't want to imagine how they got their hands on the American M16s, but we keep finding M16 empty brass casings all over the place. The 3 Vietnamese companies we are advising all have the old M1 and M2 carbines, Garants and an assortment of VC and European weapons. So, this isn't too cool, having the VC running around with M16s while our guys have the crappy old carbines. The Care Packages are great, Dad.*
*Bob*

JULY 2, 1969
Diary Entry:

*Operation to WR345913.° Negative contact.*

WR345913 is Vĩnh Lôc hamlet, located three kilometers northwest, at the intersections of the Cái Be and Cái Nhum Rivers.° We swept on foot along a trail next to the Cái Nhum and encountered no enemy. Returning, however, Hogan and I were forced to ride back by sampan, the very dangerous practice we were repeatedly warned to avoid at all cost.

As civilian farmers traveled along the canal from Vĩnh Lôc to Vĩnh Thanh, our soldiers fired shots in the air to make them pull over, and then ordered them to give us all a free ride back to Vĩnh Thanh. I knew that was dangerously wrong and asked why we were doing that, instead of going back on foot.

The 780 sergeant in charge feebly tried to assure me that once cleared, the canal was a safe means of travel. When I asked about the possibility of an ambush by Vietcông who were smart enough to wait for our return after we had already swept the banks of the canal, his reply was, "this cannot happen."

He and his men then boarded the sampans. We could either stay there by ourselves, go back to the pagoda on foot by ourselves, or ride in the dangerous sampans. We had to take the sampans.

I made a mental note to myself to never go out on another operation with that particular sergeant again.

JULY 3, 1969
Diary Entry:
*Six RD Cadre teams arrived. Large force of VC was ambushed by 781 Company and retreated to the south toward Nha Sĩ. One friendly wounded by hand grenade.*

In broad daylight the 781 Company caught some VC moving toward Vĩnh Thanh on foot. A firefight ensued, the Vietcông threw a hand grenade, then broke contact and headed back down toward Nha Sĩ. The returning 781 wounded soldier proudly strutted around the area of our pagoda, showing off the bleeding steel fragment wound located exactly on the cleft of his chin. "Doc" Parson pulled out the piece of metal with tweezers from his medical bag, and I joked to the soldier that he would now resemble the famous cleft-chinned movie star, Kirk Douglas. It went right over his head. He had no idea who Kirk Douglas was.

JULY 5, 1969
Diary Entry:
*SSgt Parson went to Cần Thơ to clear up his finance records. RD Cadre were attacked by small force of VC at WR358883. No casualties.*[P]

WR358883[P] was only 400 meters from the pagoda. We could hear the brief exchange of gunfire. By the time we got down there, it was over. The VC from Nha Sĩ were trying to make their presence felt by coming up to Vĩnh Thanh to pick on our relatively defenseless RD Cadre. It was time to plan some aggressive operations into Nha Sĩ.

JULY 11, 1969
Diary Entry:
*Operation to WR355860 because of reports that last night 40 VC slept at those coordinates.*<sup>Q</sup>

Coordinates WR355860 was the edge of Nha Sĩ Hamlet.<sup>Q</sup> We swept on foot along the canal without making contact. When we arrived, we met up with some elements of the 770 Company and took a break for lunch. I was successful in convincing the platoon leader not to return to Vĩnh Thanh by flagging down sampans.

JULY 12, 1969
Diary Entry:
*Night ambush in heavy rain - 1800 to 2100 hours.*

Winters and McFadden (Mac) left the pagoda area just after supper and helped our soldiers set up their early evening ambush site. But by 9:00 p.m. the squad leader called it off because of the intense downpour. The monsoon season in South Vietnam was fully upon us.

The biggest impact the monsoons had on our night ambushes was not the amount of rain, but the heavy cloud cover. Although it was still light enough in early evening for an ambush patrol to see its way down a trail and get set up, making the mistake of trying to return in pitch blackness created an unnecessarily dangerous situation. Our Vietnamese counterpart foolishly decided to abort the ambush and head home because of the rain, but the dense clouds blocked any starlight and even moonlight, making it impossible to see even the hand in front of your face. Worse, it increased the likelihood of becoming ambushed ourselves. It was a lazy and potentially deadly habit that was difficult for us to break, one that often put us at much greater risk than necessary.

Part of my job was to critique every operation with my counterpart. I'd take the time to explain what they were doing, right and wrong. But often, again, in the translation of mere words, I was never sure how much of an impact my thoughts were having on actually changing anything.

JULY 13, 1969
Diary Entry:

*Two Vietcông "Chieu Hoi's" with two SKS Chinese communist rifles surrendered to RD Cadre this afternoon. Night ambush, 1830 - 2100 hours. No contact.*

JULY 14, 1969
Diary Entry:

*Received intelligence report from the Buddhist monks in the village of impending VC attack. One battalion of Vietcông in the area. Supposedly are carrying B40 Rockets.*

Our two companies beefed up security. If the report by the monks was accurate, a battalion outnumbered us, and our position in the open area at the pagoda lacked any obstacles to being overrun.

JULY 15, 1969
Diary Entry:

*John Sloan arrived for inspection of RD Cadre progress. Vietnamese battalion commander returned from a nine-day absence. Virtually no work done on the outpost for several days. Sgt. McFadden (Mac) had to leave unexpectedly to return to the U.S. on a compassionate leave.*

Mac revealed to me privately, and then to the entire team, that he had some "wife trouble" at home and had put in for a Compassionate Leave. It had been granted and he said he'd return after hopefully resolving the issues at home. Many veterans "in country" experienced similar problems. It was difficult to maintain a healthy relationship so far from home and for so long.

This was Mac's third tour of duty. He was the oldest on the team and one of the best liked because of his constant injection of humor. He had seventeen years in the Army at that point.

When he arrived back on the team after his leave, I remember the night Mac and I had a long talk about his Army career. He told me he would not be extending his enlistment and would be leaving the Army after this tour of duty, before his twenty years was up. I tried desperately to talk him out of it.

"Sarge," I said, "you've only got three more years, 36 months to go, don't blow your pension now. Try to stick it out. You don't want to throw it away now."

"Sir," he replied, "this man's Army is ruining my marriage. You've got to understand something, LT. This is the third freaking time I've been sent here. And if I stay in, they'll find a God-damned way to get my ass over here a fourth time. I love my wife and I've got a family, believe it or not, outside of this man's God-damned Army. I don't want a divorce and I'm afraid she can't take anymore of this Vietnam stuff. Don't forget, it's worse for them than it is for us. At least we know what the hell is going on. But *they* have to sit home night after night wondering if the God-damned doorbell is gonna ring with two officers standing there wearing their Class-A's. I'm getting out, sir."

I respected Mac too much to offer any further rebuttal. In a war that consumed an awful lot of nineteen-year-olds, it also took a heavy toll on career people who had already given far too much of themselves.

JULY 17, 1969
Diary Entry:
*Sgt. E-5 Griffin arrived to fill in for SFC McFadden. 781 Company Commander was summoned to Rạch Giá because company is stealing chickens from the local farmers.*

Sergeant Griffin joined the team as a temporary replacement for Mac but wound up staying with us for the next two months. He was a nice young man from a troubled past, and now the Army was the only home he knew. He was pleasant and polite and he always pitched in. Like everyone else, he was a "team player."

But Griffin had a dark side. He had been sent to us from the "Big Red One," the 1st Infantry Division. He had been in Vietnam a long time. Too long, I was to find out.

On his first day, he bragged to us about killing "gooks" and what they did with the bodies.

"What we'd do, sir, is, we cut off their ears and wear 'em around our necks – and I would take my knife and carve a big One right in the middle of their chests, you know – for the Big Red One!"

It was imperative that I get something straight with Griffin right then and there: I wasn't going to allow body mutilation on our team.

"Listen, Sarge, I'm aware of that stuff in some of the big American units, but we can't be doing that out here, okay?" The rest of the guys were sitting at the table looking alternately at Griff and me.

"We're advisors to the Vietnamese, and I don't think they'd think much of us if they saw us doing that, you know what I mean?"

"Oh, yeah, sir," he acknowledged. "Just sayin'... I didn't mean I'd be doing it out here, working with the dinks like we have to and all." Griffin obviously had a problem with the Vietnamese and was not beneath denigrating them both physically and racially.

As he sat at the table, he showed us where he'd been shot while he was with the 1st Infantry Division. The bullet had passed cleanly through his left triceps. By the time they got him to Japan, the surgeons couldn't save most of the muscle, so they cut it out. This left his left arm emaciated and undersized to the point of appearing peculiar. In a man's world, it was a constant reminder to him. He didn't talk about it much after that, but one could tell he carried a grudge about it. I still liked Griffin very much. I actually felt sorry for him. He had no life before the Army and probably wouldn't have much to look forward to after the Army. And now, in 1969, Vietnam was his whole world. I decided to keep a close eye on him.

JULY 18, 1969
Diary Entry:
*Intelligence says 30 Vietcông are preparing to attack us from a distance of only one kilometer away.*

JULY 19, 1969
Diary Entry:
*379 Company replaced 780 and 781 Companies. I was awarded the CIB (Combat Infantryman's Badge).*

The Dai Úy in charge of 780 and 781, the one who initially refused to stay in Vĩnh Thanh because there were "too many VC," finally got his wish thirty days later. He had been up at headquarters for nine days speaking with his battalion commander, who now favored him by rotating him out. And I knew why. Kick-backs and bribes were commonplace throughout the Vietnamese chain of command.[15] Easy, low-risk assignments, like guarding an airstrip for example, could be bartered for or purchased.

JULY 20, 1969
Diary Entry:
*Commanding officer of the new 379 Company spoke with village people concerning the actions of our soldiers.*

The 780 and 781 companies had been stealing chickens from the local farmers, prompting some of them to get together and go up to Kiến Bình District to protest to the District Chief about it.

The new 379 Company Commander, Thiếu Úy Thuyet, held a meeting with some of the village elders to assure them his men would not be stealing anything. I liked that he did that. I couldn't win "hearts and minds" while tolerating that behavior.

But what I really liked was that the 379 Company was not Hoa Hảo, but "straight" Buddhists. They'd be a better fit, I hoped. And they were a beefed-up company, about 90-100 men strong. The most encouraging thing about them was, they had been trusted enough to have been issued M16s. We were back in business again with a "real" Vietnamese rifle company who could finally offset the M16 firepower that some of the Vietcông had.

The only drawback was, they lacked experience and were as new to the field as the other two companies who just left. The 379 RF Company had been formed only six months prior and three of those months were spent in basic training. One private I talked to was about thirty-five years old and had been driving an Esso truck at Tân Sơn Nhứt Airport. He proudly showed me his truck driver's license, trying to impress me. But I needed experienced infantry, not truck drivers.

JULY 21, 1969<br>Diary Entry:

*379 Company finally moved into compound. Sgt. Griffin left for R&R.*

We were all finally in our new outpost!<sup>M</sup>

JULY 22, 1969<br>Letter Home:

*Dear Folks,*

*Well, yesterday we finally moved into our new outpost.*<sup>M</sup> *It's a relief to move out of the pagoda. The new outpost is safer but there's about 6" of water in it. We set up our prefab teamhouse about 12" off the ground, so we're dry except the tin roof leaks a little. It's raining cats and dogs. We're fully into the rainy season now. We've got homemade rain gutters to catch the water and we can fill two 30-gallon garbage cans in one day for drinking water.*

*About 4 days after the rest of our team got here, our old outpost in Hóa Quản got hit in broad daylight by 2 companies of VC - about 100 men. I guess they figured when the Americans pulled out, they didn't have to worry about helicopter gunships.*

*It started about 9 AM and I heard Đại Úy Hoa on the Vietnamese radio calling for gunships. They got there about an hour later. I don't know how many casualties they took.*

*I have all my pay going into the "Soldiers Savings Deposit" program. I don't need any cash out here in the field, so they don't pay me directly... they deposit it into an account that spins off 10%! So far, I've saved about $3400 and I have $500 a month going into it. So, I should come home with about $6,000 as a down payment on a house!*

*Well, the weather is briefly clearing here today and I have to go out and take care of "business." We have no outhouse set up yet, so I use the same bathroom the Vietnamese use - the watery rice paddy area about 50 meters north of the outpost. I squat like they do while standing in water up to my shins! Zero privacy! Don't worry about me though, everything's fine here.*

*Love, Bob*

The attack on the outpost at Hóa Quản was inevitable because, after our departure, the VC knew they had an advantage. And it didn't help that the Hoa Hảo-religion 398 rifle company, led by my racist "friend," Chuẩn Úy Khome, was a poor fit for a Buddhist, darker-skinned, Cambodian village. They were also known for stealing anything that wasn't nailed down.

So, it came as no surprise that the old outpost was hit by so many VC. Without us there, and without people in the village warning the 398 of VC activity, the VC operated freely. No doubt they probably even recruited some of the angry farmers whose chickens had been stolen!

JULY 24, 1969
Diary Entry:

*In Nha Sĩ, three clicks to the south, the 770 Company was attacked at 0330 by estimated VC company and took twelve wounded and three killed. Enemy losses unknown.*[R]

Without warning, the VC in Nha Sĩ Hamlet hit the 770 real hard. 3 KIA and 12 WIA: the heaviest fighting so far in Vĩnh Thanh.[R]

At 3:30 in the morning I awoke to hear the violent beginnings of the attack that was to consume the early morning darkness until approximately 6:00 a.m. Using heavy mortars, the VC initially pounded the 770's position while most of them were still asleep. From our distance of only three kilometers away, some of the explosions were so loud that at first I thought it was artillery instead of mortars. The noise was bouncing off the thick, black, low-lying clouds. By the time the 770 could react, they had already sustained serious casualties.

In the blackness to our south, we could see the eerie glow of the parachute flares. The sudden flashes of light reflecting off the bottom of the rain clouds looked like lightning strikes.

The 770 opened up from their defensive positions, but their muzzle flashes gave away their positions, and the Vietcông then fired B-40 rocket propelled grenades directly at these defensive positions. I imagined the lazy 770 had not "dug in" properly either, not enough to withstand a direct frontal assault. The VC opened up from three sides with automatic rifle fire, with more B-40s, and began their ground assault on the weakest side. Once inside the perimeter, it became a free-for-all. People shooting people at point-blank range.

Over the Vietnamese radio came the panic-stricken shrill of the 770 Company commander screaming for help from us. His voice was filled with such terror it was difficult for even our Vietnamese radio operator to understand him. I remember hearing the loud explosions through the radio and hearing the same explosion again as it reached us through the jungle to our south. It was much louder over the radio, right on top of him. I could hear the din of rifle fire in his ear as he screamed to be heard over the noise, spine-chilling testimony to the close fighting. If his soldiers were firing their rifles from his command position, the VC were close in on top of him. Too close.

Our radio operator relayed a normal Vietnamese "SITREP" (situation report) to Kiến Bình, followed immediately by the 770 commander again repeating that he needed immediate assistance. Kiến Bình couldn't help, they said, cloud cover prevented the dispatch of helicopters. He begged my counterpart, Thiếu Úy Thuyet, to dispatch troops immediately down the canal to his location.

Of course, that was impossible. Sending men down the pitch-black trail along the Dường Xuồng canal to traverse the three klicks[16] to Nha Sĩ at 4:00 a.m. was suicide, something one would do only if he wanted to waste the lives of his men. The 770 were on their own; I only hoped they had prepared their positions well enough.

We lost contact with the 770 commander after twenty minutes or so, though sporadic firing and individual skirmishes could still be heard. Most of the 770 Company turned and ran for their lives, the company commander included. They scattered around Nha Sĩ in the darkness, hiding anywhere they could until daybreak.

After the Vietcông were satisfied they had done enough, they disappeared before dawn, off to hide their weapons and work the rice paddy as the sun came up, as if nothing had happened.

The 770 Company commander, still alive, was back on the radio at dawn talking with our RTO. After Thiếu Úy Thuyet still refused to go to his aid in Nha Sĩ, we lost radio contact with the 770 Company completely. The 770 had been overrun, and we hadn't helped them.

I don't know what happened to the 770 Regional Forces Company in Kiến Giáng Province after that night. They left by sampan with their dead and wounded, fifteen in all. They had been terribly mauled. Their unit designation, "the 770," never surfaced again after that night. At the end of my tour, I went back to Thời An, their former village, thinking they eventually re-grouped there, but they weren't there or anywhere else in Kiến Giáng. The 770 Regional Forces Company was gone. They had been wiped out.

JULY 25, 1969
Diary Entry:
*267 Company came in by helicopter to reinforce 770*

Company. *They will stay with us one day and then move into Nha Sĩ. Received emergency resupply for 770 - ammo, hand grenades and Claymore mines.*

At the time of this diary entry, I was unaware that the remnants of the 770 had run off. The emergency resupply I obtained for them on only twelve hours' notice did them no good. With much bravado, the 267 told us they'd be going into Nha Sĩ in the morning. They would have with them all of the resupply items for the 770. The 267 was also unaware of the annihilation of the 770 Company when they announced they would reinforce them. They thought they'd be joining the battle-weary 770, not replacing them!

JULY 26, 1969
Diary Entry:
*Operation into Nha Sĩ to insert 267 Company. 770 Company had already left.*

More fanfare as we conducted an operation into Nha Sĩ with Thiếu Úy Thuyet and the 379 Company to "escort" the 267 Hoa Hảo rifle company into the hamlet. When we arrived there, the 770 was long gone. Some villagers recanted to us the gory details of the 770's demise two nights ago. The 267 commander was upset that the 770 was gone and suddenly his bravado disappeared.

We left the 267 Company in Nha Sĩ Hamlet to set up a defensive position and returned to the outpost at Vĩnh Thanh. But realizing they were now alone and fearing what happened to the 770, they stayed only twenty-four hours and returned back to Vĩnh Thanh to camp in the jungle just outside our outpost. No way were they staying there.

JULY 27, 1969
Diary Entry:
*Intelligence report of 6 VC to the southwest. 15-man reaction force with myself and Sgt. Parson captured one VC.*

In the afternoon, Parson and I accompanied fifteen soldiers reacting to the above report. We headed southwest, winding up in Vĩnh Lói along the Cái Be River. We hadn't been there before.

We moved into the hamlet looking for the six VC. The Thiếu Úy began interrogating some of the males in the village. One of the men didn't fit in with the village, couldn't identify his home, and for reasons best understood by the Vietnamese, he was now a VC suspect.

Thiếu Úy Thuyet brought him back to Vĩnh Thanh for more questioning. "What do you think, Binh?" I questioned, the man being the first "Vietcông suspect" in our new outpost. "Trung Úy, I don't know for sure, but I think he VC," he said.

The man's arms were bound at the elbows, and he was blindfolded. Thuyet had him thrown in a 5' x 3' mud pit filled with water in the middle of the outpost. His blindfold was then removed.

There I was again, witnessing more water boarding and torture, much the same as in Hóa Quản. This First Sergeant had a new twist though. From behind, he karate-kicked the young man at the base of his neck, then lifted on the ropes to drive him face-first into the mud. He repeated this, but the suspect was still not giving credible answers.

Thiếu Úy Thuyet was out of patience, uncommon among Vietnamese. Running to his bunker, he emerged with his M16 in one hand and a magazine in the other. With great theatrical production, he held the M16 in the air as he inserted the twenty-round magazine, then chambered the first round. He wanted our prisoner to view his every move.

He put the barrel of the loaded M16 to his face, screaming at him while poking him in the cheeks with the barrel of the rifle.

"What's he saying, Binh?"

"He say the man die for not telling the truth. He is going to shoot him."

Thiếu Úy Thuyet held up the rifle and flipped the selector lever from safety to fully automatic, all the while explaining in Vietnamese, with a high-pitched shrill, exactly what he was going to do. Then he motioned those behind the suspect to clear out of the way.

The suspect was in tears, crying hysterically and begging for his life. I turned away as the tip of the barrel was being pointed at his face again, and I saw Binh do the same. Then I heard the entire 20-round magazine being fired!

I looked back as the final rounds were leaving the weapon. The Thiếu Úy had moved the barrel at the final instant slightly to the left, sending all the rounds past the man's right ear. There were powder burns on the right side of his face, not to mention what that must have done to his ear drum.

"*Chet roi, Chet roi*," (I'm dead already) the man screamed, uncontrollably crying and sobbing. He was shaking so involuntarily, it looked like a seizure.

"Yes," he would tell Thuyet everything. "Yes," he was a VC. "Yes," he had a weapon. "Yes, Yes, Yes."

After obtaining as much intelligence as we could, we sent him up to headquarters the next day for more interrogation.

JULY 29, 1969
Diary Entry:
*Operation to south with 379. Sporadic sniper fire produced four friendly casualties. Hogan and I burned a VC house.*

We headed south toward Nha Sĩ again, single-file down the trail that runs along the banks of the Dường Xuòng canal. The purpose of the operation was to try to re-insert the 267 again, and this time, coax them into remaining there.

Our brave point man, Private Dzu, led the way, followed by the rest of the 1st Platoon and ourselves. Thiếu Úy Thuyet, Hogan, Binh, and I took up the middle of the column, our typical arrangement. I carried the PRC-25 portable radio on my back. The 267 Company, not thrilled about their battalion commander's direct order to go into Nha Sĩ and stay there, was content to lag behind. They didn't want anything to do with Nha Sĩ and had been procrastinating for days.

Before entering the hamlet, Thuyet decided to have Dzu

head east first, crossing the Duòng Trâu Só canal, which brought the lead element into Nha Sĩ from the east. This provided an avenue of approach that was less likely to be anticipated by the Vietcông.

After we forded the canal, I could see that point man Dzu came upon a clearing, an open rice paddy area approximately 100 meters across. Dzu held up the column and knelt down at the edge of the clearing. We came up to join him, and paused there, observing the other side for any signs of the enemy. Dzu was an excellent point man, patiently positioning himself there for many minutes, staring at the jungle for anything unusual. "I look for movement," he hand-gestured.

Satisfied that it looked benign enough, Thuyet dispatched our point man across the open area. I watched Dzu cross the open area alone and enter the woodline on the other side, as a squad of soldiers now entered the open area. A couple of them reached the other side. Hogan and I readied ourselves to move out.

We stood up and immediately dropped back down as intense gunfire erupted on the other side. Some of the 1st Platoon, caught in the middle, came dashing back, while others, already committed, entered the woodline to take cover. One of our guys in the middle of the clearing was hit by rifle fire and dropped in a pile. He wasn't moving, and I remember hoping his wound was minor; that he was just laying still to play dead and avoid more fire.

The gunfire on the other side picked up in intensity, but some of it was M16 fire. I remember hoping it was our guys returning fire and not those three VC running around with stolen M16s. Lieutenant Thuyet was now faced with the classic infantry dilemma. With a man down in the open and some of his men already in the woodline across the way, he couldn't direct fire in there without fear of hitting his own men.

While he worked on a solution, I called up our outpost for a medivac request. Even though I couldn't see the extent of the wounds, I knew I had at least one WIA already and the possibility of others. I could hear the two-way conversation to Kiến Bình as the guys in the outpost relayed the medivac request. This was followed by Kiến Bình's conversation with Rạch Giá, of which I could only hear our side.

When we had been in Hóa Quản, we were fortunate to be close enough to Rạch Giá to have direct communication with them. Now, at Vĩnh Thanh, everything had to be relayed through Kiến Bình. And from my position in the field, calling from my portable PRC-25, my message was thrice removed. I listened to the radio operator in Kiến Bình authenticate to Rạch Giá that, indeed, this was a Vietnamese wounded in action, not U.S. The fire on the other side was subsiding as Thuyet directed two volunteers to go after the wounded man.

In combat units, ARVN units included, there exist individuals who volunteer for this sort of thing. To witness such an act of extreme courage is a remarkable remembrance. During my one-year tour of duty in the field, I saw it many times. I had seen it with the 168 rifle company at Hóa Quản and every man who volunteered to walk point on all of our patrols and night ambushes into dangerous areas.

Within that group who live by the sword, die by the sword, there are those that want to be recognized by their peers as the most daring of the daring. They want to face death unscathed and then live to brag about it. It's a "man thing" among young men who daily face death at some level anyway, and they take it to a higher level to exhibit their courage to everyone. That level of courage can occasionally be born of a simpler, less complicated motive: a wounded buddy laying in the middle of an open rice paddy who needs to be saved. On that morning I witnessed it again, firsthand.

The volunteers ran out into the open and dragged the wounded 379 soldier back to our position. He was shot in the upper leg, with a grazing wound across his hand. The fire on the other side had stopped now and based on the lack of enemy fire drawn by the rescue, Thuyet sent out the rest of the platoon again. Most of them were entering the woodline as Hogan and I dashed across the clearing. We entered the other side and were met by some of the 1st Platoon, who announced to me that we had two more wounded.

We advanced forward and located the other two WIA's, neither one of which was point man Dzu. The WIA's had wounds that didn't appear to be life threatening. I called the outpost and upped our medivac request to three WIA's. Lt. Winters called Kiến Bình, Kiến Bình called Rạch Giá, Rạch Giá called Cần Thơ, etc. I left the wounded with the Vietnamese medics and moved forward with the others. No rifle fire now.

Ahead, in a small clearing, we came upon an uninhabited shelter, a lean-to, open on several sides. Thiếu Úy Thuyet's attention was immediately drawn to the area surrounding the lean-to, as he barked to some of his men. He pointed around to the remains of a campfire, a make-shift bunker, and some kernels of white rice on the ground.

"Trung Úy," Binh turned to me, "VC sleep here last night."

"Have you seen Dzu," Binh?"

"No," he replied. I was wondering how he had fared, walking point when the gunfire erupted. Where could he be?

As we approached the edge of Nha Sĩ, we came upon the first of the inhabited houses near the Duờng Xuòng canal. The rest of the 1st Platoon had fanned out and secured the area around the house. There were soldiers crowded around the doorway of the house.

As I approached, I could see that a crowd had gathered inside the house as well. One of Thuyet's men ran up to inform us that point man Dzu was inside. I translated the *"bị thường"* (wounded) part myself, as the private pointed to various parts of his body with his index finger.

Hogan and Binh were both sometimes squeamish about seeing the wounded, especially any of the soldiers they knew. It greatly upset them. Rather than enter the house, they parked themselves at the base of a coconut tree along the edge of the canal. I wasn't particularly fond of dealing with it either. In fact, I was sick of it. I had already seen enough suffering, and the thoughts of them often kept me awake. I took off the heavy radio and left it with Hogan in the shade of the tree. I put down my M16 and ammo and asked him to keep an eye on it as well.

I was already catching the aroma of the Vietnamese cigarettes in the air, the sickeningly sweet synonym of death for me. There was always so much smoking immediately after a firefight, and my senses linked the aroma with the sight of the dead and dying. The nausea began to well up at the same time I inhaled the stink of the Vietnamese tobacco. My stomach had that same, queasy feeling again. I began sweating. Nervous, butterflies in the stomach-type sweating.

"Come on, Binh," I said, as he reluctantly looked up into my eyes. I could tell he had the same feeling in his stomach. At the entrance to the house the crowd was so thick that at first, I couldn't get in. When they realized it was Binh and I, the crowd parted, then filled back into the doorway. The smoke was thick in the room, and the sudden difference in light had us squinting to see anything but shapes. In the corner of the one-room house was a wooden-slatted Vietnamese bed, and I could make out the shape of a man on his back. As I approached, it was Dzu, his head propped up by a cylindrically shaped Vietnamese pillow. Thiếu Úy Thuyet was at his side, as was a Vietnamese medic. One of Dzu's buddies was also next to him, holding a cigarette to his lips.

As my eyes adjusted in the dark smoky fog, I moved in close. Dzu recognized me and smiled, then defiantly took a drag on the cigarette. I had seen that sort of cavalier nonchalance before. Vietnamese smile when embarrassed. It was his way of dealing with the sight of me, or rather, me of him. It was his way of apologizing as if to say, "I'm embarrassed that you have to see me this way. I hope I'm not an inconvenience to you." My eyes wandered the length of his body, which had been stripped to his shorts.

The extent of his wounds told me the Vietcông had been waiting for us on the other side of the clearing, or perhaps we had surprised them while having breakfast at the lean-to. Either way, they set up a hasty ambush and were ready for us. They waited until Dzu was almost upon them. Perhaps he even paused when he saw them, standing immediately to their front. When they fired, they shot him while he was fully erect. They shot to kill him instantly, to eliminate his threat completely, and thus concentrate their firepower on his friends 50 to 100 meters behind him. Dzu had taken the bullets meant for the rest of us.

I had never seen a man with that many gunshot wounds. Both of his arms were shot. One was broken, by the way it lay askew at his side. He had a sucking chest wound, which the medic was correctly addressing immediately. He had several more bullet holes in the midsection and a few more in his thighs. I remember the leg wounds to be peculiar. In dreams I can still see the leg shots; I stood closest to his legs. They looked like someone had taken a ball-point pen in their fist, and punched the pen into the flesh. The puncture wounds were hardly bleeding – just big, red welts. Of course, the medic was doing the best he could. Dzu had to be in immense pain; I couldn't imagine the pain.

Thiếu Úy Thuyet was speaking to me, and Binh was translating: "Trung Úy, you can get medivac now?"

"I already have one coming," I said. I turned and left the smoke-filled room. I had to get out. I was close to vomiting.

Out by the coconut tree, Hogan asked me how bad Dzu was. I knew he had a special, joking relationship with Dzu. Hogan liked him and sometimes shared his rations with him. Now I had to tell him the truth.

"He's bad," I said, reaching for the handset. Hogan stared at the ground in despair. It had already been a half-hour since I placed the medivac request. Maybe it was on the way.

"Foxtrot one-one this is Foxtrot one-zero, over." I wanted Bob Winters to push the system, accelerate the process. Lieutenant Winters again made the call, adding a fourth wounded, and stressed the urgency as well as I could have done, had I not been so far removed from those on the other end.

"Roger," they told Winters, "be advised they'll be at your location ASAP. Anything further, over?"

"Negative," Bob replied, "out."

A half-hour later, we received the same response. I sat in the shade of the coconut tree with Hogan, staring at the stagnant water in the muddy canal. Vietnamese privates began trying to bum Salems from me, and when I wouldn't give them one, they expressed displeasure. "Binh, get these little bastards out of here. I don't need this crap right now."

After more minutes, Thiếu Úy Thuyet was at my feet again, ranting to Binh.

"Trung Úy, when helicopter come?" Binh asked for him.

"They told me soon. I'm so sorry. I'll call again now, Binh," I replied. After two hours, Thuyet was impatient, and I couldn't blame him. I looked in on Dzu. He was no longer smiling. Most of the Vietnamese had left the room except for Dzu's buddy and the company medic. I tried repeatedly to get the medivac, and we waited, and waited. I was disgusted.

Three hours from the time I first placed the medivac call, the ship finally arrived. I popped smoke and guided the ship in, and Hogan helped load the three wounded on board, plus the dead body of our brave point man, Dzu. It was the longest response time of any medivac I ever summoned. And the longest afternoon of my tour of duty.

"Hey, wait a minute," the pilot yelled at me through the window, "the fourth one, is he dead?"

"No," I lied. "Take him to the hospital."

We retraced our steps as we moved out of Nha Sĩ. When we got to the clearing where the Vietcông nipa-thatched shelter was, Thuyet had his men tug at the support poles to topple the roof. They left it dangling there as they began to move out.

I took out my Zippo lighter and held it up, saying to Hogan, "What do you think, Sarge?"

"Yeah," he replied, "let's burn the mutha-fucka to the ground." We held the Zippos at the edge of the nipa leaves until they started burning. "Just a little payback for Dzu," Hogan said.

On the way back, I didn't have much to say to anybody. I felt that I had failed again. It was getting to me and making me feel despondent. To this day, looking back, I still wish I could have done more. I hoped there wouldn't be too many more days like that one. I was stressed and mentally fatigued beyond words.

Sergeant Hogan had an understanding, empathetic way about him, and he could tell on the trip back that I was down. "Hey, LT," he said.

"What?" I replied.

"That mutha-fuckin' place is nasty."

I didn't reply.

Upon returning to the outpost, Hogan told everyone on the team what had happened down there. As he put on the finishing touches, he told the rest of the guys, "And that mutha-fuckin' place shouldn't be called Nha Sĩ. That mutha-fucka should be called Nas-ty."

Everyone couldn't help but crack up with laughter. And from then on, the rest of the team adopted the new name. For us, Vĩnh Thanh's most southerly hamlet would forever go by no other name. Nha Sĩ was to be known as "Nasty" from then on.

CHAPTER SEVEN

# Sitting Ducks

JULY 30, 1969
Diary Entry:
*Made our outhouse and worked on frame of kitchen.*

The completion of our outhouse took precedence over all, even the kitchen. We had been squatting in the jungle, at the edge of the rice paddy, along the canal, anywhere we could find privacy. It was embarrassing to be an American in the field when nature called. And the Vietnamese always found humor in watching us for some reason. The indignity, I suppose.

Within a few days we discovered that the Vietnamese were using our new "facility" at night. They squat when they take care of "business," and we found muddy footprints on either side of the hole we had cut in the plywood. One morning, Parson came back from our outhouse, thoroughly annoyed about having to wipe mud off his butt after his visit: "That's it, damn it! I'm gonna get us a flip-top toilet seat." I wondered how he was going to "requisition" that one.

Parson got his chance during his next visit to the province capitol at Rạch Giá to attend a medical meeting. He rose extra early one morning, and, using an adjustable wrench, removed the toilet seat from the only commode at the non-commissioned officer's billets. He stuffed it into his duffle bag and returned to the bathroom to shave. Within a short time, a sleepy-eyed NCO wandered into the room to use the facility, and nearly fell in.

"What the Hell?" he yelled, as he caught his balance.

## Sitting Ducks

Then, looking at Parson, he said, "Do you freaking believe this? Some sorry Son-of-a-Bitch stole the freaking toilet seat!"

Parson, still nonchalantly shaving, and at 6' 2" tall, an imposing man in excellent physical condition, looked in the mirror and calmly said, "Well I'll be dipped!"

Once the contraband was safely back at the outpost, Parson attached it to the plywood platform with the hole in the middle. Now we could sit on it, and then flip it up for the Vietnamese to use. It was easier than pulling guard duty.

The seat was only half the project, though. Plywood was near-impossible to come by, but we still wanted to cover the sides of our outhouse. We had a pile of heavy canvas mailbags kicking around in the corner. We never threw things away because we never knew when we'd need something. The mail sacks were supposed to be returned after every delivery of mail. But sometimes we forgot or the guys on the Swing Ship didn't ask for the bag from the previous drop. The large, heavy canvas bags were great for covering the outhouse because of the reinforced metal eyelets. We cut them open along the seam, stretched them out, and nailed the mailbags to the frame to make the walls. There was only one problem. The mailbags had warnings written all over them.

Our outhouse was located directly adjacent to the "front gate," between the outpost entrance and the helipad. Every high-ranking visitor that landed at our new Vĩnh Thanh outpost for the coming months would have to walk directly past the outhouse when entering.

One of the blessings of being in the field (and there were few), was that the "brass" usually left us alone. We decided to take a risk and hope for the best, because, plastered all over the light grey mailbags in bold, black, stenciled letters, was written, "UNITED STATES GOVERNMENT PROPERTY," and "PROPERTY OF U.S. MAIL - DO NOT DESTROY."

AUGUST 2, 1969
Diary Entry:

*LTC. Stanberry, Major Harrington, and Major Night visited by Swing Ship to force commanding officer of 267 to go into Nha Sĩ. Received sandbags for bunker.*

The 267 Company had returned from Nasty again and this time parked themselves in Vĩnh Thanh near the pagoda for safety. Stanberry arrived with his counterpart, Colonel Tài, to have a face-to-face with the company commander of the 267 concerning his refusal to go to, and stay in, Nasty. When Stanberry stepped off the helicopter, he fired his initial questioning at me, "What's the problem with the 267, Lieutenant Amon?"

I wasn't going to present the colonel with the same feeble excuses the Vietnamese had given me, so I spit it out: "Sir, I've been talking to them 'till I'm blue in the face. We've even run two special operations to escort them down there, but they turned around and followed us back up here again. When I talk to the company commander, he comes up with more excuses than Carter's got pills! They're just scared of Nha Sĩ after what happened to the 770 Company last week, and I haven't been able to get anywhere with the company commander."

"Alright," Stanberry said, "take us over to where the 267 is. Colonel Tài will straighten this out right now."

They followed me to the edge of the woodline and we entered Vĩnh Thanh, looking for the company commander. After some difficulty, one of the soldiers finally found the company commander, a young Thiếu Úy. He sheepishly approached us, knowing full well what we were doing there.

LTC Bill Stanberry, Ambassador William Colby
and LTC Nguyen Van Tai.

It didn't take Tài very long to lose his temper. Bình wasn't around to translate, but I didn't need him. The gist of the conversation was obvious. The Hoa Hảo company commander tried to offer some of his silly excuses to the colonel, which only enraged Tài even more. I remembered the sound of Tai's shrill voice on the radio the day we were inserted into Vĩnh Thanh, but watching and listening to him vent his anger publicly in person was almost comical. He got red in the face, ranting and raving, arms waving in the air. His public tirade sent others scurrying, and eventually the company commander stood alone in the clearing taking the full brunt of the ass-chewing. Abruptly, Tài walked away, steaming for the helicopter. Stanberry and I followed, leaving the company commander humiliated and looking for all the world like a little boy whose mother had scolded him in front of all his schoolmates.

"Whoa, sir," I said to Stanberry, "I guess that takes care of that."

"Let me know if they don't go back down to Nha Sĩ," Stanberry barked.

"Yes, sir," I replied.

I wasn't going to waste any more time watching over the 267. After witnessing the embarrassing public ass-chewing of the Thiếu Úy, I was confident they would be going back down there. And if they didn't, all I had to do was call LTC Stanberry, and the Thiếu Úy knew it. There was no way he wanted to come face to face with Tài again! Facing Nasty was the lesser evil!

AUGUST 3, 1969
Diary Entry:

*Worked on bunker all day. Completed about half of it. Tonight, I sent Lt. Winters and SSgt. Hogan on night ambush. They made contact with 3 VC. They fired at the VC, and had one hand grenade thrown at them. No one was hurt. Intelligence says 1 battalion of VC will attack from the area of pagoda in Nha Sĩ.*

As hoped for, the 267 Company departed the pagoda in the direction of Nasty in the morning. A small element of our company accompanied them to make sure they stayed in place.

But the ambush at our location on that night was a close call for Hogan and Winters. It was as close as any of us came to getting shot while out on night ambush, and it concerned me. The VC came up the trail from Nasty to harass the RD Cadre again, who were still working and sleeping in the village. They must have already known the 267 was in Nasty and not Vĩnh Thanh with the RD Cadre. But our 379 soldiers were waiting for them, along with Winters and Hogan.

The ambush on the VC tripped early however, before they had them in the kill zone to their front. As a result, gunfire erupted at one end of the ambush. Winters and Hogan fired their M16s into the darkness as the VC fled south back toward Nasty. But before they left, they threw a hand grenade at our guys. The grenade exploded at a distance far enough away from our party that it wounded no one.

"Do you think you hit any of them, Hogan?" I asked.

"Shee-it," he replied, "I don't know, LT. They took off runnin' down toward Nasty and we got the hell out of there!"

AUGUST 13, 1969<br>
Diary Entry:

*I went to Rạch Giá for team business. While I was away the outpost was attacked: 2 rounds of incoming mortar fire at 2355. One RD Cadre was wounded by friendly fire.*

I went into Rạch Giá on the Swing Ship to scrounge around one more time for anything that wasn't nailed down. I talked the S4 (supply) sergeant into letting me have an empty 55-gallon drum, some pieces of threaded pipe, a valve, and a shower nozzle. I had a plan: we would cut the bottom open and flip it upside down on the roof of our bunker, screw the pipe thread into the opening in the lid, hook up the plumbing, let the rain help fill it up, and presto: a real, functioning shower with an on-off valve!

While I was in the mess hall at lunch, I was told Col. Stanberry wanted to see me in his office that afternoon. I couldn't imagine why, but I didn't let it interfere with my second Sloppy Joe and two bricks of ice cream for dessert. I can think of no one stationed in the field most of the time who didn't like coming back to the "rear" once in a while just for a little taste of comfort.

I arrived at the open-air building at the senior advisor's compound and once again climbed the same stairs I had climbed back in February. It was hard to believe I had been in the field for six months already. A specialist fourth-class escorted me to Stanberry's office.

"Sit down, Lieutenant Amon," Stanberry said, after we exchanged salutes. "You have a Sergeant Griffin on your team, right, Bob?" he questioned.

"Yes, sir," I replied. Stanberry began telling me about a recent "incident" that occurred while Griffin was passing through

Rạch Giá on his way back from R&R.

The colonel pieced together the details for me as he knew them. In late July, while hoisting more than a few at the bar, Griffin started an argument with a Vietnamese captain. The hostility escalated and Griffin punched the Dai Úy several times in the face before someone broke it up. There had also been another similar incident prior to that one. The colonel had not initially been informed of the first one because some NCOs had been able to keep it under wraps. But this time, Stanberry's counterpart, Colonel Tài, was told of both fights by his Vietnamese officers, and Tài wanted an accounting of it.

I told Stanberry I had no knowledge whatsoever of either fight, but I would be sure to counsel Griffin and make certain it never happened again. Unfortunately, my attempt to get Griff off the hook wasn't quite good enough to satisfy the colonel.

"Specialist Banks," barked Stanberry, "bring me Sgt. Griffin's 201 file. I want to take a look at this character." After thumbing through Griffin's personnel records, the colonel said to me with a frown, "For goodness sake, are you aware of how long Griffin has been in-country, Bob?"

I didn't have an answer for him, but as Griffin's team leader I should have. The only thing I could think to say was, "Well, sir, I know he was with the Big Red One for a tour before he was sent to MACV, but I don't know for sure his total time in-country. He never told me."

"Randy, take a look at this," he said, as Banks looked over his shoulder. "Yes, sir, that's something. And it looks like he's trying to get still another extension... unbelievable, sir," Banks added.

"Bob," the colonel said, "What kind of a soldier is Griffin?"

"I haven't had any problems with him, sir," I said, adding, "he's been fine in his performance on the team. He fits in well and works hard to help train the company. He does everything I ask of him. He's a good man and never complains, but I had no idea this had happened. He never told me. I know he was hit in the arm when he was with the 1st Infantry Division. Maybe that's a hang-up of his with the Vietnamese, I don't know."

"Aside from his R&R time, Griffin has been in Vietnam for almost four consecutive years!" Stanberry went on, "Apparently every unit he's been with has granted him one 6-month extension after another. I don't think I've ever seen this many back-to-back 6-month extensions."

In its boundless wisdom, the U.S. Army allowed 6-month extensions of combat tours of duty in Vietnam. Not only did they allow it, they offered rewards and incentives to anyone extending: a pay bonus, an extra in-country R&R to Vung Tau, and another shot at promotion. Unit commanders had quotas placed on them for such extensions because the Army was so short on experienced people.

Each time Griffin volunteered to stay in Vietnam, the first sergeant in whatever unit he had been reassigned to jumped at the opportunity to make the commanding officer look good. Of course, no one had ever taken the time to take a good look at his 201 File from beginning to end, or to counsel him to find out if he's still wrapped tightly. At the end of my own tour, Stanberry himself approached me with the offer. I would make captain, get an additional R&R, and be assured of a safer job in Rạch Giá working with the RD Cadre at province level, all for signing up for a six-month extension. The extra combat-duty pay in Vietnam was not to be discounted either.

Griff was nearing the end of 48 months of non-stop combat assignments. He had applied for yet another extension the same week he involved himself in the altercation with the Vietnamese Dai Úy. Had Griff not made that mistake, Stanberry himself probably would have routinely signed the papers approving yet another extension for him to stay, which would then have kept him in Vietnam for 54 months straight!

"Lieutenant," Stanberry decided, "when you get back to Vĩnh Thanh, you tell this Griffin character that you got your ass chewed out by me over what he's done. We can't have our NCOs running around punching out Vietnamese officers. My counterpart is fit to be tied. Tell this Griffin if it happens again, I'll see to it we court-martial his ass. In the meantime, I'm not approving his extension. You don't have to tell him that, let him wonder. He'll eventually find out from the first sergeant. I'm sending this kid home. He's been in-country too damned long!"

AUGUST 17, 1969<br>Diary Entry:

*Major Dowd visited by swing ship. Told us to prepare for visit by Major General Wetherill. Sgt. Lloyd came in by Swing Ship to join the team.*

Today Sergeant E-5 Lloyd arrived, probably as a replacement to fill the slot soon to be vacated by Griffin. Lloyd proved to be another valuable asset to the team, and he was with me for the rest of my tour. He was a sharp, spunky black kid from Detroit if memory serves, and from the first moment his feet hit the mud at Vĩnh Thanh, he was raring for action. I liked him from the start. Hogan and I decided we would "take him under our wing" at first, for just a little while.

AUGUST 18, 1969<br>Diary Entry:

*Major General Wetherill visited. Commented on exceptional appearance of the team.*

Major General Roderick Wetherill replaced Major General Ekhardt as commander of IV Corps, Mekong Delta. He was making the rounds, visiting selected outposts in contested areas of the Delta. The general was accompanied by Col. Stanberry and an entourage.

Hogan and Lloyd put a spit-shine on their jungle boots, which prompted Parson, Winters and me to do the same. And the new outpost was looking good... nice deep moat, solid berm walls with good, notched-out firing positions. We even had wire crisscrossed across the moats to make it more difficult for attackers to come through the water. The general stepped out of the UH-1D and followed me through the front gate. We walked directly past our new outhouse, mailbags proudly proclaiming, "PROPERTY OF U.S. MAIL - DO NOT DESTROY."

In our new team house, I briefed the general on the situation at Vĩnh Thanh. Besides the successful completion of this outpost, we had another government outpost under construction to the north at Cái Nhum, on the banks of the river. To the south in Nha Sĩ, the 267 finally settled in with several RD Cadre teams and had started construction of an outpost there. With the exception of enemy harassment during the past several weeks, things were looking better in Vĩnh Thanh.

"Are you getting full co-operation from your counterpart, Lieutenant Amon?" the general questioned.

"For the most part, yes sir, but I'm a bit concerned about company strength. There seems to be a lot of absenteeism lately with the 379 Company."

"You'd better address it with your counterpart," General Wetherill said to me. "If you don't get results, let Colonel Stanberry know. Perhaps Colonel Tài should have a talk with your company commander."

Seven days from this date, the front page of a Connecticut newspaper carried a UPI article that the 18B Regiment (about 2,000 troops) of the 1st North Vietnamese Army Division had deployed into the Mekong Delta. Major General Wetherill is quoted in the article as saying, "I think they came down here to shore up a deteriorating situation. It's an indication of Hanoi's growing concern with what's happening down here." The article pointed out that "The Delta is the richest prize of the Vietnam War. More than half the nation's 17.5 million people live there and most of the rice is grown there."[17]

### AUGUST 19, 1969
#### Diary Entry:
*Went on roving ambush with Lloyd. No contact.*

Lloyd was itching for his first night ambush, eager to finally be "in the field" and a part of the team. This was his third night on the team since joining us. I took him out to break him in. We left at dusk with a squad from the 379, and quietly took up a position near the pagoda. At 11 p.m., the sergeant had us move again, this time along the trail coming up from Nasty. We were close to the area where Hogan and Winters exchanged gunfire and had the hand grenade thrown at them. We waited there as the rain began to fall. Lloyd and I put on our ponchos, trying to keep as dry as possible.

The rain got heavier and the clouds now completely covered any moonlight. It was pitch black. Lloyd sat patiently next to me. After an hour or so, the Vietnamese had enough. Without ponchos, they were soaked and shivering. "We go back now, VC no come here tonight," the sergeant announced. Lloyd walked behind me for the dangerous return to the outpost, rain pelting off our ponchos.

On nights like that, everything you wear gets soaked and muddy, even your rifle and magazines. It all has to be cleaned. When we got back, I let Lloyd take a shower first. We rinsed off our muddy gear and left our boots suspended upside down in the kitchen.

Hogan turned the volume down on the radio. It was late and we were all tired. "Congratulations, Lloyd, how'd you like your first night ambush?" Hogan asked sarcastically, laughing at the cold, wet, shivering newcomer.

"Oh, that?" he said, giving it right back to him. "Shit, I was expecting to stay out all night. I was beginning to enjoy myself out there."

"Yeah, right," Hogan laughed, and then addressing me, he said, "Hey, LT, I'll go on the operation with you tomorrow," referring to the 379 Company operation the following morning.

"We've got an operation tomorrow?" Winters queried, from the sanctity of his warm sleeping bag.

"Yeah," I replied, "Thuyet wants to send half the company back up north again, up to Vĩnh Lôc."

"Shee-it," Hogan contributed, addressing Winters' question, "Vĩnh Lôc's where they made Lieutenant Amon and me ride in those sampans to get back to the outpost." I remembered

# Sitting Ducks

it too, and it was good that Hogan reminded me.

"I'll tell you what," I announced to everyone, "they don't need us tomorrow. Let them ride in their sampans. It's late and I want us to get some rest. And from the looks of it, it's gonna be raining like a son-of-a-bitch again tomorrow. I'm gonna tell Thuyet to count us out."

"You won't get any argument from me," Winters called out from beneath his mosquito netting.

"Yeah," Hogan said, "got that right."

I just had a bad feeling about that one, like a voice in my head telling me not to send my guys out.

Sometimes in life, luck is all one has. In Vietnam, luck was a big thing. Some had a great deal of luck. Most had a little from time to time. Some had none. We were about to get lucky. Or maybe it wasn't luck at all.

I have recurring dreams to this day about certain events in Vietnam. In one of the dreams, I'm aware that I'm still the older man that I am today and I'm in Vietnam. But I'm not on the ground as was the case in 1969. Instead, I'm looking down at a young Army lieutenant in Vietnam and he has a lot on his plate. He's responsible for peoples' lives.

I can't make out his face and I don't know who he is, but I can hear what he's saying. I even know what he's thinking and the decisions he's about to make. I'm inside his head, trying to warn him, yelling at him, but I don't know if he can hear me or if he's even paying attention.

In the dream, it's raining and the visibility is very poor, so I swing the camera around to his front and zoom in to get closer to warn him to not ride in sampans the following morning. As I focus the lens on his olive-drab fatigue shirt, I notice the sewn-on cloth tape above his left pocket reads, "U.S. ARMY." I swing the camera over to his right pocket and the name tape above it has my last name on it, "AMON."

Good Lord, the young man I'm trying to warn is me!

Not knowing if I'm getting through to him, the dream usually startles me so that I wake up at this point. I lie in bed thinking that perhaps I actually did get through to him, or rather, to myself, fifty years ago. I'm convinced that I did. Extrasensory perception? Divine intervention?

Clairvoyance is supposedly the ability to perceive things or events in the future or beyond. I wonder if it works in reverse or traverses time. Welcome to The Twilight Zone.

AUGUST 20, 1969
Diary Entry:

*An element from 379 was ambushed while returning in sampans.*[S] *Two killed and one wounded. Later, when they were taking the bodies to Kiến Bình, they tripped a booby trap. One civilian was killed instantly and two more soldiers were wounded.*

Everyone on the team slept in except me. The water-logged ambush with Lloyd the night before knocked the heck out of my sleep and I really didn't have any physical energy. But it was more than that.

The bad premonition I had after the ambush… that voice in my head telling me to stay back at the outpost, was still jarring me. As soon as I opened my eyes, I went over to Thiếu Úy Thuyet's bunker and told him we wouldn't be going with them up to Vĩnh Lộc. I was really tired of putting myself and my men at risk with the Thiếu Úy's lazy and hazardous commandeering of sampans to get back to the outpost.

Lloyd was already up helping Hogan make coffee. I could hear him telling Hogan about the ambush, the amount of rain, the pitch-black visibility, etc. Parson and Winters slept until about 11 a.m. Outside, water was coming down sideways, a good day to catch up on sleep and write a few letters home.

At about 2 p.m., in the pouring rain, intense gunfire erupted to the north, halfway to Vĩnh Lộc.[S] From the sound of it, the part of the company that had gone to Vĩnh Lộc had made contact on the way back. As abruptly and violently as the gunfire started, it ended.

I put on my wet boots and poncho, put together some dry M16 magazines for my rifle, and headed over to Thiếu Úy

Thuyet's. His radio was already crackling. I heard the words, *"Phục kích* (ambush), and *"bị thương"* (wounded) and I had a good idea what happened.

Within minutes, the lead sampan arrived at the outpost. The Vietcông had set up an ambush along the Cái Nhum canal leading to Vĩnh Lôc after the patrol had swept the area. Now feeling safe about returning in sampans on the Cái Nhum, they got hit. It was raining, they were getting wet, and they wanted to take the easy, lazy way back.

The sole sampan arriving at the outpost had been lucky enough to pass through the kill zone in front of the main ambush. Unscathed, they knew very little of what happened behind them. They simply gunned the motor and got out of there, leaving the rest of the patrol behind. It was a classic VC ambush tactic - hit the middle (hoping for the officers, possibly an advisor or two), then *"di-di mau"* (go, go quickly) out of there.

Thuyet stood next to me at the edge of the canal and chewed out the men in the lead sampan for returning to the outpost instead of doubling back to engage the VC. Another sampan emerged from the bend in the jungle, followed by a third that had been in the middle.

The third sampan was a grizzly sight. Lloyd stood wide-eyed next to Hogan and me as it pulled up at our feet. Lloyd was about to receive his "Welcome to Vietnam" indoctrination. On his fourth day in the field, just like my first time with Guerrero, he was about to get his first look at the fresh kills.

Two of our soldiers from the 379 lay dead in the sampan, piled on the floor in a heap. They were shot at point-blank range with multiple bullets. They were soaking wet. A third lay in the sampan, still alive, but badly shot. There had been a fourth, a civilian, who was shot and killed while standing up in the rear of the sampan. He was knocked off the boat first, causing the sampan to go out of control into the embankment. They all eventually wound up in the water.

My mind flashed back to January 31 again: Chuck Emery and I, sitting side by side, both laughing, the hilarious Trung Úy

De reiterating, "You tell counterpart he full of shit! Always want to ride in sampan, easy way. Numba ten. *Sáu lam* (very bad)."

The ambush was intended to kill all the occupants of the middle sampan, the central command. It's where Thiếu Úy Thuyet rode, and consequently where I would have been with Hogan. I breathed an internal sigh of relief. It would have been the two of us laying in a muddy pile on the floor of that sampan. The voice in my head had been right.

Then my mind played tricks on me: I was looking down at me and Hogan. Our large American bodies were stretched out in the middle of the sampan, side by side, arms flopped over each other as if embracing. In death, bodies touch and reach out for one another. I was looking down at the floor of the sampan, at my own corpse reaching out for Hogan. I blinked, then looked up at Hogan to make sure he was still standing on the bank with me.

Parson worked on the wounded 379 soldier while I called for a medivac. Thiếu Úy Thuyet directed the men who arrived in the first sampan to take the two bodies of their friends to Kiến Bình, and to carry them on foot this time, until they got to the Cái Be River.

Later in the afternoon, we received word that the body-carrying patrol tripped a booby trap in route to Kiến Bình. Another civilian was killed instantly and two more of our soldiers were wounded.

Additionally, an M16 had been shot in half at the stock, and only the rifle butt had been retrieved. Thuyet had to send two more squads back up the canal to dive for the rest of the M16, which sank in the canal. After an hour of swimming, they found the "business end" of the M16 and brought it back to the outpost. We didn't want the VC to fetch it. They were too good at repairing anything usable and they were already using captured M16s against us in their ambushes.

Our casualties at Vĩnh Thanh Village totaled 7 that day: 2 KIA, 3 WIA, and 2 civilians killed. That voice in my head... I still don't know what that was. I don't believe in the supernatural, but maybe there is something like mental telepathy between yourself as an older man and yourself as a young man. Or perhaps divine intervention.

I often tell my wife I don't know why I survived in Vietnam. My destiny was probably to die in the mud there. Then she always asks me… "How many grandkids do we have?"

I tell her seven.

Carrying our wounded out to the helicopter pad to the arriving medivac.

Many of our new recruits were quite young.

AUGUST 21, 1969
Diary Entry:
*LTC Stanberry and Major Dowd visited by Swing Ship to inform us of expected visit tomorrow by the Under-Secretary of the Army.*

AUGUST 22, 1969
Diary Entry:
*Under-Secretary of the Army Siena visited with Mr. Vann. I gave them a briefing.*

I was to find out the reason behind all the recent hoopla and briefings, but it would be years before the pieces of the entire puzzle revealed the complete composite, one of the rewards for having kept the diary and matching it years later with other recorded history and research on the subject.

First, on the 17th of August, we had a visit from Major Dowd to announce the visit by the IV Corps Commander, Major General Wetherill, on the 18th. Then my briefing to the general on the 18th. That should have been the end of it. In our world, at that God-forsaken mud-hole, they didn't come any bigger than the commanding general of the entire Delta. Topping that, however, was another visit on the 21st by Major Dowd and Stanberry for another briefing, followed by the announcement of the visit by the Under-Secretary of the Army "and some high-ranking civilians."

"What is going on here?" I thought. "We just had seven casualties here two days ago, four of which are dead. Don't they know I have more to do than prepare for briefings? And why bring the Under-Secretary of the Army, *here?* Are they nuts?"

Years later, piecing together events, and after having read much on the era, including Neil Sheehan's brilliantly researched and documented 862-page book, *A Bright Shining Lie*, I discovered why the intense interest in Vĩnh Thanh late that summer.

Major General Wetherill had come to Vĩnh Thanh outpost at Stanberry's suggestion, eager to see for himself if my briefing would meet his high standards and be positive enough.

## Sitting Ducks 175

MAT 88 had been selected, among other teams in the Delta, by the general for the ultimate "show and tell." I was going to be briefing people higher up than the general, even higher up than the Under-Secretary of the Army.

Mr. Siena's official job title in August of 1969 was Deputy Under-Secretary of the Army, Specializing in International Affairs. He reported to Under-Secretary of the Army Beal. But more important and influential than Siena were the other civilian visitors to our teamhouse, and none more outspokenly influential in higher circles and among his peers than Mr. Vann, mentioned in the diary. On August 22, 1969, I had no idea who Vann was, much less why I was briefing him and the others dressed in civilian clothes.

John Paul Vann strode off that helicopter like he had lived in Vĩnh Thanh Village all his life. He was wearing civilian slacks and a white short-sleeve shirt, covered by a windbreaker. It was odd to have someone get off a chopper dressed that way. I led the way from the helipad, exercising my Pied-Piper routine past our mailbag outhouse and our sentry sitting in the machine-gun bunker at the "front gate."

Inside, Hogan, Winters, Lloyd, and Parson all stood in the back of the room at "parade rest," wearing clean jungle fatigues and spit-shined boots.

I didn't know who was in charge. Standing in front of them with a pointer in my hand, I addressed them, referring to our topographical map. I assumed the civilians were the heavyweights, so I made sporadic eye contact with them. I had learned from previous briefings to avoid self-inflicting booby-traps, such as mentioning the 770 getting their asses waxed in Nasty, or the refusal of the 267 to go down there, or the ass-kicking our own 379 Company took two days ago. Such negativity would only lead to a barrage of difficult questions.

Besides, there were good reasons for optimism. What we had accomplished in Hóa Quản had been rewarding. And now, at Vĩnh Thanh, we had been thrust into the most difficult of challenges and met them head on. The VC had not driven us from

Vĩnh Thanh, or Nha Sĩ, or anyplace else. All the threats of impending attacks, even the presence of the heavily armed NVA with the Chinese advisors passing within 300 meters on the first night, had not deterred us. The weather and the ambushes had not slowed the building of the outpost, which we accomplished in one month. The outposts and pacification plans in the other hamlets, including Nha Sĩ, were progressing nicely.

When I had finished, I ended with, "This concludes my briefing." I then found out who was in charge. It was Vann who spoke first. "Are you using your RD Cadre teams to your fullest advantage, Lieutenant?"

"Yes, sir, we are," I slapped back. "RD Cadre teams 18 and 30 were here even before the completion of the outpost, working on the pacification. They've also been gathering information from informants on the local VCI (Vietcông Infrastructure) for the Phoenix Program."

"Make sure you personally monitor them to be sure they submit the names through their channels," Vann said.

"Yes, sir, I will," I replied.

"Your team is doing an excellent job, Lieutenant," he spoke again. "Keep up the good work."

"Thank you, sir," I responded.

Sitting directly in front of me, John Paul Vann was forty-five years of age. He had been in Vietnam throughout the '60s, first as an Army officer, then as a civilian, returning to the place he loved, the war he loved, the killing of communists in Vietnam. Because of his feisty demeanor and positive effect on the war effort, Vann was notorious in military and political circles, having done remarkable advisory work throughout Vietnam. The CORDS director in charge of Vietnam, William Colby, was so impressed with Vann that he convinced him in February of 1969 that his talents were better served in the Delta, where the VC had traditionally drawn so much of their manpower and tax revenues.[18]

Additionally, Vann was needed in the Delta because the VC were managing to "retain strongholds south of the Bassac (river) in the U-Minh Forest of Ca Mau, in Kiến Giáng and Chương Thiện provinces. To accomplish that, Hanoi had to infiltrate four NVA regiments into IV Corps."[19] They were the NVA that passed by us on June 20.

During 1969, through persistence, John Paul Vann gained access to the highest of inner circles. His aggressive, optimistic plans for winning the war in Vietnam eventually reached Henry Kissinger, and from there, the Oval Office. Throughout the latter part of the summer of 1969 and into the fall, Vann campaigned for, and eventually achieved, an audience with President Richard Nixon. At 12 noon on December 22, 1969, Kissinger introduced Vann "with unstinting praise" to Nixon, the man who had recently told Congress, "I will not be the first president of the United States to lose a war."

Nixon talked with John Vann for nearly an hour that day. After Vann briefed him on pacification, including his visits with advisors in the field in many provinces of the Delta, Nixon questioned Vann on how he had seen the war change over the years, seeking to learn why Vann had arrived at his current opinions. "He appeared to accept with some confidence," Vann's memo writes, "the judgments I gave him as to the now favorable situation (in Vietnam)."[20]

Nixon had narrowly won his election as president. A widening distrust for him had made it difficult to achieve victory. At the last minute, he had pulled out all the campaign stops "by giving the (American) public the impression that he had a secret plan to end the war. Nixon admitted in his old age that he never had any such plan."[21]

In some small measure, my optimistic briefing that day reached the ears of the most powerful policymakers of our time through Vann, telling of the efforts of the advisors he had interviewed, reinforcing "Vietnamization" and hope for "peace with honor," as Nixon put it.

By comparing the time frame of my briefing to Vann, and Vann's audience with Nixon, I could see my little piece of the puzzle meshing with the total picture: the diary entries fitting in with recorded history, from the teamhouse to the White House, from Nasty to Pennsylvania Avenue.

Tragically, Vann was destined to become one of the statistics of his own beloved war. On June 9, 1972, after serving the advisory effort for a decade, the crusade of the tragic Don Quixotic-like champion of South Vietnam's quest for freedom, their impossible dream, ended unceremoniously in a grove of tall trees near the Montagnard hamlet of Ro Uay in Pleiku Province. Vann's capable and daring pilot, Lt. Ronald Doughtie, pushed to his limits by Vann and flying at night in a mist of darkness, experienced vertigo and flew into the only group of trees for hundreds of yards. Vann's broken body was sent flying from the wreckage, landing face down in the mud.

Neil Sheehan wrote of his death: "A patrol of ARVN Rangers who had arrived (first) from a nearby fire base exacted payment for the danger of being sent to fetch him at night in an area where they had been fighting with the NVA. They stripped him of his wristwatch and wallet and his Rutgers class of 1954 ring before they carried his body to Anderson's helicopter."[22]

He was laid to rest at Arlington National Cemetery. Those in attendance included Senator Edward Kennedy and General William Westmoreland, one of the pallbearers.

AUGUST 24, 1969
Diary Entry:

*Had a sector operation into Chương Thiện Province east of Nha Sĩ. We fired our 60mm mortar at retreating Vietcông. Chuẩn Úy Duc arrived to replace Thiếu Úy Thuyet.*

Chuẩn Úy Duc became the company commander of the 379 Company after 2LT Thuyet was transferred to another company. His control over the company had been slipping, as more of his men seemed to be deserting the outpost, afraid for their lives. And although I was still annoyed with Thuyet for allowing some of his subordinates to force us to ride in the dangerous sampans, I had mixed emotions about him being replaced.

However unorthodox, Thuyet had a lot of experience.

And with thirteen battle scars on his body, he also had remarkable, almost suicidal courage. He would stand up in the middle of a firefight and use a walking stick to whip his men into advancing. During our infrequent drinking sessions in which everyone drank far too much *bá xi dé*, he would remove his shirt, theatrically point to each of the thirteen scars and, one by one, exclaim, *"bị thương"* (wounded), *"bị thương!"* He attributed the fact that he was still alive to a tiger's tooth he wore around his neck. He claimed the tiger's tooth brought good luck and that the wearer could only be wounded in battle and never killed.

I wondered if our new replacement, a *Chuẩn Úy* (an aspirant, the equivalent of an officer candidate) had enough experience, leadership and courage to lead the company in a place like Vĩnh Thanh.

I bid farewell and good luck to Thuyet. He had not been my favorite counterpart (no one could ever replace Hungl, my first 168 Company counterpart), but we had been together for some time and I had helped his men through some very difficult times. As a token of his appreciation, he removed his tiger's tooth and presented it to me for luck. I wished him well and gave him my wristwatch, wondering what fate would befall him now that he no longer wore the tiger's tooth. He could now tell time. But maybe now I could count on not being killed.

### AUGUST 26, 1969
Diary Entry:

*Parson and Hogan went on operation to WR367890.*[T] *No contact except for exchanging rifle fire with 168 Company.*

*Sgt. Griffin returned by Swing Ship, not being allowed to extend his tour.*

Parson and Hogan accompanied the new Chuẩn Úy Duc on this patrol and got into a brief, accidental firefight with my old friend, Thiếu Úy Hungl and the 168 Company. They were out on one of their roving patrols along the border between Kiến Giáng and Chương Thiện Provinces.[T] Fortunately no one was hit by the "friendly fire." It was a shame that I wasn't on that operation as I would have loved to visit with Hungl and chat.

Meanwhile, in the afternoon, Sergeant Griffin returned to the team from a trip to Rạch Giá and told us that the first sergeant denied his request for yet another extension of his tour of duty in Vietnam. Of course, I already knew the denial was imminent, but I had followed Stanberry's advice and said nothing to him about it.

AUGUST 27, 1969<br>Diary Entry:

*Six soldiers went AWOL. This lowered company strength below 50%.*

The new Chuẩn Úy Duc arose this morning to discover six more of his men missing. During the night they simply decided to leave. He was honest enough to tell me about it immediately. Hogan and I each took a physical head count of every soldier in the outpost, before any more of them had a chance to wander off somewhere during the day. We each came up with 22. We were down to 22 ARVN defenders in the outpost.

In the morning I would be going into Rạch Giá to attend one of Colonel Stanberry's monthly team leaders' meetings. I intended to bring it up with him. Twenty-two ARVNs and the five of us was a total of twenty-seven inside the outpost, not enough manpower if we got hit with even a small company of experienced Vietcông fighters.

AUGUST 28, 1969<br>Diary Entry:

*Went to MAT leaders' meeting in Rạch Giá. Hit wires.*

I waited for the Swing Ship to take me to the teamleaders' meeting. I popped smoke as the chopper approached. The pilot identified the color of my smoke and landed, and I climbed in and buckled up in the right web seat along the rear wall next to the open doorway. I enjoyed the cool, early morning breeze as we landed at our second stop. I introduced myself to another lieutenant who climbed on board, and we chatted briefly as the pilot revved it back up for takeoff.

Like most outposts, this lieutenant's outpost was situated next to a canal. Our young helicopter pilot lifted off the small pad, and skillfully hovered us sideways until he was clear of the embankment and out over the middle of the canal. Then, nose down, we began our forward momentum for takeoff over the watery tunnel. There were tall trees on both sides of the canal, so he was using the canal as a "runway."

I was still looking to my left, talking to the other team leader, when a change in the sound of the helicopter engine alerted me that something didn't feel right. When I looked up, I saw black wires immediately to our front, which slapped the windshield at eye level and shot upward between the main body of the ship and the rotor!

The RF's in this outpost had taken it upon themselves to twist two double strands of black communication wire together and string it at tree-top level across the canal between two coconut trees. The wires ran to a field telephone at a listening post on the other side of the canal so they could communicate with one another across the brown span of water.

As we hit the wires, the ship decelerated and immediately drifted sideways. Because the body of the ship was being held back and the forward momentum slowed, the force of the tail rotor blade pulled the tail around to the side. I looked out of the side door as the trees approached, the transmission and engine whining at our backs. The pilot looked like he was having a seizure as he danced on the pedals to steer the ship in the other direction to keep the tail away from the trees. He made the drastic correction immediately, but when it stopped the drift to that side, the overcompensation brought the tail back the other way, now swinging the tail rotor quickly toward the trees on the other side!

"No," my mind screamed, "don't let the tail rotor hit the trees and shear itself off. I don't want to die here, this way, careening into a muddy canal like this." If the force of the crash didn't kill us, we might drown as we spun wildly out of control into the brown water below.

The wires finally snapped after being stretched, but we were still overcompensating on our third swing toward the trees. The pilot controlled it one more time and got the ship straightened out as we resumed acceleration down the canal "runway."

The nightmare wasn't over yet. When I looked forward at the pilot, he was turned around and pointing at the open side door.

"The wires," he screamed, "bring them in." I didn't know what he was talking about until I looked out my door and saw the commo wires were still with us, flapping in the breeze past both doors, threatening to entwine themselves around the tail rotor. The wire hadn't snapped in the middle as I had assumed, but rather at both coconut trees. The other lieutenant and I unbuckled, and now at considerable risk of falling out of the door because we weren't tethered, we leaned out and tried to grab ahold of the wires to pull them inside. I was finally able to grab mine, and I pulled the wire into the chopper hand over hand. The pilot lifted up and over the trees and set it down with the two of us holding onto all the wires.

The pilot shut down the engine (which I thought was highly unusual) and radioed Rạch Giá to tell them what had happened. I wasn't familiar with this part of the province or VC there, but I wasn't taking any chances. We were sitting ducks out there in the open paddy, with unfamiliar woodlines in all four directions. It would only be a matter of time before the VC came for us.

I climbed into the door gunner's seat and fed a belt of ammo under the cover of the M60 machine gun as Chuck Emery and I had done at Advisor School. I chambered a round, removed the safety and sat there patiently, ready to fire if necessary.

As the blades slowed to a stop, the young warrant officer climbed out of the cockpit and took off his helmet. He barely looked old enough to shave. He came around to the right door where I sat in the gunner's seat and tried to light a cigarette. His fingers were trembling so badly he had trouble keeping his lighter steady, so I took out my own Zippo and helped him light it.

# Sitting Ducks

"Was that your outpost?" he nervously asked me, his hand still shaking uncontrollably.

"No," I said, "it's his," nodding in the direction of the other lieutenant. "Wires are bad, huh?" I asked him.

"Bad?" he said, "Shit, wires are the worst. Hitting wires, Jesus! You don't want to run into freaking wires flying in one of these."

"I'll talk to my counterpart about this when I get back," the new team leader told the pilot.

"Yeah," the pilot said sarcastically, "I guess you better," adding, "what the hell would they want to put wires there for anyway?"

The pilot climbed up on top of the body of the helicopter to inspect the rotor area and did the same at the tail rotor before firing the machine up again. We uneventfully picked up the rest of the team leaders and flew to Rạch Giá for the meeting.

In 1985, I attended a camping trip with my son and Boy Scout Troop 42 to Cheesequake Park in New Jersey. The Air National Guard landed a helicopter in an open field for the boys to look at. One of the choppers was a vintage UH-1D Vietnam-era chopper, and the pilot appeared to be about my age. After striking up a conversation, I learned that he flew in the Mekong Delta in 1969. I told him I was in Kiến Giáng Province.

"A buddy of mine and I flew in Kiến Giáng," he said. I told him I operated on the ground in Kiến Binh District, to which he replied, "You're kidding! We used to do the Swing Ship runs in that area." Then I told him about the commo-wire incident.

"Was that you?" he said. He went on to relate that his friend of many years told him about the day he ran into the commo wires with his Swing Ship. "He talks about it all the time. You guys almost bought the farm that day."

"Yeah," I said. "You might want to tell your buddy to stop doing that!" I joked.

It felt good to know that the skillful young warrant officer that saved my life back in 1969 had made it home from Vietnam.

SEPTEMBER 4, 1969
Diary Entry:
*This day I left for my R&R in Hawaii.*

I finally got my R&R! I was to meet my wife in Hawaii on Saturday night! I had so looked forward to that since I arrived in Vietnam, but little did I know the trick it would play on my psyche. How do you flip a switch from living in hell to being in paradise? I remember hoping that I would act normal to her. I was worried that Vietnam had changed me in the eight months I'd been in country. I didn't want to be changed. I wanted things to be the way they were, the way I was before Vĩnh Thanh. Before Nasty. Before Quang accidentally blew himself up with the hand grenade. Before witnessing all the death and suffering.

My wife and I enjoyed a stroll through the International Marketplace. We rented a jeep and drove across the island and I stopped and picked sugarcane for her to sample, and we had our pictures taken. The first forty-eight hours was like being in heaven.

But after two days of that, rather than being able to savor each remaining day in paradise with my wife, I found myself counting down the days until I had to flip the switch again.

SEPTEMBER 10, 1969

My wife and I spent the day quietly lying on the beach in front of the hotel. It was our last day together. I closed my eyes, the gentle tropical breezes blowing across my body. The sunshine and saltwater had been medicinal for my skin. Seven months of insect bites had pretty much cleared up and the rice-paddy bloodsucker marks around my ankles were disappearing. But in a day, I had to head back to the mud again, and without mercy, my thoughts turned there.

What was going on in Vĩnh Thanh? I wanted to know how the rest of the guys were doing. Were they okay?

And, I didn't want to think about it. I didn't want to go back to the suffering. I didn't want to go back to the dying, the near-crashes, the dangerous sampan rides, the "mistakes" by the gunships, the incoming. I had been out in the field too long. Seven months was long enough. I didn't want to become like Darden, like Griffin. I had a life other than Vietnam. I wanted to go back to the civilian world, a world where people say "Goodbye" at the end of a conversation instead of "Roger, Out."

And I didn't want the pressure of being in charge of the team anymore. I didn't want to be asked, "Are they Uniform Sierra, or Victor November personnel, over?" I didn't want to send anybody out on night ambushes anymore.

I wasn't myself the last night of R&R. I almost felt like the Army had played a cruel joke on me. There was a part of me that wished I hadn't even met my wife in Hawaii. The R&R was not a good idea. I'd waited eight months for it and then I had to go back to the killing, the mud, the pressure and the unbelievable responsibility.

### SEPTEMBER 11, 1969

I tried to act as normal as possible as we had breakfast on that last morning. I couldn't tell my wife what was going on in Vĩnh Thanh... what I had seen, how it might change me, maybe, for the rest of my life.

Although we're no longer together, I'm still glad I spared her the worry. But inside, I knew I had to talk to somebody, just to confirm my own sanity. Being in Hawaii with normal people made me question my sanity. Only a madman would willingly return to Vĩnh Thanh to live the way we were living - going on operations and night ambushes all the time, discarding personal safety as easily as one discards a cigarette butt.

My plane took off in the late afternoon and I proceeded to get completely shit-faced on the flight to Saigon.

### SEPTEMBER 12, 1969

I arrived at Tân Sơn Nhứt airbase and bought a ride on a cyclo for some sightseeing in Saigon. I had the driver take me over to the Saigon Air Force Officer's Club. I'd been told it was a place worth seeing: Total REMF Headquarters. They had tennis courts and even an olympic-sized swimming pool.

I couldn't believe the bar area at the club! It was early Friday night, and the REMFs already had the weekend partying in full swing. Inside the huge, air-conditioned building was a dance floor, bandstand, and a padded bar! It was just like being in the States. Well, almost.

A Vietnamese band was destroying a perfectly good Beatles number as I ordered a "Seven and Seven" and took a walk around. I noticed an entrance to a small, separate room, partitioned off by beads suspended across the entrance. I parted the beads and carried my drink into the room. It reeked of cigar smoke, and I saw several card tables. I walked over to one of the tables and couldn't believe my eyes.

Sitting at the table were very high-ranking officers. One of them was a full-bird colonel. They were playing poker with real U.S. dollars on the table. But I knew it was illegal to possess, much less gamble with, United States currency in Vietnam. Upon arrival, everyone had to surrender their U.S. currency and were instead issued MPC (Military Payment Certificates). We called it "Monopoly money." But there I was, looking at piles of American greenbacks, some in large denominations! "How the hell are they getting away with this?" I asked myself.

Just then the Air Force colonel looked up and saw me standing there. I was wearing my green U.S. Army jungle fatigues, displaying my 1LT rank, my jump wings, and my Combat Infantryman's Badge.

"What are you doing in here, Lieutenant?" the colonel asked, cocking his head while removing the cigar from his lips, exhaling the smoke in my direction.

"Just looking around, sir," I said. "I'm on my way back from...," and that was as far as I got.

"Get out of here, Lieutenant! This room is major and above, and I mean NOW," he blasted, sitting up in his seat.

So much for having some fun at the Air Force Officer's Club. I left thinking, "Screw these guys. Everyone else has to obey the rules except them." I wouldn't have had anything in common with them anyway. I was only a ground-pounding, Delta dog-face. And besides, my R&R was over. Tomorrow I had to fly back to my team.

## SEPTEMBER 13, 1969

While still in Saigon, I did some last-minute shopping for the team - supplies we couldn't get through normal channels but would mean a lot to us out at the pigsty. I found a mess hall and figured I had just enough time for a delicious lunch before I caught a flight to Cần Thơ. I took my tray to a table facing the door. Just as I sat down, my old friend, Chuck Emery, walked in!

"Bob," he yelled out. "What are you doing here?" he asked.

"I'm having lunch." I said, "What does it look like I'm doing? I came here to do some bowling?"

And instantly we were kibitzing again. It was as if our friendship at Advisor School had never been interrupted. He got a tray-full of food and joined me. We talked non-stop. I told him about the REMFs in the Air Force Officer's Club, and we caught up on what our lives as advisors had been like for the past eight months.

I remembered why he was so much fun to be with. He had a great sense of humor and wasn't afraid to talk about "unmanly" things like feelings, fears, and emotions. He asked what Hawaii was like and I told him about my R&R. "Wow!" he said, when I showed him a picture of my wife. Never one to hold back, he said, "You're really lucky. What's it like being married?"

I remembered earlier personal questions back at Advisor School, questions about my formative years and family life, questions asked in such a way that they now made me curious: Why would someone have such an intense interest in what (to me) seemed a normal upbringing? He seemed to have an insatiable thirst for anything family- and relationship-related.

At Advisor School, we never quite had the time to casually talk. But there, in that quiet mess hall, we just leisurely sat and chatted, one on one. Fielding his personal questions, I felt obligated to ask questions of his background also. But when I did, he quickly changed the subject back to Vietnam, so I went with it.

"I'm a team leader in An Xuyên Province," he said.

"An Xuyên?" I exclaimed, "No kidding! I'm on your border, I'm up in Kiến Giáng at a place called Vĩnh Thanh Village. Nasty place. Matter of fact, we nicknamed one of our hamlets 'Nasty.' The place is crawling with VC."

"We've got a ton of Charlie where I am too," he said, "but it's great being an advisor, isn't it, working with the South Vietnamese like we talked about? We're seeing it all from the *Rice Roots* level alright! Those REMFs you saw last night don't even know there's a war going on!"

He asked me when I was planning on returning to the team, and I told him I really had to catch a plane that afternoon. I remembered Lt. Darden getting his ass chewed out by Major Bonner for coming back late from R&R.

"Oh, come on, go back tomorrow," he said, "we'll go find us a fancy Vietnamese restaurant and have some lobster." I thought about it and told him I really couldn't be away from my team that long.

"Listen," he continued, "you saw for yourself last night how these REMFs live in Saigon. Don't you owe yourself one extra day? One more day here is one less day you'll have to spend in Vĩnh Bang or Bing Bong or wherever your freaking outpost is. Besides, really, what are they gonna do if you're late getting back? Send you to Vietnam?"

He was right. *Screw it*. We found the most expensive Vietnamese restaurant in town and had lobster dinners. Actually, it was crayfish, flown in from Rạch Giá in my own Kiến Giáng Province.

After dinner we saw the 1968 movie *Romeo and Juliet* about two "star crossed lovers" of enemy families. I would have preferred a Steve McQueen action movie, but Romeo was the only one playing in the nearby Vietnamese theater. Chuck again displayed his softer side, fascinated with the story line and eager to discuss the plot. I didn't think much about that at the time, only that it was an interesting side of him in our world of violence. And I wasn't to think that much about that side of him again, until many years later.

### SEPTEMBER 14, 1969

I had breakfast with Chuck before making an early break for Tân Sơn Nhứt. It was then that he told me he had applied for a 6-month extension of his tour. I shook my head and said, "I'm going home, Chuck."

"That's good, Bob," he replied. "You've only got three months left and if you're careful, you can make it out of here in one piece. You can do it," he said.

I told Chuck about the sampan ambushes. He agreed that riding in them was really dangerous, although, as advisors, we did what we had to do. I told him Major Bonner himself had me take a sampan all the way to Kiến Binh for district team leaders' meetings. "Yeah, I know," he said, "sometimes they have me doing that too."

"Take care, Chuck," I said as I shook his hand.

"You too, Bob," he replied, adding, "Good Luck."

I looked back over my shoulder as I swung the heavy duffle bag onto my back. "You too, man."

From Tân Sơn Nhứt I caught an early flight into Cần Thơ and, without wasting time, tried to get another flight on a military plane to Rạch Giá. I didn't want to have to spend the night in Cần Thơ. All the flights for the day were booked solid, so I took a chance and wandered out onto the flight line where the Huey choppers were parked. I ran into some Spec 4 aircraft mechanics who introduced me to one of their pilots, and I bummed a ride an hour later into Rạch Giá on a supply flight.

I made it to the chow hall just in time for one more hot meal. That night it was Chicken Chow Mein ala Mess-Sergeant Jackson. It wasn't the cuisine of Waikiki Beach, but it was better than what I knew I'd be eating for the next three months. I went to the O-Club and then to the Chinese funeral parlor for my last undisturbed night's sleep.

SEPTEMBER 15, 1969
Diary Entry:
*Returned today to the team. We utilized an O-1 bird dog to look at the Nha Sĩ area from the air.*

SEPTEMBER 17, 1969
Diary Entry:
*RD Cadre completed the training of fifty PSDF from Vĩnh Phu hamlet. 379 Company captured 3 VC suspects and took them to Kiến Binh.*

SEPTEMBER 20, 1969

The days following R&R became a blur. I found it difficult to focus on my work. The psychological adjustment to Hawaii had been easy; it was adjusting back to Vĩnh Thanh that gave me a problem.

Acclimation in February to the realities of Vietnam had been sudden. But old-timers like Guerrero were there for support as I slowly grew accustomed to seeing the horrors, dealing with the suffering, doing the dangerous work of an advisor without fear of death. The more operations and night ambushes I participated in, the more I slipped away from serenity and sanity.

I had gradually prepared myself for not going home. The longer I remained in the field, the greater my chances of being shot or killed. Without beauty, peace and love in my life, I had gotten to the point where it didn't matter what happened to me. If I died, I died. I couldn't worry about it. The ones dying were both cautious and careless, concerned about danger and unconcerned. It didn't seem to matter. And worrying about everything probably made it worse. It was easier to not worry about the danger and just go about your business.

After seeing my wife in Hawaii, I realized there was something to live for, something to go home to, a reason to be more cautious. I had a terrible time being back in the field. I didn't want to slip back again into the "if I die, so what" mentality. I wanted to be more careful. That meant thinking about being careful again, which meant worrying and watching what I was doing every moment. Forget about it!

That feeling of hope lasted only two to three weeks after R&R. Vietnam once again swallowed me, grabbed my ankles and then slowly pulled me back under, neck-deep into the quicksand of death and horror.

"Come on, Bob," Vietnam whispered, "you're back in Vĩnh Thanh again. Get into it, stop worrying. Vĩnh Thanh is our real world – our world of death. This is where you're supposed to be. It's not so bad. Hawaii was only a dream. Come back where you belong. This is what life is really supposed to be. There is no such thing as love and peace. Rather, witness all that I have on display for you here. Take in the whole show, and after you do, I'll arrange for you to die here as well. It won't be so bad, trust me."

SEPTEMBER 21, 1969
Diary Entry:

*Harassed by VC at 2300 hours. Discovered early the next morning that a 14-round grenade launcher had been deployed in the woods 75 meters away by the VC, but for some reason they were unable to fire it. Had a night ambush.*

At 11 p.m. some local Vietcông began shooting at us from the closest woodline to our north. We returned a heavy volume of fire into the jungle and that quickly put a stop to the harassment. The next morning, we discovered the mechanical contraption mentioned in my diary. The VC had planned a large-scale attack on our outpost, but their plans were foiled when the grenade launcher malfunctioned. Out of frustration, they decided to take some potshots in the hopes of killing someone, and we laid down such a heavy volume of bullets that they ran away immediately, leaving their homemade device behind.

SEPTEMBER 22, 1969
Diary Entry:
*Sgt. Griffin departed for Deros. Two doughnut dollies*

*visited the team by Swing Ship, they stayed about five minutes on the pad. RD Cadre were harassed by a VC grenade launcher like the one we confiscated yesterday.*

Sergeant E-5 Griffin was finally going home. Actually, to clarify, he was going to the United States, which, for Griff, was not necessarily home. Vietnam had become his home. By returning to the States, he was *leaving* home. After a one-year tour, and six half-year extensions, the Army was finally forcing him to return to the States.

I walked the young man with the gun-shot emaciated arm to the helicopter and helped him put his gear on board. He had been in-country four years, almost exclusively with combat infantry units. But he was clearly upset about having to leave the combat zone.

"Just think, Griff," I said, trying to make it easier, "three squares a day and all those round-eyed girls waiting for you back in the Real World."

"I don't like stateside duty, sir," he said, stepping onto the skid and sliding onto the floor of the chopper, "and those round-eyed, stuck-up bitches don't do anything for me. I'll take a short-time dink any day. Maybe when I get to my duty assignment in the States, they'll let me volunteer to come back again."

The helicopter began its liftoff, and Griffin sadly waved to me from the open door, his legs dangling in the breeze.

I wondered to myself what would become of him after the war. Surely there would be a day when the war would end, and guys like Griffin would be turned loose on Main Street in Jerkwater, U.S.A. He had been such a part of this horror show for four years that he loved being here, loved the excitement and the rush. I flashed back to our first conversation, the wearing of the ears around his neck, the mutilations of dead enemy soldiers. Without counselling, how did the Army expect people like Griff to adjust back to civilian life?

The tragic answer is that the lingering WWII military mentality of the 1960s didn't concern itself one iota with its soldiers' transitions back to civilian life. The warriors that it trained so efficiently and brainwashed so effectively to do its dirty work weren't worthy of a second glance when the time came to discharge them. It would be on them to find a way to assimilate back into society and to function as mentally healthy, productive citizens. There would be no programs, no counselling for guys like Griff, just turn 'em loose to join the ranks of the alcoholics, the wife-beaters, the barroom brawlers, the drug addicts, the incarcerated, and the suicide victims. The tragic truth is a lot of Griffins never truly did go home. The VA hospitals in the States turned their attention to the physically wounded, and rightfully so.

But only limited psychiatric counselling was available, and with a mile of red tape attached to it. And guys like Griff wouldn't avail themselves of it anyway. Hell, he didn't have any problems. He didn't need that shit.

SEPTEMBER 24, 1969
Letter Home:

*Hi Folks,*

*We've been in this new location for about 3 months now and we haven't made much progress. We knew this was a Vietcông communist stronghold, but this is ridiculous.*

*There is still no government here because the elected village chief is afraid for his life, so he lives up in Kiến Bình. The company I'm advising right now just graduated basic training in June, so they're not much help.*

*The area 3 kilometers to the south is still infested with Vietcông. Ever since they pounded the 770 Company down there, our troops are afraid to go there. Supposedly they're going to send another company down there again next week. Meanwhile, the Vietnamese officers have been promising they'd do that for weeks.*

*My counterpart put up more wire, so now we have 4 barbed wire fences. The VC will never overrun us now because they'd have to come through the wire, get across the moat, which is 12' deep and 12' across, then climb the mud wall, all the while exposed to 3 machine guns, 2 grenade launchers and our M16's on fully automatic.*

*So, don't worry about me, because now that I'm getting SHORT, I am looking forward to getting out of this hell hole without a single scratch. Coming back after Hawaii blew my mind though. Everything was so nice and peaceful there and then I come back to this pigsty.*

*I have a Chinese communist SKS rifle that some VC had hidden next to his house. I'm planning to take it home with me.*

*Love, Bob*

SEPTEMBER 27, 1969
Diary Entry:

*Operation to WR344860 with Chuẫn Úy Cao. Company captured 1200 rounds of small arms, 7 mines, and field equipment. Also sank 4 sampans and burned 5 houses.*

Chuẫn Úy Cao was a new replacement to the 379 Company. He also spoke very good English. He and Binh had much in common as they were both raised in the same neighborhood in Saigon. They talked of families they knew, mutual friends they had. Cao had known Binh's brother, the ARVN soldier, who died from his wounds after having his legs amputated. He offered Binh his condolences.

CHAPTER EIGHT

# Blackest of Days
*"ask not for whom the bell tolls, it tolls for thee..."*[23]

SEPTEMBER 28, 1969
Diary Entry:
*Major Harrington visited with counterpart. Hogan and Winters went for a visual reconnaissance.*

This date had no importance to me at the time. Nothing happened in Vĩnh Thanh Village on that Sunday. But it has since become a date of very somber significance to me and to friends and family members of Chuck Emery.

It's the day he died.

Provinces in the Delta didn't share information about KIAs over the radio. We didn't even share radio frequencies. I therefore had no idea on September 28th that a fellow advisor had been killed until two weeks later, when Major General Wetherill visited us again and informed us of the death of a first lieutenant in An Xuyên Province. He could not recall his name.

It haunted me then and still does. I left Vietnam without knowing if it had been Chuck. When I finally mustered the courage to visit "The Wall" in Washington, DC in 1986, I carried with me my diary and began looking up names. And there, on a sunny fall afternoon, in that quiet little park just off Constitution Avenue, I found his name in the directory. And that was all. I knew nothing else.

It took me many decades to piece together the details. For years, I reached out in the VVA Magazine's "Locator" section for any information on the circumstances of his death. Nothing for a long while.

I even dialed information one night and got the phone number of a Charles H. Emery Sr. When I called the number, the gentleman who answered told me he had no son who had served in Vietnam. When I hung up, the brevity of the conversation left me with an uneasy, suspicious feeling. Charles H. Emery Sr. and Jr. is too much of a coincidence.

Finally, a fellow veteran responded to my ad and said he had a "Deceased Personnel File" on 1st Lieutenant Charles Emery, something he had gotten from the bureau of records by mistake. It had arrived along with information on another soldier that the man had known, and he had no interest in keeping Chuck's records. The file is very graphic, right down to the burial arrangements.

I was also contacted by a soldier who served on Chuck's advisory team. He had first-hand knowledge of what occurred on September 28, 1969.

In 2018 I wrote a memorial on a "Virtual Wall" website in Chuck's honor. Thereafter I was contacted by Chuck's niece and subsequently by Chuck's sister, Helen Emery. We arranged a meeting in St. Augustine, Florida that fall.

The following information is from the 50-odd pages of U.S. Army files, from the subsequent conversation I had with Chuck's teammate and from several interviews with Chuck Emery's sister, Helen Emery.

Very early on the morning of September 28, 1969, the Vietnamese rifle company Chuck was advising was to surprise a Vietcông encampment. They were acting on an intelligence report on that rainy Sunday morning. They left their outpost in pre-dawn blackness and made their way to Tân Lộc Village, five kilometers west of Phông Thanh Tây in Thời Bình District, An Xuyên Province.

Monsoon season in full swing, visibility was extremely limited due to the heavy black clouds, clouds so dense that not even moonlight penetrated the blackness. Not even daybreak provided much relief.

Chuck's group is believed to have been traveling in sampans to reach their destination. The medical examination supports this. Chuck was shot at extremely close range by automatic weapons fire coming from his left. One bullet nicked his left wrist before entering the left side of his chest. A second bullet grazed his left shoulder before penetrating the left side of his forehead. Major Foster, the medical examiner at the 29th Evacuation Hospital in Saigon who signed his death certificate, determined his death to be "immediate."[24]

Staff Sergeants Chavers and Blackford were serving in the NOK (Next of Kin) Primary Notification Unit in Saigon at the time. Blackford had already received the Report of Casualty.[25] The soldier was Emery, Charles Henry Jr., 1LT, INF, 05346761, U.S. Army.

"Killed in action in Vietnam at 0625 Hrs on 28 Sept 69. He was on a combat operation when a hostile force was encountered and engaged in a firefight. Cause of death: GSW (gunshot wounds) to the chest and head."

Following the ambush, a good portion of the day passed before Chuck's body could be recovered. He was transported back to his teamhouse by sampan and positively identified on the ground by Chuck's teammate. Chuck was then air-lifted to the 29th Evacuation Hospital. The following day, Monday, he was delivered to the U.S. Army Mortuary in Saigon. By Tuesday morning, September 30th, the death certificate and official casualty reports were issued to Blackford and Chaver's Notification Unit.

They were charged with starting their notifications as soon as they got the reports. But they immediately encountered their first obstacle. 1LT Emery had no addresses listed for his mother or father. In fact, he had no family listed for NOK - not even a brother or sister.[26]

"Was this poor guy an orphan?" Blackford wondered.

Back on February 8, 1969, Chuck and I were summoned into the mess hall to fill out "paperwork." Since we were heading to Vietnamese combat infantry units, one of the sobering forms we had to complete was DA Form 41, RECORD OF EMERGENCY DATA. The form had blanks in which to list family-member contact information in case they had to notify our next of kin in the event we were wounded or killed. I sat next to Chuck as we filled out the form and assumed he was filling in names to be notified, as I was doing.

But on September 30th, almost eight months later, Sergeant Chavers shook his head as he read Chuck's entries:

Religion: *None*
Mother: *Unknown*
Father: *Unknown*
Adult NOK To Be Notified: *NONE* (in capitals)
Beneficiary for Unpaid Pay and Allowances: *Shirley McGill (friend), 50%*
Location of Will: *None*
Insurance Data: *SGLI*[27]
Remarks: *I do not desire my NOK to be notified in case I am slightly wounded.*
Signature and Date: *Charles H. Emery, 8 Feb 69*

All Blackford and Chavers had to go on was the name and address of Chuck's friend, Shirley McGill. But it was improper for them to notify a friend before notifying NOK relatives. They requested Chuck's commander to go through his files and belongings for any information on a mother or father. By 1745 hours on the second day, the reply came back: *"Unit has checked records and personal effects of the deceased. All records in 201 file have father and mother unknown. Officer's Section reports NOK only shows Shirley McGill."*

Just before midnight, while working the night shift, Major Whitley broke protocol, instructing all:

*"Go with friend ... Shirley."*

They could wait no longer. The following morning, in Stevens Point, Wisconsin, Army Major Leister pulled his car into the parking lot of an apartment building which bore Shirley's address. He and 2LT Anderson made their way to unit 439A and pushed the door buzzer marked "McGill."

Shirley McGill, undoubtedly heartbroken, explained that Chuck Emery bounced around foster homes since the age of nine. She stated that Chuck did have a father and a mother and also a brother and two sisters who might still be in the Long Island area, but that he was estranged from his parents.

She said that Chuck had not even seen or spoken to his mother in over two years and had not spoken to his father in over ten years, since the age of thirteen or so. Chuck had no relationship with his father or mother, nor did he want a relationship with either. No explanation was furnished as to why Chuck was placed in foster homes at such an early age.

Chuck never wanted to talk about it very much. He certainly never revealed his past to me, nor to his college friends at Buffalo State College.

Shirley McGill told Leister that she first met Chuck when he was sixteen. He was in the foster care system in the Sheltering Arms Children's Placement Center in New York City. From the age of nine, he had been in and out of four different homes over a period of seven years, but she only knew of the last couple that had him for a while, a Mr. and Mrs. Werner in the neighborhood. She explained that she had befriended Chuck in that neighborhood and that he had gotten himself a Kiwanis Scholarship to attend Buffalo State while a student at Freeport High School. But when the money ran out, he enlisted in the Army. At one point, Chuck had asked Shirley to marry him but she declined because of the age difference between them.

As soon as Major Leister got back to his office, he passed this on:

*"Emery was supposedly in the Sheltering Arms Foster Children's Placement Center in New York City, NY. Call 1st Army – give them entire case and have them check out the above 'establishment' for any info on parents or other relatives of Emery."*

Things kicked into high gear after that. That afternoon, Sheltering Arms furnished the contact information on the Werner family and also Chuck's mother, Lillian Schneider. Mrs. Werner notified Chuck's sister Esther (Helen) Emery at work. Helen then visited her sister who was living in Brooklyn at the time and their other brother living on Long Island.

By mid-October, the Army had been digging into the divorce records of Chuck's parents because there had been no will. They had to be positive about where to send the $10,000 SGLI life insurance money. Chuck's records clearly stated on DA Form 41 that 50% should go to Shirley McGill. And on his SGLI form he also indicated 50% was to go to the Sheltering Arms Foster Children's Placement Center. Lillian Schneider had clearly been granted custody of her son, but did that mean that any of the life insurance proceeds and his back pay should go to her? Not according to the SGLI form.

Besides all that, there was considerable contention already brewing over a number of other things. Even in death, Chuck couldn't escape the unfortunate family dysfunction that plagued his youth.

A friend of the family, who was also serving in the Army at the time, was called upon to escort Chuck's remains back to New York. Specialist 5th Class Royal E. Klein (Roy, as known to the Emery family) was dispatched from his duty assignment at Ft. Bliss, TX.

From the outset, Roy Klein was besieged with the assignment's disarray. Shirley McGill had been on the phone with Major Leister, asking him if she could handle the funeral arrangements. She told him she was sure that that is what Chuck would have wanted.

The Army refused her request. Arrangements had to be made by immediate family. The Army informed Lillian Schneider that Chuck could be buried at no charge at the Long Island National Cemetery in Farmingdale, Long Island if they so desired.

It is obvious in the files that by now, Roy's head was spinning. He had known of the family's problems for years but never expected so much consternation. During the three days SP5 Klein spent with the family members, he encountered other problems besides the difficult family relationships. Questions were thrown at him that he couldn't answer, questions regarding the disposition of Chuck's substantial $10,000 SGLI life insurance proceeds, his back pay, his medals and even his personal belongings.

And there was the squabbling Klein tried to quell: "What do you mean, family members were not listed as next of kin in his paperwork?" Immediate family couldn't believe Shirley McGill was the only one Chuck wanted notified. And Chuck's father, the man who hadn't seen his son in over ten years, not even as he was leaving for Vietnam, became outraged that his ex-wife had stipulated that "Jr." not be on the gravestone. He privately lambasted Klein over this and also over the fact that his ex-wife did not want a cross engraved on his son's gravestone. After all, other military grave markers had some sort of religious symbol on them!

But Chuck had written "NONE" for a religious belief and signed the form without including "Jr." as a suffix.

Klein became entangled in the third-party bickering, trying to keep the situation as calm as possible, but knowing even more trouble was brewing.

Following the funeral service and burial, SP5 Royal Klein was thankfully released from his assignment. His records indicate he caught a flight out of JFK the following morning and filled out his "Military Escort Debriefing" form while on the plane. On line 9, it asked for "remarks or constructive criticisms." Klein filled in this line as follows: "Persons who are departing to a combat zone should receive legal advice with respect to legal definitions, i.e., Next of Kin. This case was very confusing."

Having been Chuck's childhood friend for many years and knowing full well the extent of the family dysfunctionality, Roy Klein's last act was a defiant one for the benefit of his old friend. An American flag draped Chuck's casket. Before presenting the flag to Lillian Schneider, he secretly switched that flag with another. He later gave Shirley McGill the actual flag that had been on Chuck's casket. He knew that was what Chuck would have wanted.

Like most advisors, Chuck wasn't carrying very much the day he was shot. Beside his eyeglasses and wristwatch, he had some military payment certificates and Vietnamese piasters in his pocket along with a cigarette lighter and a Geneva Convention Card.

In a list of what was recovered in his footlocker back at his outpost, he had the usual worldly possessions of an advisor in the field, including one bundle of letters.

It was that last item on the list that Shirley McGill was most interested in and had asked Roy Klein about. She had been writing Chuck regularly and kept all the letters Chuck had sent her. She asked Klein to see what he could do about obtaining the letters she had sent Chuck. She wanted to know if Chuck had received the last letter she had written to him. That was very important to her.

First Army received a call from Chuck's father on October 21. Mr. Emery and his "new wife" (as the report reads) wanted to know why "Jr." could not be engraved after Chuck's name. He was also adamant about having a cross engraved above his son's name, a cross just like all the others. A clerk promised someone would get back to him.

On October 22, Colonel Munt from the Memorial Division wrote to Charles Emery Sr.: *"We have rechecked to see if Mrs. Schneider is firm in her request that there be no religious emblem on the upright marble headstone. I'm sorry to say her decision seems final. Additionally, your son indicated "none" when asked about his religion. Also, the inscription on the headstone will only have his name, state, rank, organization, war service, date of birth and date of death."*

On October 24, Lillian Schneider received a U.S. treasury check in the amount of $444.65. "This comprises funds which were recovered to date belonging to your late son." The Army apparently disregarded Chuck's wishes as stated on the form the two of us filled out on February 8, 1969 while at Advisor's School.

It was clearly time for Shirley to get some help. Chuck's

desires were being trampled upon - a complete disrespect for the wishes of a young man who gave his life in service to his country.

She called Major General Wickham's office, Office of the Adjutant General. She wanted to know if any of the letters she had sent Chuck had been recovered, especially the last, very important one. They informed her they had no way of knowing whether or not Chuck had received her last letter.

But there was the "bundle of letters" that had been listed in Chuck's possessions. That bundle was among his personal belongings that had been shipped to Lillian Schneider.

That afternoon, Shirley sought the help of a local attorney in her area. On the afternoon of October 29, the attorney sent the following letter to the Honorable Melvin Laird, Secretary of Defense, with a copy to Major General Wickham, Adjutant General of the Army:

*"Miss Shirley McGill of Stevens Point, Wisconsin has requested our assistance in securing certain items of personal property due to the death of Lt. Charles H. Emery.*

*It appears this young man was born and raised in New York, NY where his divorced parents still reside. From age 9 on, he was shifted from one foster home to another. Since the foster homes were in the same area, Chuck soon became the adopted boy of the entire neighborhood.*

*During these years, Charles and Shirley became very close friends. She was, in her own words, as much a mother to him as anyone could be. She is not related, however, to Mr. Emery in any way, by blood or marriage.*

*Charles named Shirley McGill as his beneficiary on his insurance policies as well as the beneficiary of his Army pay, allowances, etc. On many processing forms Charles would usually write "none" where the form requested family information. Miss McGill does not know if Charles left a will. She traveled to New York for his funeral and no mention of a will was made at that time.*

*Miss McGill is confident that Charles would not want his mother or any other member of his family to have his personal effects or any medals or honors which the Army might bestow on him. She is very grieved by his loss and I really believe she loved him as her own son.*

*The primary purpose of this letter is to request the assistance of your office in locating Charles Emery's personal effects and to determine the Army's plan for disposition of the same."*

Well now, Shirley was finally pushing some buttons!

The Army phoned Lillian Schneider to find out if she had any letters that Miss McGill might have sent to her son and if so, would she mind forwarding them to Miss McGill. But Lillian Schneider immediately denied receiving any such letters, even though the list of personal effects clearly stated "one bundle of letters."

Shirley McGill was denied access to any of Chuck Emery's personal effects and medals. And she never recovered the one thing she wanted the most, that "bundle of letters" listed on the RECORD OF PERSONAL PROPERTY – COMBAT AREA dated October 14, 1969.

But one final letter from early January 1970 remained in Chuck's file. It was the reply to Shirley's attorney from Major General Wickham, Adjutant General:

*"An examination of Lieutenant Emery's records reveals that Lieutenant Emery designated Miss McGill as beneficiary to receive 50% of his insurance proceeds as well as 50% of any unpaid pay and allowances to which he was entitled. As soon as Miss McGill returns the insurance claim form which was forwarded to her, payment will be made to her in the amount of $5,000. Your interest on behalf of Miss McGill is appreciated.*

*Sincerely,*

*Major General Wickham, Adjutant General."*

With the above determination, the Army had reviewed Chuck Emery's files and, just as he had instructed in his paperwork, 50% of his $10,000 SGLI life insurance policy went to Shirley McGill, and the remaining 50% went to the Sheltering Arms Children's Placement Center in NYC.

In death, his last act of kindness was to help the one person who cared most about him and the one organization to whom he was forever indebted. I wish he could have known the impact he had on my life. I finally understood why Chuck had so many questions for me about family. He wanted to know what a normal childhood was like.

Chuck Emery's high school photo – Freeport High School, Long Island.

Long Island National Cemetery, Farmingdale, Long Island. Note the absence of a cross or any religious denomination engraved above Chuck's name, nor is there a "JR." at the end of his name. This was all in accordance with his wishes.

CHAPTER NINE

# Brownwater Navy

SEPTEMBER 29, 1969
Diary Entry:
*VC fired mortars at us at 1850 hours. It was still light out.*
Bob Winters and I were standing outside the teamhouse enjoying the cool evening, working on our second cans of warm Carling Black Label. We were commenting on the outrageous sunset unfolding to the west. During the rainy season in Vietnam, late-day clouds blend with spectacular shades of pink, black, blue, orange, and purple as the sun sinks beyond the jungle.

I was considering going inside for my camera when we both heard a mortar tube in the distance: *Whump!*

"Where's that coming from?" Bob said.

A mortar landed on the other side of the berm. The round sent up a geyser of water and smoke into the air. By the time the second round left the tube, we were dashing the twenty feet to the bunker, beer cans still delicately balanced in hand.

Fortunately, the "incoming" landed in a variety of spots around the outside of the outpost in the sloppy rice paddy where they caused no harm. Of concern to Chuẩn Úy Duc and myself was the brazen hour of the attack. A mortar has to be fired from a clearing to allow the rounds to clear the trees.

The VC attack that evening was to exact revenge for the burning and ransacking of their little base camp outside of Nasty two days prior. In broad daylight, they didn't care who saw them as they let eight or ten rounds fly. They had balls, I gave them that, and they did come fairly close to hitting us. Actually, they were much better marksmen than our own mortar crew was. Winters and I had quite a laugh over not having spilled a drop of our beer!

### SEPTEMBER 30, 1969
Diary Entry:

*Had operation to Xẻo Sáu area. Returning, one aspirant officer from the company was killed in an ambush. Two of our soldiers and one civilian were wounded.*[U]

The recently arrived Chuẩn Úy Cao, Binh's friend, was sent on his first operation today by Duc to lead an element of the company back up to the outpost at Xẻo Sáu for a check on things. He was the same young aspirant that knew Binh's family back in Saigon.

In what was almost an exact repeat of the previous ambush, one of the sergeants in the company convinced the new Chuẩn Úy Cao to have the small group commandeer three sampans and take the easy way back to the outpost. It was as if the VC could predict their repeated disregard for the danger. Worse, it was as if the VC had an inside track on the company's movements, some way of obtaining inside information. They riddled Cao's middle sampan but good.[U]

Now I had two more wounded soldiers and another wounded civilian to medivac, and Chuẩn Úy Cao's dead body to deal with. He had been in the field with us for three days. I wondered how his family, the family Binh knew from Saigon, would react when they received the dead body of their son after having just sent him off to his first duty assignment in this decade-old war.

I felt bad about Cao. I liked him, but in three days I really hadn't gotten to know him very well. Binh, on the other hand, was in complete shock at the sight of Cao's bullet-ridden body, having been much closer to Cao than I was. I walked Binh to the canal as the body came in by sampan, accompanied by the other three wounded. As Parson helped dress the wounds and Winters called for the medivac, Binh said to me, "I can't believe Chuẩn Úy Cao is dead already, Trung Úy, only three days."

Binh was somewhat taken aback at my callous words to him and everyone else within earshot. I blew my stack. "Well, I'll tell you what, Binh," I said. "What the hell does anybody around here expect when they insist on riding in these stupid freaking sampans? Tell them, go ahead, Binh, tell them what I said."

Binh just looked at the ground, thinking of Cao's family, probably thinking about the grief of his own family upon hearing the news of his ARVN brother's death. Tears welled in his eyes as he mumbled, "I know, Trung Úy, I know, you right. This war getting very old."

Then he put his hand to his face to cover the embarrassment of publicly shedding tears, a socially unacceptable occurrence in Vietnam.

OCTOBER 2, 1969
Diary Entry:

*SFC Stevens arrived to join the team as our new medic. Hogan went to Rạch Giá for dental work.*

Sergeant First Class Stevens replaced Parson as our team medic. Parson's tour of duty as an advisor was over, and he was leaving the next day. Stevens was a powerfully built man, strong and stocky, with tattoos on his arms. He had several tours of Vietnam under his belt, and I had no doubts as to his capability as a medic. We threw a going-away party for Parson in the evening and all of us put down a considerable amount of beer.

OCTOBER 11, 1969
Diary Entry:

*Operation to WR387887.[V] Two Sergeants from 379 were ambushed by VC and were killed. Six water buffalo were killed by gunships flying over Chương Thiện Province. Received intelligence of impending VC attack.*

OCTOBER 13, 1969
Diary Entry:
*563 supposedly will move to Nha Sĩ on 14 Oct. MG Wetherill visited. I gave briefing on situation. Night ambush.*

After I briefed General Wetherill, it was on this date that he told us of the death of the combat advisor two weeks prior. "He was a 1st lieutenant," the general said. I asked him for a name, but he couldn't recall it.

"Colonel Stanberry tells me you've had some activity here lately - some setbacks," the general stated.

"Yes, sir," I said, "we've had our share of casualties since you were last here with Mr. Vann."

"Well," he said, "by having Tài insert another company to the south, that should help spread the load. Keep up the good work, Lieutenant."

I saluted as they walked past our U.S. government mail-bag-enclosed outhouse on their way to the helicopter pad. I gave thought to the part about "keeping up the good work." Were we doing good work? How good were we doing, really? It seemed to me we'd been getting our asses kicked lately. The place was really starting to get to me.

After the general departed it concerned me that he was unable to tell me the name of the lieutenant that was killed. I turned to Bob Winters and said, "I've got a friend in An Xuyên. Chuck Emery's his name. I went through Advisor School with him. I hope it's not him!"

Bob did his best to put me at ease:

"Aw, An Xuyên's a big place - there's probably lots of teams down there."

OCTOBER 14, 1969
Diary Entry:
*563 Company was inserted into Nha Sĩ with Captain Delgado and MAT 45. RD Cadre were moved to Nha Sĩ, leaving none here.*

Captain Delgado, the Mexican-American I knew from

my days back at Hóa Quản and Thời An outposts, moved into the outpost at Nasty along with his MAT team 45. The 563 Company he was now advising was relieving the jittery 267, the worst company we had ever advised. With two Mobile Advisory Teams in Vĩnh Thanh now, we were putting more pressure on the VC. Maybe the general was right, maybe that would finally help pacify the place, to "spread the load" in the untamable Vĩnh Thanh Village.

OCTOBER 16, 1969
Diary Entry:
*SFC Stevens went to Vĩnh Phu hamlet and treated approximately 50 people in a small MEDCAP.*
Letter Home:
*Hi Everyone,*
*Getting shorter now. Yippee!*
*The other day we had an operation just a little to our south and lazily, I decided to leave my steel pot and flak jacket behind.*
*Well, it turned out to be the worst firefight I've been in yet. We were in the middle of an open rice paddy when about 8 VC pinned us down with AK-47's and a machine gun. I thought I was watching a John Wayne movie. The water around me started splashing in the air. I pointed to the woods to our left and told my interpreter that's where the fire was coming from.*
*Binh said "no sweat," and then I saw splashing around him and we both dove behind a berm. They had us pinned down so bad I couldn't even get my head up. Every time I did, I was looking at water splashing up in front of me. Then what really got me pissed was, the cigarettes in my pocket got soaked and I cursed in Vietnamese and Binh thought that was pretty funny.*
*The company commander decided to move off to our right and head into the woods to get into the cover of the jungle, but then he just keeps going off to the right. He was whipping along so fast I couldn't catch up with him. He avoided making contact with the VC on purpose and that really got me angry because we*

*had them outnumbered by about 5-1. Ridiculous!*

*Anyway, that was the first time in months that I didn't wear my flak jacket and now that I'm getting short, I'm going to wear it and my steel pot all the time. I'm gonna wear it every day until I step foot on that airplane in Saigon.*

*I'll try to write again soon. Love, Bob*

### OCTOBER 18, 1969
#### Diary Entry:

*Went on operation to Cái Nhum and spent the night.*

### OCTOBER 19, 1969
#### Diary Entry:

*Outpost in Cái Nhum is being constructed. Sixty PSDF have been trained there.*

### OCTOBER 21, 1969
#### Diary Entry:

*LTC. Stanberry and Province Chief visited. Discussed strength problem of 379 Company.*

We still averaged only twenty to twenty-five men in the outpost on any given night. Colonel Stanberry told the new company commander that if the 379 Company couldn't provide better security for MAT 88, he'd consider pulling my team from Vĩnh Thanh.

LT Amon with interpreter Trung Si Binh in Vinh Thanh Village.

OCTOBER 22, 1969
Diary Entry:
*Gunships on an operation in Chương Thiện Province killed two civilians only about one kilometer from here.*

From our position at the border, I used my field glasses to watch helicopter gunships blasting away at something a half mile to our east.[W]

That afternoon, I watched as men from the hamlet piled logs in a slightly-elevated plot of rice paddy between us and Chương Thiện. They laid down several logs in one direction, then several more on top of them, crisscrossing them as they stacked them. Through my field glasses, they looked like a colony of ants carrying the logs, carefully building a tower in Lincoln-log fashion. After many hours, they had constructed an open cube measuring twelve feet square by twelve feet high, with dead branches and tinder underneath—a cube of combustible material out in the middle of the open rice paddy.

Binh came over and climbed on top of the bunker with me to get a look through the binoculars. "What the hell are they doing, Binh?" I asked, showing him how to focus the field glasses.

"They build a funeral fire Trung Úy, you know, to burn the body."

"You mean a funeral *pyre*, for cremation?" I asked.

"Yes, someone say helicopters killed civilians today. I don't know whether civilians or VC, but two men dead," he said.

We watched as they carried one of the bodies out to the Lincoln-log pile. The dead man was on a homemade stretcher of bamboo and nipa palm leaves. Climbing while lifting the body to the top of the funeral pyre, they placed the remains at the very top.

After the funeral service, the group of mourners returned to the village, while two men with torches circled the base of the pile and ignited it. It was early evening, and the fire soon started to build as the sun began to set. It became a raging inferno, lighting the dusk and sending up a thick plume of smoke that could be seen for miles. Eventually we lost sight of the body on top as it became engulfed by the smoke and bonfire. With the sun completely gone, it continued to light up the distant rice paddy, burning on into the dark Vietnamese night.

OCTOBER 23, 1969
Diary Entry:

*Navy Lt. Stover, a doctor, pulled a Medcap and spent the night. Received intelligence of impending 200 VC attack.*

Stevens' earlier MEDCAP's were practice runs for the main event on October 23. Doctor Stover and Stevens did an excellent job of attending to every kind of ailment, including a very pregnant woman who looked like she was ready to deliver right there. What made me feel good, and was equally rewarding for Stover and Stevens, was that we were finally doing something positive in the village. I hadn't felt that way since Hóa Quản.

Although the turnout was not as large as the MEDCAP

we performed in Hóa Quản, we probably treated a larger percentage of the village population. Vĩnh Thanh was not as populated as Hóa Quản had been, the result of firefights and ambushes. Many families left when the heavy fighting and shooting began. A contested village loses population quickly as families flee the area to get away, not wanting one of their children to become the next innocent victim. So, we were pleased with the somewhat meager turnout.

As usual, Hogan enjoyed playing with the children, who always seemed to gather around the likeable man with the basketball player's build. It was as if they wanted to play, but were afraid at the same time, shoving one another toward him. Occasionally, the mere sight of Hogan, the 6'5" African American, would send a young child screaming toward the safety of its mother in fear, only to return again, enticed by his smile. Hogan was in charge of the candy disbursement, with interpreter Binh assisting him. Stevens had managed to obtain packages of Life Savers, Charms, and Tootsie Rolls on his recent trip to Rạch Giá.

"Maybe this will help turn things around," I thought. "We can win here in Vĩnh Thanh. Not with bullets, but with Tootsie Rolls!"

Interpreter Trung Si Binh giving out candy in Vinh Thanh Village.

OCTOBER 24, 1969
Diary Entry:

*Lt. Stover completed Medcap. RD Cadre returned to our location. We held a small village meeting. Company went on a night ambush.*

After the MEDCAP, the village chief invited Binh and me to his home for dinner. Most of the hamlet chiefs had come as well, including the hamlet chief from Nha Sĩ, which really surprised Binh and me. I couldn't help thinking he might be one of the Vietcông that had helped overrun the 770 Company. He couldn't possibly be the senior South Vietnamese Government representative of Nha Sĩ Hamlet and still be alive in Nha Sĩ – the VC wouldn't stand for that. We surmised he was a "token" government official, probably a Vietcông affiliate, sent to the meeting by the VC as a representative of the hamlet.

"Oh well," I thought, "one big, happy family." It probably wasn't the first time I had broken bread with a Vietcông soldier. And it was not to be the last. Before long, the meeting became a party as we tried to conduct business interspersed with drinking. One by one, they asked me to have a solitary toast with them.

"Trung Úy!" Binh said as he smiled. "The Hamlet Chief of Nha Sĩ wishes to have a small glass of *bá xé de* with you." *Bá xé de* is an extremely strong spirit distilled from rice. It kicks like a water buffalo and goes right to your head. I remembered Major Bonner's advice: "Just drink it even if it tastes like shit."

Would I drink with the hamlet chief of Nasty? Of course! I pretended I didn't know what they were up to. "Tell him I'd be glad to have a drink with him, Binh." I said.

Some of the wives brought out steaming bowls of pig ears and rice. There were other pig body parts mixed in as well, none of which looked anything like my mom's ACME pork chops. The men continued around the table, one by one, challenging me to a toast of the liquid napalm.

After they had all taken their turn, Binh announced, "Trung Úy, the Hamlet Chief of Nha Sĩ says he wants to have another toast with you." They all began laughing at me. My cheeks were already red and my lips were numb.

"*Không, cám on* (No thanks)," I said. Then, waving my arms circularly and slurring my Vietnamese, I added, "*Xin, chúng ta uông* (Please, let's all drink)!" If they were going to get me plastered, I'd take them all with me.

It was well after dark when Binh and I finally embarked on the trail back to the outpost, he unarmed and hiccupping, and I with my WWII Remington Rand .45 pistol on my hip, which, if drawn from its holster in my inebriated condition, would have blown my foot off.

If it is true that there is honor among thieves, then it's certainly true that there is honor among soldiers. Binh had received word on that night that there would be no shooting. He said it was a temporary cease fire, and we stumbled back on that dark trail unharmed. An hour after passing out on my bunk, I woke up knowing that whatever was in my stomach had to come out and come out immediately. The entire outpost was spinning as I ran out behind the bunker and heaved all the liquor and "delicious" pig ears into a pile.

But if I accomplished anything in Vĩnh Thanh that night, it was to convince the elders we were there to help, not dominate. They were tired of the communist domination they'd endured for so many years. For once in their lives, a five-man team of men wanted to help them and asked nothing in return. No tax dollars, no chickens to feed their troops, no retribution. They saw progress in their village, they saw organization, and a doctor to turn to. Politics didn't matter, peace in the village mattered. They wanted to get on with their lives, to have the killing stop.

I left the meeting revitalized and thought about conversations I had with Chuck Emery. Maybe our instincts were right. Maybe we had a shot at winning the hearts and minds. The meeting and subsequent declaration of a cease fire taught me that people in Vĩnh Thanh just wanted the same thing that everyone everywhere wants: peace.

OCTOBER 30, 1969
Diary Entry:
*Worked on plans for hamlet mobile defense plan. 379 Company has 50% of personnel missing from the outpost.*

Hogan and I took another head count today and came up with 23 South Vietnamese manning the outpost. In case of attack, that would only give us a total of 28, hardly enough against a large force.

South Vietnamese were much more likely to be Absent With-Out Leave (AWOL) than Americans in Vietnam. Since most Regional Forces companies were recruited from the same region they were defending, their homes were relatively close by. During rice harvest, for example, their family's livelihood and subsistence depended on being able to quickly reap the harvest and get it to market. By 1969, the war in their homeland was more than a decade old and showing no signs of letting up. For the average ARVN, that was half a lifetime. From their perspective, there was no urgency to prosecute the war with vigor. It was there last year and it'll be there next year. Let the crazy Americans knock themselves out trying to end it quickly.

I understood all the reasons why the outpost was half empty and why they were AWOL. Chuck Emery and I had been told at the outset that the life of a military advisor was not for the faint-hearted or those prone to insecurity issues. But I was more than a little concerned about the small number of defenders. The lives of my team-members were my responsibility, and I again made a mental note to bring it up with Colonel Stanberry. If Colonel Tài couldn't force the company to retrieve its AWOLs, perhaps it *was* time for us to move.

OCTOBER 31, 1969
Diary Entry:
*379 Company had ceremony with a pig in memory of the dead. Went to party with counterparts. The Navy had one PBR destroyed by VC B-40 rocket fire. Eight Americans were wounded, two very seriously.*

The United States Navy operated a flotilla of PBR's (military nomenclature: Patrol Boats, River) out of Cần Thơ to our east. The Vietnam-era PBR is best recognized as the 31-foot, heavily armed, olive drab boat that Martin Sheen was aboard in the movie *Apocalypse Now*. On the front deck was the forward gun position, manned by a gunner sitting in a depression in the deck. The front guns consisted of two .50 caliber machine guns mounted on both sides of a 40 mm grenade launcher. All three were mounted on a tripod, and could be fired individually or, by pushing up on a bar, the gunner could fire all three at the same time. Wherever aimed, this contraption hurled a steady stream of exploding grenades and half-inch diameter .50 caliber bullets capable of cutting down trees.

On the evening of October 31st, our radio crackled as we heard the call from Kiến Binh to Rạch Giá for several medivacs. It was late at night, and these boats had been operating on the Cái Nhum river to deny the Vietcông the use of the river to transport weapons, ammo, medical supplies, etc.

The Ho Chi Minh Trail, a misnomer, was actually very rarely a single trail. It was any means of transporting supplies from the communist north to their comrades in the south, be it by boat, truck, wagon, bicycle, or on foot. And it was rarely the same routes for long, a constantly changing number of roads, trails and waterways. Maps of the trail indicate that even the South China Sea was considered part of the Ho Chi Minh Trail.

On some of our night ambushes, we set up along a canal, waiting for a sampan to come along. And in the silent night air, I often heard boat motors in the distance, even though the population was well-warned that night travel was prohibited.

On this particular night, the PBR's had been ambushing along the Cái Nhum, not far from our Cái Nhum Outpost. The young Naval officer in charge was a very aggressive lieutenant, the Army equivalent of a captain. Kendrick was an Annapolis graduate. His five PBR's had been sent into our area on a temporary assignment to eliminate night traffic.

From the shoreline, a Vietcông soldier managed to get

close to them on the banks of the Cái Nhum in the darkness. He carried with him a B-40 Rocket, also referred to as an RPG (Rocket Propelled Grenade). His target was the bow of one of Kendrick's PBRs. When he fired the rocket at almost point-blank range, it detonated on the front tripod of the twin .50s, literally in the face of the young sailor manning the guns. The force of the explosion gravely injured him and one other on board, and sent shrapnel flying into six others. It all but destroyed the boat, setting off a fire that was extinguished by the other four boats amid the confusion and chaos of returning fire. His mission accomplished, the Vietcông soldier slipped off into the darkness.

The PBRs were unable to medivac the eight wounded from their exposed position on the river, and aware of the considerable risk of sitting there much longer, they loaded all eight WIAs on the other four boats and blew back to Kiến Bình town. Over the radio, I heard Major Kone making sure Rạch Giá understood that they were "Uniform Sierra, November Alpha Victor Yankee (U.S. NAVY) personnel."

## NOVEMBER 1, 1969
### Diary Entry:

*Went to Cái Nhum with McFadden (Mac) to go out on an ambush with Patrol River Boats (PBRs) operated by the U.S. Navy. We ambushed VC and killed two in a sampan traveling on the river in the dark.[x] Returned early.*

Early in the morning, Major Kone's voice was on the air calling my call sign. I scrambled out from under my mosquito net and grabbed the handset. Sergeant First Class McFadden, an early riser, and recently back with the team after returning from his Compassionate Leave, sat listening and drinking a hot cup of coffee as I took the call. The major wanted to know if I could assist the Navy PBR people.

He handed Navy Lieutenant Kendrick the mouthpiece as Kendrick asked if we would "help him out" with a night ambush later that day. I agreed. I was to meet him with 8-10 of our 379 soldiers at the Cái Nhum outpost at 1900 hours.

"Roger," I replied. "We'll be there. Anything further, over?"

He cut it short with a brief, "Negative, out."

"Mind if I come along, lieutenant?" McFadden asked, "I don't think I've ever seen one of those PBRs up close." I always liked Mac's company. His sense of humor made the time pass quicker, and besides, he asked first.

"Sure, Sarge," I told him. When Lloyd and Hogan found out Mac was going with me on some kind of mission with the Navy PBRs, Hogan couldn't contain himself.

"Sheeit," he lamented to Lloyd, "we'll probably have to go down to Mutha-Fuckin' Nasty today while Mac gets to go for a Mutha-Fuckin' boat ride. Now ain't that some sheeit?"

"Hey, Hogan," Mac said, unable to resist rubbing it in, "maybe I'll do a little water skiing while I'm up there."

"Yeah, right," Hogan laughed.

McFadden and I left the outpost at 3 p.m. for the three-kilometer hike up to the Cái Nhum river. I brought along a handful of the most reliable men I could find, the remnants of Dzu's fairly competent 1st Platoon. Even though we didn't have to meet them there until 7 p.m., I wanted us to be there early enough to not keep the big boats waiting. And we didn't want to be hanging around there after dark.

By 6 p.m. we got to the banks of the Cái Nhum. Mac and I broke out C-rations for dinner while the 379 boiled some rice mixed with con chuát (field rat) over an open fire. The pre-arranged meeting time of seven o'clock came and went, as did eight o'clock. The mosquitoes moved in for a meal as the last light of day disappeared.

At 9 p.m. we began hearing a low, droning sound in the distance. Soon the noise was unmistakable: it had to be them coming down river. The first boat appeared around the bend, and it looked awesome.

"Holy shit," was all McFadden could say. The boats were quite visible in the moonlight, silhouetted against the dancing black water. In short, we had the same view of the boats from the bank that the VC had the night before. I didn't say anything, but I now realized the reason they had been ambushed. Mac's "Holy shit" had said it all.

McFadden and I stood up and waved our arms frantically while we watched all four boats go right by, not even slowing down. At half past the hour the PBR's could be heard coming back upstream. This time all of us were on our feet, waving. The lead boat swerved toward shore, temporarily shining an extremely bright searchlight into our eyes, causing us to lose our night vision. As the boat approached the shore, it had to maneuver to parallel park. This meant throwing the boat into reverse and revving the already noisy engine, then forward, more revving, reversing one more time, then forward again. Finally, the right side of the boat was as close to the clearing on the bank as it could get, three to five feet at best.

"Lieutenant Amon?" Lieutenant Kendrick called out.

"Yes, sir," I acknowledged.

"It took us awhile to find you. Did you see us go by before?" he questioned.

"Yes, sir, we were right here, waving," I replied, thinking to myself, "If you missed seeing us, no wonder you missed seeing the VC that wounded eight of your men last night!"

"Get your men on board," he said, annoyed that things weren't going smoothly and probably reading my mind.

The mud shelf on the bank of the river was the closest thing to a "dock" we had, but it was for sampans. From the embankment, McFadden and I had our hands full lifting the Vietnamese up and out to the outstretched hands of the sailors on board. The boat bobbed up and down, making it even more difficult. Once we accomplished getting them on, I helped Mac get on board, handed him my M16, and made a flying leap to grab the handrails of the PBR. With everyone on board, we took off from Cái Nhum and headed upstream.

With Mac at my side, I asked Kendrick about the ambush the night before. He spoke of the explosion in a sterile, factual way, completely devoid of emotion. It was as if he were a third party describing someone else being ambushed. I sensed he was embarrassed and humiliated by the fiasco and made to look inept and incompetent in front of his men. Now he chose to go back out on the same river in the same area the very next night, exposing his remaining four boats and sailors to yet another ambush. The men on board looked anxious.

As minutes passed and Kendrick rambled on about the importance of ambushing sampans at night to cut off the flow of munitions, it became obvious to Mac and I that Kendrick was a man obsessed with demonstrating what he'd been taught at the naval academy. None of the other sailors on board spoke. Lieutenant Kendrick was in complete control, the only opinion allowed. He seemed to be a young naval commander imagining himself to be a Vietnam version of John F. Kennedy, the PT-109 legend. Mac and I said very little, somewhat taken aback by his arrogance.

"Which brings us to why I asked Major Kone to give you a call," he rambled on. "We're going to be ambushing here," he said, pointing to his combat map. "When we get in position, we'll park along the riverbank and you and your ARVNs will get off the boat and perform half-moon security on land."

"Half-moon security?" I squintingly asked.

"Yes, that's right, lieutenant," he said. "You'll get off onto the shoreline and fan your men out in the shape of a half-moon to protect the boats from attack from land. I don't need any VC sneaking up and tossing hand grenades on board or firing B-40s at us point-blank like last night."

McFadden glanced at me with a frown and walked to the back to sit on the deck with our Vietnamese soldiers from the 379 Company. I read Mac's mind but decided to let it play out and see what developed. I had to give Kendrick the benefit of the doubt.

Soon we entered a horseshoe bend in the river and all four boats followed in single file as we slowed down at the bottom of the "U." Jockeying the boat along the outboard side of the bend, he worked the boat closer to the shoreline. I had never been along this section of the Cái Nhum before. We were out of our area of operation and well into Chương Thiện Province. The river in that remote area was wild and raw, the heavily overgrown brush and undergrowth on the bank hung a full twenty feet out over the water into the river. There appeared no reasonable place to disembark.

"Here, lieutenant," Kendrick said, handing me a long pole, "stick this in the water to check the depth, I can't get the boat any closer to the bank." Mac came forward and watched as I sank the pole six feet deep into the muck. We were still twenty feet from the shore. All four boats were making so much racket so close to shore, it prompted Mac to finally speak up.

"Christ, no wonder these guys got ambushed last night, LT. Charlie can hear this shit for miles." I looked at him and didn't say anything, but I knew he was right. I thought our ambushes were risky business, but this guy was begging for trouble.

"How's this spot, lieutenant?" Kendrick wanted to know. I told him it was too deep. Annoyed, the Navy commander gunned the motor in the darkness and moved downstream another hundred meters to look for another spot. When he pulled over, it was the same depth. Mac spoke up, saying he didn't think it would be possible for us to get off anywhere along that section of the river. Kendrick ignored his remark as he moved the entire entourage of boats another two hundred meters.

This time he pushed the bow of the boat directly into the heavy branches and brush protruding from the shoreline. The nose of the boat parted some of the undergrowth as the motor churned loudly to push the bow into the mud of the embankment.

"Here," Kendrick said, handing me a flashlight, "get up on the bow and look to see if you can get your men off from the front. I can't get any closer. I don't want to run aground."

"Sir," McFadden said to me, "this isn't a good idea. You know how much trouble we had getting on this freaking thing at Cái Nhum. Even if we can get off here, there's no way we're gonna be able to get back on again. And if the shit hits the fan, we're on the riverbank and shit outta luck. Besides, these boats are attracting so God-damned much attention, Ho Chi Minh himself can probably hear us."

I went up on the bow of the boat past the sailor sitting in the forward gun position. He gave me a dirty look as I clumsily made my way past him to the front. I shined Kendrick's flashlight into the wall of bushes and branches to my front.

"Hey," the gunner said nervously, "what the fuck are you doing? Put out that fucking flashlight. Are you nuts?"

"I'm just trying to find a place to...," I started, as he cut me off.

"I don't give a fuck what you're trying to do," he blurted out. "Put out the flashlight, you asshole. This whole idea is fucked up."

It snapped me to my senses. Had I completely lost it? Maybe I was in country too long. I had been out on many night ambushes during the past eight months, and never lit a single light. Why was I doing it now? Just because Kendrick told me to? I was nuts for doing that. I was nuts, Kendrick was nuts, the whole idea was nuts.

"You know what?" I said to the sailor after his disrespectful remarks. "You're absolutely right. This *is* fucked up."

I walked back past the gunner and climbed down into the cockpit and handed Lieutenant Kendrick the flashlight. "Was it okay up there?" he asked.

"No," I told him, "the drop is too steep. If we jump off, we'll be neck deep in muck and stuck in the middle of thick branches."

"Well, you've got to get off somewhere," he said. "Why don't you have them jump off the side into the water and swim ashore?" he questioned.

"Swim ashore?" Mac laughed, as he came closer to my side. "Did you say swim ashore? Shit, the deepest water our guys have ever been in is six inches, and you can't learn to swim in a rice paddy. With all their equipment, these little fuckers'll drown in six feet of water."

Mac's brief tirade evoked laughter from the enlisted men on board who had been listening to the conversation. After what they'd been through, they appreciated the brutal honesty and levity from the salty, old Army dog. His slight lack of respect for their naval officer probably amused them as well.

"Look," I added, "even if I can get them off here, I don't know how I'm going to get them back on. You can see how loaded down they are."

"Major Kone told me I'd have your full cooperation, lieutenant," Kendrick pressed one more time. But before I could speak, Mac interjected again, trying to get me off the hook.

"Shit, sir, all due respects, but you know these little bastards'll be more fuckin' trouble than they're worth once we get 'em overboard. Their fuckin' equipment weighs more than they do!"

That evoked even more laughter. Kendrick's men were apparently fond of anyone handing out disparaging remarks about the Vietnamese. Mac used the humor as a tool to get Kendrick to reconsider. Fortunately, it was just enough to get the Annapolis graduate to change his mind.

"Alright," he conceded, "we'll get away from here and ambush up toward the other bend in a fresh spot."

With the same fanfare, he moved the noise machines to a new location further into the horseshoe.[x] Finally the motors were off, and the only sound was an occasional break in the squelch on the radio. The four boats waited. McFadden and I sat in silence in the darkness, waiting to ambush.

Waiting in the night air. Waiting to kill.

All the times we set up along the dangerous VC-traveled trails leading to Nha Sĩ, we luckily hadn't tripped one ambush. "Lucky," I said to myself, "I've been lucky. Tonight won't be any different," I told myself. "No one ever comes into the kill zone on my night ambushes 'cause I'm lucky."

"What time you got, LT?" Mac whispered. When I finished telling him it was quarter to one, I heard a muffled purr in the distance. Mac and I sat staring at the floor as the unmistakable sound of a sampan motor got faintly louder in the distance.

"I think we got company," Mac finally said.

"Oh, come on," I said, "don't tell me."

The radio squelch on our boat broke silence as the end boat announced the approach of a sampan. "Roger," Kendrick replied, "hold your fire until they're front and center. On cue, out."

The sampan seemed to take forever to reach the bend in the river. Our 379 soldiers sat looking at one another, knowing what was about to take place. I rolled over onto my knees and Mac followed suit as we peered over the side of the PBR in the direction of the sound.

A sampan containing two figures rounded the bend in the darkness, silhouetted by the moonlight glimmering across the black water. As it approached our forefront, the motor suddenly dropped in RPM, and then just as suddenly, stopped, as the occupants cut the motor off. They had seen what they thought might be an outline of a PBR. Gliding directly to our front, the occupants sat frozen as they realized what they were looking at.

"Maybe Kendrick will just stop them and question them… take them in for interrogation the way we sometimes do," I naively thought to myself, not wanting the adventure any more, hoping it was all a bad dream, not wanting to see any more death.

At that moment, one of the boats opened up, followed immediately by all of the boats. Our entire PBR vibrated as the sailor in the front spewed out death like a fireman directs a firehose. All of us were awe-struck as the inhabitants of the boat were blown and shot to pieces. Chunks of the boat and body parts were thrown into the air mixed with geysers and columns of water. The 40mm grenades continued to detonate on the debris on the water while the eight .50 caliber machine guns chopped everything into small pieces. The gunners continued to exact revenge for the previous night until Kendrick called for the cease fire. It took less than a minute; it seemed like hours. Mac and I didn't have to fire a shot.

If anyone for five miles didn't know we were there before, they certainly knew after all that gunfire. The PBR boats started up and smartly made a run for the district compound at Kiến Binh to drop us off. No one had much to say as we sped up the Cái Nhum. Mac, with all his experience, turned to me and said, "Maybe one of these days they'll get these God-damned peace talks going to the point where we can all leave this fucking place." The look in his eyes said he'd had enough of the killing and my look back reflected the same.

"We ambushed VC and killed two in a sampan traveling on the river in the dark," was my exact diary entry for November 1, 1969. The memories of the flying body parts will always be there. And yes, *we* killed. I helped kill, facilitating that one and all the other ambushes. I always said I didn't want to be part of the killing. But I was. We all killed, me included. At last, I finally admitted it in the diary. *We* killed two complete strangers. It wasn't Major Bonner's kill, but we had killed all the same.

Silently waiting to kill someone is a cowardly thing, not a brave act. I always worried about having to kill and I didn't want to live with the memory of having done that. But the reality was, just being with a group that was killing passed on the guilt as if I'd pulled the trigger myself.

NOVEMBER 2, 1969
Diary Entry:
*Returned by swing ship. Checked outpost defenses.*

Back at the district teamhouse at Kiến Bình, Mac and I got little rest. They had a generator powering a dangling light bulb in the sleeping area and kept it on all night. Visions of the ambush plagued me as well. Within no time, after we finally dozed off, Gannon was up assembling combat gear and making coffee, readying himself for yet another operation.

At 5 a.m., someone knocked on the back door and Gannon opened it to greet Vĩnh, his interpreter. "Vĩnh!" Gannon exclaimed. "You remember Lieutenant Amon?"

"Of course, I remember," Vĩnh said in perfect English. "How have you been, Lieutenant Amon?"

Vĩnh always amazed me. His command of the English language was incredible, given he had never set foot in America. We reminisced about the first time we met back on February 16 during my very first "official" operation - the futile chase after the VC who had kidnapped the father of one of the Kit Carsons. For me they were the early days. The days of innocence, days of adventure. They were the days when I looked forward to the field duty, not realizing the horror that was in store: the killing, the death, the maiming, the suffering. For Vĩnh there were never days of innocence, having grown up in the midst of the war.

I asked him about the outcome of the kidnapping. "We never found his father," Vĩnh said, "the VC must have killed him. But the scout still works with us. He hates the VC."

"I can just imagine," I said.

Vĩnh and I chatted more as he helped himself to a bowl of Quaker oatmeal, a perk for the privileged district interpreter. He and Gannon were headed out the door into the black Vietnamese morning. Their mission was to patrol the shoreline on foot while the Navy boats moved down the river looking for more Vietcông to engage.

"Gannon, listen," I said, "those Navy guys - they're a wild bunch. And that Kendrick is one gung-ho son of a bitch. Be careful out there!"

"Cairful?" Gannon grinned, with his Cajun drawl. "Shee-it, Charlie's the one who's gunna hafta be cairful today!"

Vĩnh laughed and nodded his head at me, and the two of them left the teamhouse for the short walk over to where the boats were parked.

McFadden and I each poured a cup of coffee, helping ourselves to the oatmeal while listening to the radio broadcast along with Major Kone. Monitoring an operation is like listening to a police band. When things are routine, it's boring. When they're not, it's hair-raising.

Kendrick's voice was the first to break squelch. He was on the radio telling the major they had VC contact. In the background, I could hear the deafening roar of the gunner on Kendrick's boat, firing his grenade launcher with the twin .50s. Unfortunately, during the time it took for Kendrick to finish his call, no one else could get through on the radio, including Gannon. As soon as the transmission ended, Gannon's booming Cajun slang could be heard over the airwaves:

"Cease Fiah! Cease Fiah! This is Broken Henhouse One Zee-ro. Ah say again, Cease Fiah! Stop yoah shootin'. Do you copy, ovah?" he screamed at Kendrick. "What the hail is the mattah with yoah men, don't ya'll know we've got friendlies ovah heah on the rivah bank, ovah?" The ensuing transmissions made our hair stand on end. It all started when Gannon and his Vietnamese RFs began receiving small arms fire from a handful of Vietcông in the rice paddy along the river. They took cover behind a small berm along the riverbank and returned fire with their backs to the PBR boats.

One of the PBR's heard the gunfire, thought the PBR's were under attack, and immediately opened up in the direction of the VC, firing past and over the heads of Gannon, interpreter Vĩnh and the rest of the RFs along the shoreline. It didn't take long for the other boats to begin firing where they saw the first boat directing its fire.

Gannon later told me he was lucky to be alive. He had never been subjected to that much "friendly fire." Some of the airborne grenades fell short and exploded in the trees over their heads. Some landed at the river bank, while the .50 caliber machine gun bullets chopped down branches and slammed into the mud around them. "And ah couldn't get them to stop on account of Kendrick's fucked-up Sit-Rep. Ah couldn't get own the daymned radio!" he later explained.

To get away from the intense gunfire to his back, Gannon dove over the berm and took cover *on the VC side of the berm.* He said the fire from the VC was nothing compared to what the boats dished out. Then as Vĩnh attempted to follow suit and dive over the berm, he was hit from behind by one of the gunner's .50 caliber machine gun rounds. Gannon was beside himself.

"Bob," Major Kone said to me, "they're going to bring the WIA here by boat. Would you go down to the river with the PRC-25 radio and guide the medivac in?"

"Of course, sir," I said, throwing the portable radio on my

back and heading out the door.

On the radio I heard Major Kone successfully divert a medivac from somewhere else and within fifteen minutes I could hear the sound of the chopper flying toward us. I popped a smoke grenade and red smoke billowed up into the bright blue morning sky. Whirling around, I saw that the boat had already arrived. Two sailors ran toward me with a stretcher. As they approached, they slowed to a walk. And once again, I couldn't believe my eyes.

Vĩnh was lying on the olive-drab stretcher on his stomach. His shirt was off and his pants were pulled down. He was very conscious and alert. He held his head up and made eye contact with me without being able to say anything. I will never forget the look on his face, as if he was silently asking me, "Is there anything you can do to make this okay?" I'll always remember his hands, which gripped the two wooden runners of the canvas-covered stretcher next to the hands of the sailor carrying it. He had a white-knuckle death grip on those two wooden poles. Sweating profusely, he was in immense pain.

When I looked down at his back, I thought I was seeing things. The .50 caliber machine gun bullet caught him in mid-air as he was diving over the berm for cover. He was perpendicular to the ground when the bullet hit him. The bullet entered the base of his spine and traveled up along his spine, coming to rest between his shoulder blades. It had actually made a tunnel. The bullet was now a visible lump under the skin. He was bandaged and bleeding from the rectum.

We wasted no time loading him. The chopper took off, leaving me and the two Navy enlisted men crouched in the flying dust and smoke. The two sailors filled me in on their version of what happened.

"We started taking fire from the side of the canal. What the fuck were we supposed to do, not shoot back?" he said.

"Who was that gook, some sort of interpreter or something?" one of the seamen asked me.

"Yes," I said, "he was Lieutenant Gannon's personal interpreter. They were together a long time."

"Man, I guess so," the sailor responded, "Lieutenant Gannon, he was pretty upset."

"I'm sure," I said.

"Man," he continued, "I never saw anything like that! I don't know how they can patch that up! A freakin' .50 right up the middle of his back! He was a pretty good interpreter, huh?"

"Yes," I said, "his name was Vĩnh. He was an excellent interpreter and a really nice guy." That afternoon Mac and I hitched a chopper ride back to the team.

NOVEMBER 7, 1969
Diary Entry:

*Lloyd and Stevens went on raid with 379 Company at 1200 hours - returned 1400 hours. Ambush to WR358892 at 1845. Returned 0020 hours - captured one VC.*[Y]

"Don't we have a night ambush tonight, sir?" Sergeant Lloyd questioned.

"Yeah," I said.

"Okay if I go, Lieutenant Amon?" he asked.

"Sure, we're goin' about a klick to the north tonight, along the canal." I said. Lloyd was still my newest guy, but by now I knew he could handle himself. At Rạch Giá, he had been told we were a "hot" team, that he'd surely see some action. But he arrived too late to experience earlier Vĩnh Thanh - the initial insertion, our living in the pagoda, and the operations to try to tame Nasty. Those were but adventure stories told to him as only Hogan could tell them. And since Lloyd's arrival, the visits by John Paul Vann and General Wetherill were, to him, a boring extension of stateside briefings and spit-shine.

E-5 Lloyd was brimming for action – that's what he came to Vietnam for. He wanted to earn his Combat Infantryman's Badge, like any good infantryman. Even though he had been on the tiring raid this afternoon in search of VC, I decided to bring him along on that night's ambush.

The 379 Company still had a few good sergeants left and

Thanh was designated to lead the ambush patrol. I'd been out with that particular Trung Sí enough times to think he knew what he was doing. We had the usual number of Vietnamese with us; seven or eight men. We selected an ambush site just north of our outpost and strung out in a straight line near a fork in two canals.[Y] Lloyd settled in to my immediate right and Trung Sí Thanh was to my left. We were three to four feet apart. "Nice quiet night," I thought. "Good discipline. Decent location. With any luck, it'll be uneventful."

Nights in rural Vietnam are no different than nights on any farm before industrialization. Except for an occasional helicopter or the distant rumble of some B-52s pounding the U-Minh Forest, it was exceptionally quiet. In the dead silence of the dark countryside, even the click of a rifle being taken off safety is a loud sound. The equipment we carried had to be secured in such a way as to prevent any noise. Even our dog tags had little black rubber bumpers around the edges to prevent them from making a clinking sound. Stealth was the goal. Silence was our friend, the best protection we had while on a night ambush.

"All we have to do now is just sit here," I thought. "Sit here and nothing will happen, and I'll make Trung Sí Thanh stay out here all night until dawn, when it'll be safe to go back."

Passing time and avoiding sleep in the pitch-black silence was a mental discipline acquired over time. Soon my mind drifted off to going home. Home! Yes!

Thanksgiving around the corner! Well, I wouldn't be home for Thanksgiving, but dream on. Turkey dinner with stuffing and mashed potatoes and peas and carrots. *And don't forget the turnips. Gotta have the turnips. Yeah. And the gravy. And the pumpkin pie with the whipped cream on top. There it is on the table!*

A slight noise snapped me out of my fantasy. What was that? There it was again! Sounded like a footstep. Faint footsteps in the mud! The planting of a foot, followed by the sucking sound, followed by the other foot. It wasn't my imagination; it was the sound of someone moving toward us from the other side of the canal. Someone was over there!

I looked both ways. Everyone else was doing the same thing, looking back and forth down the line. They all heard it. A few heads nodded up and down and one of our guys pointed his index finger across the canal. We all began breaking the incredible silence, me included. Broke the silence with that deafening roar of the little selector lever on the side of my M16 as I switched it, not one, but two clicks, from "safety," past "semi-auto," to "auto." CLICK - CLICK. Fully automatic.

Trung Sí Thanh touched my left arm and pointed his finger toward the approaching sound. "*VC*," he whispered, "*Tói di chô dó*."

"What did he say?" Lloyd wanted to know. I thought I caught the "I go" part, but that couldn't be right. As I turned back to my left, Sergeant Thanh was getting up.

"*Khome* (No)," I whispered, as he began to move toward the canal.

I tried to grab Thanh but missed. I couldn't imagine what was going through his mind, but I was not about to go after him. I watched him as he silently slid feet-first into the water. Lloyd looked at me in disbelief. With his M16 above his head, our sergeant was chest deep in the canal before we knew it. His upper body was fully exposed to enemy fire from the other side as he waded toward the opposite shore, toward the footsteps.

Lloyd and I moved closer, shaking our heads. We covered his entrance into the jungle on the other side as he struggled out of the water with the rifle still over his head to keep it dry. Silently and slowly, he disappeared into the black jungle on the other side. Lloyd and I kept our M16s pointed at the jungle wall fifteen feet in front of us.

Thanh had unexpectedly turned things into a very dangerous situation. "Great," I thought, "if a figure comes in view now, how will I know the difference between a Vietcông soldier or Thanh until it's too late? Maybe Lloyd or I will be shot in the time it takes to discern who it is. Or do I shoot the target and take a chance on killing Thanh, a South Vietnamese non-commissioned officer? Wonderful... kill a friendly before I go home."

I silently cursed the little bastard for putting us all in that situation. I knew Lloyd was thinking the same thing. Our stateside ambush training taught us to stay put and shoot to kill the enemy, then quickly leave in the opposite direction. You don't move around in the kill zone.

I heard someone speak. Then I again heard footsteps, several of them this time, coming directly toward us. They got louder until I could tell they were almost to the spot in front of me where Thanh had disappeared into the jungle. My eyes saw the branches and nipa leaves moving at my direct front as my gaze bored a hole into the blackness, trying to see who it was. I stared directly down the gun sights of my M16, my finger touching the trigger.

"Ever take a human being in your gun sights before and watch him drop?" Major Bonner was once again asking me.

My next image was that of a man in the jungle on the other side. It wasn't Thanh because the man had no shirt on. With my M16 sights in the middle of his chest, I readied myself to take his life. As the man came closer, I saw his arms were over his head, so I held my fire.

Thanh's voice called out, "*Không bán* (don't shoot)!" A young man was on the other side being ordered into the water by Thanh. Thanh told him to keep his hands on top of his head. He came up out of the water directly in front of me. The only article of clothing he wore was a pair of gray boxer shorts. He had no weapon.

We packed up and made the dangerous half-hour midnight walk back to the outpost with our "guest" nestled in the middle of the column. Back at the outpost, he was tied at the elbows and spent the night on the ground in front of the guard shack at the front gate. The initial interrogation of the prisoner was fruitless. His alibi for walking around at midnight was that he was looking for crabs in the dark, something that the Vietnamese sometimes did. But Thanh pointed out that he had no lantern with him, no crabs, and no pot to contain the crabs he was supposedly gathering.

A couple of Thanh's men beat the man for a short while and he confessed he was trying to observe our ambush location, to see where we were. He was a "spotter" for the local VC. By establishing our ambush patterns or favorite locations, they hoped to be able to predict where we would set up the next time and then ambush us as we moved into position. The information would have done them little good – we never ambushed at the same spot anyway. But his capture told us something we had long suspected. There were informers and observers everywhere whose job it was to find out where our ambush patrols went, where we set up, and what routes we took.

We sent our prisoner up to Rach Gia on the next swing ship. They had interrogators there that were good at extracting information and generating intelligence reports.

As for Thanh, I told him the next day that while I admired his courage, he could have gotten himself killed. And I told him not to ever do that again on an ambush with anyone from my team. Moving around and taking prisoners while on a night ambush is just plain stupid.

NOVEMBER 9, 1969
Diary Entry:
*Mac and Lloyd checked fighting positions and claymores. 1930 hours, unknown number of VC fired on RD Cadre, no one injured. 379 Company fired 60 and 81 mortars at withdrawal routes. Intelligence reported 200 VC at WR386912.[2] Spat flew a visual recon there - saw nothing.*

We hadn't patrolled the Nha Sĩ area for three weeks, having relinquished control of it to the 563 Company and MAT 45 led by Captain Delgado. Under his direction, the construction of the outpost in Nasty, which had been started by the 770 on June 25, was now near completion. It had taken four months, compared to the thirty days it took us to build ours in Vĩnh Thanh - an indication of how menacing the communists were there. Delgado and MAT 45 moved into the uncompleted outpost. The mud berm walls and moat were there, and the ramparts and firing positions in the berm were in place. The outpost still lacked barbed wire, but it provided better security for the advisors than being in the open.[N]

On one of the evenings around November 9 we heard the sounds of an attack in Nasty, sounding exactly like the attack on the 770 on July 24. We were awakened at approximately 2 a.m. by the sounds of rockets and mortars exploding to our south. Our teamhouse radio was always left on, and within seconds, Delgado was on his radio calling me. The muffled, in-coming explosions we heard to the south were amplified through our speaker as a background to Delgado's transmission, partially drowning out his voice: "Red mustard one-zero this (whumpf) Final Checkbook one-z (whumpf), we (whumpf) under heavy attack (tack-tack), over," he screamed.

"Roger, one-zero, I am calling Kiến Binh now with the sit-rep, over," I told him. I didn't have to hear a word of his transmission to know he was in trouble.

The next twenty minutes were heart-stopping. The VC were attempting to do to the 563 what they had done to the 770, to soften them up and then overrun them. It was a little different this time. The nearly-completed outpost had high, thick mud walls. It was one of the newer designs with four sides, the first four-sided outpost I had seen. Each corner featured a good strong bunker with a roof, and all four had an M-60 machine gun in it. Delgado's advisors also had their M79 grenade launcher, and some M72 Light Anti-tank Weapons (LAWs). And his team knew how to use the tools of their trade.

When the barrage subsided, the 563 Company didn't wait for the VC to take the initiative. They let loose with their M16s, grenades and LAWs into the jungle. Delgado's heavy weapons advisor dropped a steady stream of illumination rounds into the mortar, sending the mortars skyward. When they reached the top of their arc, they turned into parachute flares, slowly descending and lighting up all the fields of fire. The Vietcông broke it off early, deciding it wasn't worth it that time.

NOVEMBER 12, 1969
Diary Entry:
*PSDF meeting in village. Divided 69 men into three groups for alternating guard duty of village. RD Cadre ambushed and killed one VC.*

I decided to hold a large meeting in the middle of the village with the People's Self Defense Force we had been training. It was "graduation day" and the RD Cadre had official-looking documents to present to the PSDF, proclaiming each as a defender of the village, a guardian of freedom and peace. Unlike the PSDF I trained in Hóa Quản, we gave the group no weapons. Vĩnh Thanh Village was making progress but handing out grease guns to that group would have to wait. Walking in their midst, smiling and shaking hands, I tried not to show any sign of the uneasy feeling I had. Some still had to be hard-core, active Vietcông communists. I kept reminding myself it worked in Hóa Quản. Maybe it would work in Vinh Thanh.

Later in the evening, the same group of VC who had fired on the RD Cadre on Sunday night, November 9, returned to harass them again. But this time our RD Cadre had previously set up an ambush at the northern end of the village along the path coming down from Xẻo Sáu hamlet. As the small group of Vietcông cautiously approached, one of our RD Cadre shot the lead man dead on his feet, much the way Dzu was shot. The rest of the VC fled for their lives in panic, leaving the body of their point man in a bullet-ridden heap on the path.

NOVEMBER 14, 1969
Diary Entry:
*One civilian wounded by gunships from Chương Thiện. Did a night check of PSDF and RD Cadre. Made emergency requisition for dapsone and morphine for our team.*

NOVEMBER 20, 1969
Diary Entry:
*IG made an inspection, this time they were from Saigon.*

*We passed very well. He got mud on his spit-shined boots.*

The Inspector General landed and asked a lot of stateside questions. They went over everything from our requisitioning procedures to the proper functioning of our equipment. After they told us we passed, they headed back to the waiting helicopter.

At the last minute, I noticed one of them pointing to our outhouse, covered with the cut-up U.S. mailbags.

"Damn," I said to myself, "maybe we should have been a little less flagrant. Now I'm going to catch Hell for that." I saw them chuckle and make a few remarks as they continued heading for the chopper. We were glad to see them go. Enough said: "He got mud on his spit-shined boots." After we were sure they were gone, we broke out a case of warm Carling Black Label.

CHAPTER TEN

# Old Guy, New Guy

NOVEMBER 22, 1969
Letter Home:

*Dear Family,*

*Well, if everything goes okay, I'll be leaving about a month from now. The way things are going, they let people come in from the field about 3 days early. Big deal, huh?*

*The Colonel asked me if I'd like to extend for 6 months to get a staff job up at headquarters, advising the Revolutionary Development Cadre at Province level. HA! Right!*

*The company I've been advising has had 4 killed and 6 wounded, plus we had a civilian walking point one day who blew himself away on a VC booby-trapped U.S. hand grenade. So, I'm really tired of this and although I don't think I'm in any immediate danger, I still don't feel like pushing my luck.*

*I've been in the field the whole time now because most advisors in the field are now required to stay out there their whole tour, compared to other combat tours, which usually rotate people out of combat at the end of 6 months. It creates morale problems with the men.*

*I'm responsible for maintaining their morale, but unfortunately, nobody takes care of mine, so I try not to have any! HA! HA! I hope I'll be home for Christmas, but if not, right after New Year's.*

*Love, Bob*

NOVEMBER 23, 1969
Diary Entry:
*Mr. White, DPSA, and LTC Stanberry visited. Main topic of discussion was move to Thời An Village four kilometers southwest of Hóa Quản Village.*

I was surprised when Colonel Stanberry told us he had decided to move us back to the Hóa Quản area. I didn't think we had completed our job there at Vĩnh Thanh. But we had been there for five months, longer than most Mobile Advisory Teams stayed in any one place. An advisory team wouldn't be very mobile if it planted itself in one village for very long. Besides, we had finished the hard part.

Unlike most advisors in the field, I had been able to see the complete transformation of Vĩnh Thanh, working in the one village long enough to take it from the dark side to the emerging flower. In the past five months, we had taken it from the village that, since before 1954, had been controlled by the communists, to some semblance of order and government presence.

Colonel Stanberry and Major Dowd explained that Thời An Village was still rough around the edges. In June, when we left that area, the 770 Company remained in Thời An. But when Captain Delgado and his MAT 45 advisors were removed and sent elsewhere, the 770 went back to their sloppy ways and actually lost ground there. The VC still hated them for being Hoa Hảo and they had stolen many a chicken and performed many a "shower" on female VC suspects. So, the failing 770 Company had been sent to us on June 25 and inserted into Nasty, only to be wiped out a month later, on July 24.

Now, there had been no rifle company in Thời An for the past five months. In my mind it would never be as bad as Nasty, but it was the place I was first sniped at in broad daylight. I dreaded moving closer to the U-Minh Forest again too, remembering our captured Intelligence Report dated May 4, which stated that the Thời An Communist Party Chapter had coordinated with the 350-man U-Minh 10 Battalion to "annihilate" our outpost.

As Dowd, Stanberry, and White left the outpost, I walked

them to the pad, and as Stanberry was about to climb on, he remembered something.

With his index finger pointed skyward, he said, "Oh, yes, and Bob? When you make the move to Thời An, do you think you could cover your latrine with something other than those U.S. Government mailbags?"

"Yes, sir," I replied, not being able to hold back a grin. The colonel grinned back, and shaking his head, climbed onto the chopper.

NOVEMBER 27, 1969<br>Diary Entry:

*THANKSGIVING DAY!*

*Received 5 portions of turkey, dressing and gravy in green metal containers by the swing ship. We reheated it and it was pretty good.*

There were rumors in the field in Vietnam that the U.S. Army always delivered turkey dinners to every soldier on Thanksgiving and Christmas, regardless of where they were or even how remote their location.

"I'll believe it when I see it," was my attitude. No one could be more remote than the five of us were in the middle of nowhere.

"No really, LT," Hogan reassured, "they really do." As the morning became the afternoon, we all waited. 3 p.m. became 4 p.m. and again I expressed my doubts to Hogan. Finally, at 4:30, we heard a helicopter approaching.

And just as Hogan had promised, there it was: sliced turkey smothered in gravy, sitting in a Mermite can. Powdered mashed potatoes, stuffing, and vegetables were in other cans. Insulated Mermite cans were designed to keep food warm, but it had been hours since that meal was prepared. Hogan was more excited than anyone. Acting like a self-anointed five-star chef, he single-handedly took command of the re-heat job.

"Everybody out of the kitchen," he exclaimed.

"Holy Cow," Lloyd yelled, "now he sounds like a freaking housewife."

"Yeah," Mac chimed in. "Hey Hogan, where's your freakin' apron?"

We all opened some warm beer and stood around talking about our families back home and what they were probably doing on that day.

We joked and talked as we ate the delicious hot meal. And sure, we missed our families. But I think something surfaced that afternoon that most of us weren't in touch with – at least I wasn't. I think we all realized that the guys on the team had temporarily taken the place of our families back home and we were a lot closer than we realized.

To the same extent, whenever I'm introduced today to another Vietnam War veteran, I still feel that same closeness. We're not blood family. But we're still certainly family.

NOVEMBER 30, 1969
Diary Entry:
*Received intelligence of 100 VC in Xẻo Sáu hamlet three kilometers north. Cái Nhum outpost was attacked by VC with small arms fire.*

The VC were at it again in Xẻo Sáu, assembling a large force not very far to the north. And the outpost at Cái Nhum came under attack by a smaller band of VC, the firefight there being nothing more than harassment by several snipers. Still, the repeated warnings of the assembly of large Vietcông units in the area had us on high alert.

DECEMBER 1, 1969
Diary Entry:
*Major Kone and myself went on a VR on swing ship to Thời An. Met Dai Úy Nhon. He is a very young captain. There is a lot of water in the outpost there.*

Major Kone was Major Bonner's replacement as district senior advisor. The VR (Visual Reconnaissance) revealed nothing as we hovered over Thời An Village, and Dai Úy Nhon greeted us enthusiastically as we landed outside the compound. I remembered the outpost well, having been shot at the first time I was there. But the outpost was in much worse shape than I remembered it being. The helicopter pad was a mud pit, not high and dry. You got a soaker stepping off the helicopter. The firing positions along the berm had gaping holes, having succumbed to the heavy monsoonal torrents during the last rainy season.

Nhon spoke excellent English - a plus, I thought. It would be nice to be able to carry on a conversation in English for a change. "Follow me," he said, "go where I go. Many mines, many hand grenades in this area," he repeated, waving his hands in a circular motion to his left and right. I found myself staring at the ground and nowhere else.

When the 770 Company had been stationed there, they had been harassed by the VC to such an extent that they mined and booby-trapped the entire area surrounding the outpost for protection. Now the 770 was gone, having been annihilated at Vĩnh Thanh, and so too were the individuals with the knowledge of where the mines were placed. Making matters worse, the Vietcông had done the same along trails and routes used by the soldiers. By December 1, 1969, it was impossible for anyone to know the whereabouts of those explosives. I didn't see any signs of the treacherous devices, but I watched very carefully as Major Kone followed Nhon and I followed Kone. Apparently, the only way Nhon's men discovered the mine fields and booby traps was to occasionally step on one.

I walked through the front gate and looked to my right at the spot along the berm where Binh and I had taken shelter after being shot at. The berm had melted like chocolate in the sun. It was barely three feet tall now, and there was six inches of stagnant water inside the outpost. The still air suspended the stench of human waste and garbage.

"These people aren't going very far to go to the bathroom, sir," I mentioned to the major.

"Probably because of the mines," he agreed. The place was like living in a booby-trapped pig-pen.

## Old Guy, New Guy

Dai Úy Nhon did his best to make us feel welcome. He dispatched one of his men to the market to fetch tall glasses of lemonade. It was obvious he was trying to convince the major and me that MAT 88 was needed there. Vietnamese commanders welcomed advisory teams. It made their job easier. With the advisors came all the bennies: faster requisitions of ammo and supplies, faster medivacs, air support, RD Cadre teams to help in the village, medical supplies, MEDCAPs and faster pay. The list was endless.

I liked Nhon. I felt I could have a good rapport with him. He complimented MAT 88 by telling the major, "I have heard Lieutenant Amon's MAT team is one of the best in the entire province of Kiến Giáng!" What a charmer! Even though I could see through the obvious schmoozing, I knew an advisor could do worse than Captain Nhon. Compared to others I had been working with for the past ten months, he was Nguyen Van Thieu!

Nhon explained what he was trying to accomplish in Thời An. "The people here don't trust government soldiers!" he explained to Major Kone. "770 Company was never liked here, constant problems with village people." I agreed and told him of my observances of the slovenly 770.

"Not good soldiers," he reiterated, "not good leadership. Vietnam cannot win this war with that kind of leadership. I run my battalion differently. I insist on chain of command. My men very disciplined." He was doing a great selling job, I thought. And if only some of it was true, he was better than some others I'd been working with. Perhaps we *could* turn Thời An Village around. Major Kone and I left with a positive feeling about bringing the team there.

### DECEMBER 7, 1969
### Diary Entry:

*Continued preparations for the move. Had night ambush with Lloyd and Stevens. 1815-2330 hours. No contact.*

Our last night ambush in Vĩnh Thanh Village! It was Stevens' turn to go out with me, but the ever adventure-seeking

Lloyd decided at the last minute he wanted to come along, so all three of us went. I didn't want anything happening, and fortunately, nothing did. I was getting pretty "short"[28] by now and hoped that would be the last of my night ambushes.

### DECEMBER 8, 1969
### Diary Entry:

*Received word we will move to Thời An on the tenth. Tore down prefab house and put it in the cargo net for pickup.*

Once again, our stenciled "Made in California" plywood teamhouse would have to be laboriously disassembled and rebuilt at a new location, something none of us looked forward to. But Winters and Hogan were both on the team with me when we moved from Hóa Quản to Vĩnh Thanh, so with our combined knowledge of how the assembly and disassembly went, we had the prefab torn down in no time. We spread out a huge nylon cargo net in the rice paddy, onto which we piled the 8' x 8' sections. The next morning, we were all up early, piling still more kitchen stuff on top of the plywood. We secured all of that and the tin roofing sheets into the nylon net and fastened it together at the top. That enabled the CH-47 Chinook helicopter to load the rest of the team and all of our equipment and then hover over the cargo net, hook it up, and take it all to Thời An in one fell swoop.

### DECEMBER 9, 1969
### Diary Entry:

*Tore down our kitchen. I moved out with Hogan as an advance party. LTC Stanberry, Major Dowd and Major Kone accompanied us to Thời An Village.*

As before, advisory team protocol dictated the fanfare of an "advance party" to mark the official arrival of our MAT Team in the new location. I would rather have stayed with the team and helped them with the last of the physical work and then all of us go in as one unit. But the way it was done, teamleader and sergeant went first. As soon as Hogan overheard "advance party," he wanted to be the one to go with me. He had been disappointed in

June when I selected Parson to go with me as part of the advance party into Vĩnh Thanh. I had selected Parson because he was the senior NCO at the time, but more importantly, he was our team medic and I knew I would need him in Vĩnh Thanh. But now that Parson was gone, Hogan didn't want to be overlooked as the first of the team to be inserted into Thời An.

He started selling me even before I could tell him he was my choice: "You know I've been to Thời An, LT, and you know I know Thời An like the back of my hand lieutenant, and I'm the senior man now." he pitched.

"You're right Sarge! And I'm not arguing!" I said. "Get your gear together!"

The next morning, LTC Stanberry and MAJ Kone arrived by chopper at 10:00 a.m. Hogan and I boarded, regrettably leaving the rest of the guys toiling in the hot morning sun to finish carrying all the last of the gear out to the cargo net. At the last minute, they'd tear down the outhouse and shower and load them on. We didn't leave anything behind for the Vietnamese.

"You look like John Wayne, Sarge," I ribbed Hogan. We were both in full combat gear.

"Come on LT, you remember Thời An," he replied.

"Well, at least it wasn't as bad as Nha Sĩ," I said.

"Shee-it, LT," Hogan chided. "You know my ass ain't gonna miss Nasty now. No way."

I told Hogan about the booby traps at Thời An. "No telling how many there are, so we're gonna have to watch it wherever we walk."

"Well, I know somebody who's getting real short," he said, looking at me with a smile. "You won't have to be watching it too much longer, LT."

"No, sir, he continued. "But that's alright, yes indeed, 'cause I ain't gonna be much further behind you. I'm gettin' short my own damned self."

It was fitting that Hogan was accompanying me to Thời An, and to the Hóa Quản area. He and I had been together for over eight months, the longest of anyone on my team. Our tours ran almost concurrently. He was scheduled to go home in March. With an "early out," his DEROS could occur as early as the end of February. He only had a little over nine weeks to go and I didn't want anything happening to him.

During the time I was in charge of MAT 88 I had many capable, loyal men serving under me and certainly Hogan was one of them. But we had also become good friends. The length of time we spent together and the experiences we shared had made us close. And though he had been spared some of Hóa Quản's early horrors, Hogan had come in right behind me as my first "new guy." I always felt responsible for any new man arriving on the team, but he was my first.

It went deeper than that, though. An inexperienced 1st lieutenant as team leader in a captain's slot is going to make mistakes, especially one who hasn't been in the Army very long and who had never set foot in a combat zone. Every call I made increased the likelihood of a mistake. I made the calls anyway, and Hogan always backed me up. For nine months, he was my best support, both to my face and behind my back. Throughout the darkest of times, he helped me keep a positive outlook. He truly loved being an advisor, as I did, working with the Vietnamese people and trying to turn the tide of the war.

During 1969, there were racial problems within the military. But Hogan would have none of it. Racial tensions sometimes caused minority soldiers to question why they were chosen for a particular night ambush or mission, for example. Not once did Hogan ever question my decisions or complain. We all had difficult and dangerous jobs to perform and plenty more to be concerned about than the skin color of the guy sitting next to us while out on night ambush.

DECEMBER 10, 1969
Diary Entry:
*Rest of team followed us by Chinook helicopter with the team supplies. Village chief and Dai Úy Nhon were very helpful in providing us with men to move the lumber.*

Hogan and I spent the night on the ground in Dai Úy Nhon's grass hut. We awoke early and followed the Dai Úy into the village for some Vietnamese *caphe* (coffee) and pastries. While that was a nice break from going on operations, getting to the tiny marketplace was another story. The 398 Company used one heavily traveled path to the market. One could be reasonably sure there were no explosives along that trail simply because it had been walked on enough to be declared safe.

"Make sure you walk right behind us," I told Hogan, "there are mines and booby-trapped hand grenades all around here." Even the process of relieving oneself was hazardous. The threat of setting off one of the maiming death-traps while trying to find a non-public spot was not exactly conducive to a normal bowel movement.

Hogan and I made it back to the outpost just in time to hear the sound of the huge double-bladed Chinook approaching. The big green machine looked awesome with all of our belongings swinging in the breeze beneath its belly. The pilot skillfully set the contents of the cargo net down in the wet rice paddy and then landed the bird and dropped the huge tailgate to let out Winters, Stevens and Lloyd. Once again, it was great to have all five of us reunited.

DECEMBER 11, 1969
Diary Entry:

*Constructed our team house. Had a brief meeting with village chief and Dai Úy Nhon.*

All five of us got an early morning start on the teamhouse and had the entire structure completed by 4 p.m. That evening, I met with the village chief about trying to help him get rid of the land mines and booby-trapped hand grenades the 770 Company and the Vietcông had promiscuously planted in the area. He told me of a little girl in the village who lost her life when she stepped on one. I assured him I would do anything within my power to help.

I didn't want to get his hopes up, but I had already inquired about what could be done. My request for a mine-sweeping team was met with disappointment. In 1969, those highly specialized teams were busy clearing major supply routes all over Vietnam and were not about to mine-sweep every little hamlet throughout the countryside.

"What else can be done?" I asked the colonel.

"Let me work on it, Lt. Amon," Stanberry said.

DECEMBER 12, 1969
Diary Entry:
*Began construction of addition to team house. Civilians worked on floor and frame of house.*

At approximately 10:00 a.m. Major Kone called on the radio to announce that province headquarters needed an Assistant RD Cadre Coordinator in Rạch Giá and Bob Winters was being offered the job. He was to be on the Swing Ship in two days to learn more.

Bob had arrived on the team on June 3 and spent six months in the field. He was perfect to fill my shoes as the team leader upon my departure, but instead they needed him at province level.

That was lucky timing for Winters. Instead of having to endure another six months of hazardous duty, he would have an office, a jeep, three squares a day and a secure place to sleep.

"Bob," Winters said to me, "I'm torn about this REMF job. As crazy as it sounds, I don't mind it out here. But Parson is gone, Mac will be leaving soon, you'll be gone in a couple of weeks, and Hogan's leaving in two months. It'll be a whole new crew and it won't be the same. I was able to put up with all the crap in Vĩnh Thanh because of the team. It was the guys on the team that made it okay. But now maybe I should take this opportunity. What do you think?"

"I think you're out of your mind if you don't take it, Bob," I said. "Who would stay in this pigsty when they could be sleeping in the BOQ getting three hot meals a day?" I told him there was something he could do for me though, before he left the team, and it had become a tradition of ours. He couldn't leave without a going-away party.

### DECEMBER 14, 1969
### Diary Entry:

*Lt. Winters departed for Rạch Giá. Binh, SFC Stevens and I went to Hóa Quản village. Village office has moved to center across from PF outpost. Three uniformed police were there and gave information to Dai Úy Nhon.*

I helped Winters get his equipment out to the helicopter pad as the Swing Ship arrived. He told me to call him on the day I was leaving and he'd pick me up with his jeep at the landing strip in Rạch Giá on my way out "of country."

"Thanks for everything, Bob," I told him, then watched him wave from the chopper as it took off in a swirl of smoke. He wasn't going home, but he was out of boobytrapped Thời An. I reflected on all the guys I watched leaving the field during my tour. Watching someone leave brings a bitter-sweet emotion. I was sorry to see them go, but always happy for them, knowing they were uninjured and out of harm's way. I always thought maybe I'd done something right if I was watching them go home.

After the chopper took off, Dai Úy Nhon wanted to go to Hóa Quản Village to check on the RD Cadre there. I looked around for Hogan because I knew he wanted to visit Hóa Quản after all these months, but he was off in the village helping the 398 Company Commander figure out how to safely approach and destroy the booby-traps. Stevens asked to go, he wanted to see for himself the Hóa Quản Hogan and I had described.

"Okay," I thought, "I'll go with Stevens this time. Hogan and I can go back one more time together before we leave to spend some time in the village and get reacquainted again with the village people." But the chance would never come, at least not the chance to ever visit Hóa Quản with Hogan again.

The three-kilometer march to Hóa Quản was another open rice paddy hike in the blazing hot sun. We walked along the straight, shallow canal that ran between the two villages. Along the way, Binh and I talked with Dai Úy Nhon about all the things we had accomplished there. Stevens listened to us describe our advisor's "prototype" village, the almost textbook pacification of the Hóa Quản area. Binh told Stevens and Nhon about the day Hungl's men killed the three VC in broad daylight; about the night we medivaced the hamlet chief's father; the afternoon we captured the five VC. I told them of the tragic hand grenade incident and the horrible day the gunships shot up the six farmers, killing three.

"But we got Hóa Quản to the point where we could arm the PSDF with about 90 grease guns," I told Stevens, "that's how far along the village was, that's how pacified it was." My memory of the forgiving way the people held me blameless for the helicopter killings stuck in my mind and made Hóa Quản's memory larger than life. It still is today.

We cut across the open rice paddy and entered the village in the middle, near the pagoda. Entering from the west, we were walking on the same trail I had walked on with Guerrero and Hungl's men on my very first night ambush. It was the same trail we were on with Major Dowd the night the drums were beating and the dog barked.

"My God," I said to myself, "that was ten months ago!" Somehow it seemed like ten days ago. What a strange perception of time, I thought. That was the first time I noticed the time warp, a curious phenomenon in the Vietnam experience. Even today, things that took place decades ago sometimes seem like days ago. I have found that to be a common thread among veterans of all wars - the wild distortion of time when it comes to war experiences.

Beyond the pagoda, in the center of the village, was a small Popular Force outpost. It was supposed to be manned by PF troops, but there were no soldiers around. I reasoned they were out on patrol or in the fields doing chores as local recruits sometimes did. The village office was located across the canal from the outpost, but not a soul was there. The hamlet chiefs weren't around either.

We finally found three uniformed police in their cool-looking brown camouflaged fatigues. Nhon and Binh chatted with them and were able to get some information about recent VC activity.

"The VC have been coming back, Trung Úy!" Binh told me. "Sometimes they come at night. The PFs are doing what they can to keep them out."

The four of us continued southward on the trail toward our old, now-abandoned outpost, past the front doors of the rows of hootches along the canal. Stevens had his M16 with him. Nhon and I wore our .45 pistols, and of course, Binh was weaponless. In all, not a lot of firepower. It was quiet in the village. Very quiet.

We passed the market area along the canal that was once bustling with sampans selling bread, bananas, ice, rice cakes, etc. I thought it strange that there were few people in the marketplace today. Looking to my right, I saw some signs of people inside their homes - mostly women and children. They peered out at us from the dark seclusion of the doorways.

Something else was missing from the picture. Usually the children would come running to us, begging for candy and soap. And absent were the little yellow flags with the three red stripes, the ones we used to see hanging in front of the doorways, the official national flag of the Republic of South Vietnam. The flags had so proudly been displayed on the mornings of the election and the big MEDCAP.

"Strange," I thought, as I continued walking, my eye catching the remains of the tree stump that was blown apart the morning the 168 killed the three VC at that spot. I started to tell Stevens about the incident.

"Trung Úy," Binh's voice called softly. I stopped, and turning around, Binh was standing twenty feet behind us. He was just standing there, looking at me with a strange expression on his face.

"Binh," I said, "What? What is it?" He stood motionless in the morning sun, looking around at the houses, then looking back at me. He shook his head as I walked back to him.

"Trung Úy, I don't know," he said in a low tone, looking over his shoulder. "Trung Úy, something wrong, no like it here. I think we should leave village."

Binh turned to Captain Nhon and they engaged in quiet conversation. Nhon frowned as Binh motioned toward the houses with a nod of his head, describing the Hóa Quản we left six months ago compared to the Hóa Quản we now stood in. The Dai Úy nodded in agreement. "Trung Úy Amon, Trung Sí Stevens," Nhon began, "maybe we take a different route back. Come with me now, please."

Not taking the trail, we abruptly left the village by turning west between two houses and through some overgrown brush, then broke out into the open rice paddy on the western edge of Hóa Quản. From there it was a straight shot across the open paddy to Thời An. The strangest part of the walk back was that Binh and I didn't discuss Hóa Quản at all as we trudged along in the scorching heat of that Vietnamese mid-day. We each knew what the other was thinking. We didn't have to verbalize it. I was trying to accept what I was thinking. Had the VC taken back Hóa Quản?

I had wanted to go back to the spot where the outpost was, where the 168 Company had been, where we used to party with Trung Úy Kanh and the mortar crew, the place from which we helped the villagers for so many months. I just wanted to see what it looked like.

Looking back, I was probably looking for more that day. I was looking for closure, to get it out of my system, to be able to stand at the outpost and reflect on what I had seen and accomplished. To say goodbye to the place called Vietnam and put it behind me.

"I'll be leaving soon," I thought to myself. "I wonder if I'll ever get to see this place again?"

DECEMBER 15, 1969
Diary Entry:
*Started work on bunker. Night ambush to WR194808.*

*1830 to 0200 hrs. LTC Stanberry and Major Kone visited.*

Colonel Stanberry flew in with Major Kone for yet one more briefing. I expressed my chief concern in Thời An: the mines and booby-trapped hand grenades. I had to help these people one last time, help them get rid of that menace.

"We won't be able to operate freely without first addressing the removal of the mines and booby-traps, sir," I explained, adding, "I also believe we'll win considerable respect from the people in the village if we could show them we're as concerned as they are about getting rid of these things."

The colonel nodded in agreement. I went on to explain that most of the mines were planted some time ago, and some of the booby-trapped areas concealing the hand grenades were now covered over with vegetation, making them virtually impossible to spot.

Colonel Stanberry reiterated the impossibility of getting a mine-sweeping team to come to Thời An, but as promised, he had inquired about the problem and told us of one method being used. It required pouring diesel fuel on the ground and igniting it. The burned area is then cleared enough to use the conventional methods of poking and digging for the mines. Sometimes larger areas can be made safer by dragging heavy logs attached at a safe distance to a water buffalo. The mines could be exploded in that manner without causing injury. Stanberry agreed to follow up on my requisition for diesel fuel just as soon as I requisitioned some. I told him I'd do that immediately.

## DECEMBER 16, 1969
Diary Entry:

*Worked on bunker. Mr. White visited and discussed village progress with myself and the Dai Úy at the coffee shop.*

Dai Úy Nhon and I decided to take Mr. White, the CORDS official, "downtown" to the increasingly popular "coffee shop" to give him a firsthand impression of Thời An. Along the way, we inspected some of the booby-trapped areas. At the coffee shop we sipped iced *caphe* and discussed what could be done. I explained that a People's Self Defense Force (PSDF) already existed. With the help of the village chief, we could identify those individuals and revive the PSDF. The RD Cadre team had already begun rebuilding the village and helping with the clearing operations. Mr. White said he had learned of Stanberry's clearing plan and promised we would be receiving diesel fuel.

DECEMBER 17, 1969
Diary Entry:

*Had a night ambush to WR201825. Departed 2030 hours, returned 0200. No contact. Noise discipline was poor. Village chief visited our team house with Dai Úy Nhon. Discussed the clearing of booby-trapped area.*

On the evening of December 17, Mac and I went on the ambush to WR201825. The Trung Sí in charge didn't get his men mobilized until 8:30 p.m. We were forced to leave the outpost at dark, with just a hint of light left. Leaving too late presented the two-fold problem of not being able to see where we were going and also subjecting all of us to being ambushed while moving to the ambush site. During my entire tour, I had been on very few night ambushes that departed after dark. Given also that the area was booby-trapped, the darkness added even more risk. And the soldiers made more noise than was acceptable. When I told the squadleader I wouldn't stand for it, he refused to speak to me or Mac for the rest of the evening.

It didn't matter anyway, as short as I was. We left the ambush site at 2 a.m. More unnecessary risk. That was my last night ambush in Vietnam. The last night ambush for the rest of my life, not counting the mental ones.

DECEMBER 19, 1969
Diary Entry:

*1st Lt. Barker joined the team as replacement for 1st Lt. Winters. Took Barker to meet Dai Úy Nhon in the village. Mac went to Rạch Giá. Hogan was sent to MAT 70 because they needed a fast replacement. Company had ambush to WR194803. They left at 1930, returned 2345 hours. No contact. In the afternoon I gave a briefing to LTC Stanberry and Mr. Wilson.*

The reality of just how little time I had left in Vietnam smacked me in the face as the above two changes in personnel took place within an hour of one another.

First, new-arrival Lieutenant Barker came in by Swing Ship. My diary entry describes him as Bob Winters' replacement (assistant team leader). But Barker was a 1st Lieutenant. Barker wasn't replacing Winters. Stanberry sent him out to MAT 88 because he was getting ready to replace *me!*

*Wait a minute. Am I ready for that? Are you telling me it's time for me to go back home now? Already? Oh, I know I'm short. Sure. I've been counting the days, in fact. But, it's time already? Go home and start sleeping in a real bed and forget about this place? Turn it all off, just like that?*

I realized what Griffin must have gone through the day he knew he had to leave. I knew his thoughts. I understood the panic on his face when he stepped onto the chopper, his eye-contact with me crying out, "I'm not ready to leave." Maybe I liked being in charge of my team of advisors, maybe I thought I was good at what I did at keeping my men alive, of winning the hearts and minds of the Vietnamese, at helping to win the war. Hell, it was working. What Chuck and I talked about… it was working. *There must be some mistake: this new, fresh, green replacement can't possibly fill my shoes!*

Or maybe it was something a lot more than that. I realized what panicked Griffin and sent him into a tailspin after four years in Vietnam. He wasn't ready to be taken, cold turkey, off the intravenous adrenaline rush of dealing with being in the field every day. *Was I?*

Was I ready to go back to a world where the most exciting thing happening was the township digging up the sewer line at the end of the street? More important than facing what I perceived as unbelievable stateside boredom, would I be able to fit in and function again in that world? I knew I was good at staying alive and doing my job in Vietnam, but would it count for squat back home? What useful purpose back in the Real World could be served by knowing how to set up an excellent night ambush? That would really impress the hell out of business associates and customers, wouldn't it? No, it would freak them out! It scared the hell out of me. And I *had* become an adrenaline junkie to boot.

To make matters worse, after taking Barker to the village to show him the booby-trapped area, I arrived back at the teamhouse to find Hogan gone.

"Gone?" I yelled. "What do you mean, Hogan's gone?"

While I was in the village, "they'd" sent the Swing Ship back and picked him up to go to MAT 70 as an emergency replacement in some far corner of Kiến Giáng Province. And it would be a permanent assignment. No good-byes, not even time for a handshake. I knew I'd never see or hear from him again; I just had that feeling. I didn't have his home address, he didn't have mine; hell, nobody bothered or took the time. Just like that: spend over eight months in the field with a guy who is rarely out of your sight for more than a couple of hours a day and "they" whisk him away without giving anyone any notice at all. "But this is *my* team!" I grumbled to myself. "Doesn't anybody check with *me* first?"

I have plenty of pictures of Hogan to remember him by, playing with the children in the outpost, swinging them around, giving them candy. He had been majorly loyal and helpful to me. Then he'd been abruptly pulled from our team and sent to MAT 70 without the chance to say goodbye. I never saw Hogan again after that morning.

"So, this is how it ends, huh?" I muddled. "Spend your entire tour in the field and then split the team up. Get replaced and go back to civilian life. Separate yourself from everything you've seen and done, from the heroic people you've known, American and Vietnamese. Just go home now, and don't look back. It's over."

This may not work for me. I was starting to panic.

DECEMBER 20, 1969
Diary Entry:

*Completed work on bunker. Went to coffee house with Lt. Barker to meet with the Dai Úy and various village officials. Received intelligence of 15 VC at WR205797.*

Barker was a very nice, intelligent young man; a good listener, a good learner. The seven short days I had to teach him and work with him weren't possibly enough time to impart everything I wanted to, and it frustrated me to turn my advisory team over to a new arrival.

I found myself talking to him endlessly to try to bring him up to speed. It had to be frustrating for him also, listening to me ramble on. "Don't forget this, and make sure you do that, and there's always a possibility of such-and-such." He must have thought I was nuts.

But Barker was patient and we both did the best to transition. I limited Barker's tutoring sessions to times when we were alone or in the village with our counterparts, never around the teamhouse or in front of the other Americans.

DECEMBER 21, 1969
Diary Entry:

*Chinook delivered 16 drums of diesel fuel to burn off the jungle where the VC have mined the area with booby trapped hand grenades. Lt. Barker and Stevens went on night ambush to WR197801. 1900-0200 hrs. No contact.*

As promised by Stanberry, a huge CH-47 helicopter landed at Thời An during the morning and unloaded the large 55-gallon drums of diesel fuel. We all pitched in with the Vietnamese and began rolling the heavy barrels from the helipad down to the area of the booby traps. It was back-breaking work on the uneven path. The relentlessly scorching noonday sun had the sweat rolling off our shirtless bodies. To traverse muddy sections of the trail, wooden poles had to be laid out as "runners," lest the heavy barrels sink in the quagmire. Wooden pry bars provided leverage to breach the worst areas. As a colony of ants would move a bread crumb, so we moved those drums into the dangerous booby-trapped area.

As the sun sank lower in the sky, Sergeant Stevens left the outpost with the new Lieutenant Barker on Barker's very first night ambush. The Vietnamese squad leader selected an ambush location that was less than a klick away from last night's reported sighting of the VC. Because of that, it would have been an ambush that I would have taken myself, were I not so short. But my time had come.

I anxiously watched them leave the front gate at 7 p.m. and couldn't help but remember my own first ambush with Guerrero, ten months prior. Just as Guerrero patiently broke in that new lieutenant, so too would Stevens show this one the ropes. "It's better this way," I thought, "let Barker learn from the NCOs." I really missed Hogan being on the team to help break in the new team leader.

DECEMBER 23, 1969
Diary Entry:
*Mac and Stevens went on operation to WRI885 with 398 Company.*

DECEMBER 24, 1969
Diary Entry:
*Lt. Barker went to the booby-trapped area to observe the burning of the jungle with the Dai Úy. Had brief meeting with village chief and Dai Úy Nhon.*

Because it was Christmas Eve, Barker and I scheduled no operations for several days. I began getting my gear ready to go. I went out to the CONEX container and retrieved my musty duffle bag and other mildewed belongings and brought them into the teamhouse. My khaki summer uniform was a wrinkled mess and in need of laundering. I wondered how I would be able to get it clean by washing it in the canal. I had a few more decorations now that I wanted to attach to the shirt.

My green airborne cap with the glider patch was still in

good shape. I took off the second lieutenant's gold bar and replaced it with my silver 1LT bar. I pinned a new metal CIB on the left side of my chest above my silver jump wings. I cleaned up my old leather Corcoran jump boots and gave them a spit-shine for the last time. I packed everything and got it ready as if I'd be receiving a call at any minute.

DECEMBER 25, 1969
Diary Entry:

*CHRISTMAS DAY*

*Received turkey in Mermite cans again by helicopter. We heated the whole thing up again and had a real nice dinner. Played cards in the afternoon.*

The food arrived after 3 p.m. and we again reheated it: turkey, mashed potatoes, stuffing, and corn. I realized I had come full circle as I looked around at Barker, Stevens, Mac, and Lloyd. Of the four, only Mac and Lloyd would have remembered Parson, and none of them would have known Ponce, Guerrero, or Darden, the original guys on Mobile Advisory Team 88 when I first arrived. Winters, Griffin, McFadden, Van Nader, Garner, Lloyd, Parson, Stevens and Hogan had all safely passed through the team on my watch.

We talked about Hogan, wondering how he was. None of us had heard from him. Since we didn't know where MAT 70 was, it was impossible to get him on the radio to wish him a Merry Christmas. I knew he was sitting in some teamhouse somewhere in the province thinking about us and the turkey dinner.

"Yeah," Lloyd chimed in, "he's probably playing Chef Boyardee again, wherever he's at." Lloyd missed Hogan as much as I did. We all did.

The team was filling up with new guys. It was time for me to get out of their way, give them the ball, let them carry on the team mission. I was glad I hadn't turned bitter toward the Vietnamese. Sometimes it was easy to do, the way Darden had, the way Griffin had done at the end. It was important to me that I leave Barker and the others with as much positive energy as I could.

On Christmas day, 1969 I never for a moment conceived of the collapse of the Saigon government that we were all to witness on nationwide television years later. The unexpected and sudden withdrawal of all U.S. commitment and support for the free government of South Vietnam was unthinkable as we sat in our "kitchen" drinking beer and eating turkey.

By encouraging the new men on the team to enthusiastically pursue the dream, the dream Chuck Emery and I so cherished to help the South Vietnamese make a better, safer life for the people in the village, I actually thought it would work. My one-year tour of duty had flown by because I stayed positive, always worked to achieve the goal, never once looked back over my shoulder. And I knew for them that their tours would be over in a flash also, if only every day was a positive, energetic one.

"LT," Stevens said, "you haven't been back in the States for a whole year. You have no idea what's been happening back there lately. There's a whole peace thing going on now with the hippies. They say we're baby-killers. They're even spitting on soldiers at the airport in California!"

I knew things had gotten worse at home; that Vietnam returnees were being spit upon. "Hell," he continued, "you should've seen what happened at Woodstock. The little bastards used peace as an excuse to have a big drug party. They were screwing in public and everything."

"Sounds like my kinda party!" Lloyd chimed in with a laugh. Hogan would have gotten a kick out of that one.

"Well, don't worry guys," I told everyone at the table, "anybody who tries to spit on my uniform is gonna get my Corcoran jump boot up his ass!"

### DECEMBER 26, 1969
### Diary Entry:

*Today I went with Lt. Barker and Sgt. Lloyd to the booby-trapped area to observe the burning off of the jungle. Progress was slow because the diesel fuel is hard to ignite and it takes a lot to destroy the thick bushes. Filled out OER on Lt. Winters and EER's on McFadden and Stevens.*

I woke up feeling melancholy. I knew I'd get the call on the radio soon to pack up and get on the Swing Ship. I should have been elated, but I wasn't. I was fidgety. I wondered what was wrong with me. I should have been happy it was finally over for me. I was going home! Lt. Barker and Sgt. Lloyd were headed to the village and I invited myself along. I had to pass the time somehow. We stopped at the snack stand where I bought them each a morning glass of caphe and a rice pastry.

Binh showed up and introduced us to his new girlfriend, a village girl from Thời An. They were holding hands. "Alright, Binh!" I jabbed, as the young couple blushed. Public displays of affection were not socially acceptable mores in Vietnam in 1969, but that never held Binh back from being quite the ladies' man.

Even though he was approximately twenty-four years of age at the time, he preferred girls in their late teens. He had no difficulty attracting them either. He was good looking, had government pay in his pocket, and used his position as interpreter for the American advisors to spin swashbuckling tales of heroic action in combat. He swept young ladies off their feet, spinning yarns of combat operations against the Vietcông.

Even though Binh was deathly afraid of the VC, to listen to him, he had single-handedly cleaned out Vĩnh Thanh Village! And the girls fell for it. I didn't think of ever telling anyone that he never once carried a weapon for fear that if we had been overrun, he could tell the VC that he wasn't a "combatant!" But in all fairness to Binh, if he had ever been captured, the VC would have skinned him alive for working so closely with the Americans.

His command of English and his connection with the Americans gave Binh a huge ace too. I'm sure young Vietnamese girls saw him as a ticket out of Vietnam, a chance to get to the United States when the war was over, to raise a family in peace and live free in the cornucopia of abundance. All would be wonderful in that new land and emigration would be no problem after the war had been won.

I looked at Binh and realized he'd been with me for my entire tour. He knew I was leaving but didn't know I'd be gone in just a matter of hours or a day or two.

Sergeant Binh was my most valuable asset and a close friend. He was much more than a good interpreter; he was a loyal ally who helped keep me alive on many occasions. I tried looking him up after the war, but the only name I knew him by was his last name, "Binh," which is almost as common as "Smith" in the U.S.

Barker, Lloyd and I continued on to the booby-trapped area. The place gave me the creeps. From a distance of fifty meters, we watched the local farmers spilling the diesel fuel onto the vegetation, attempting to keep it burning while hacking at the wet brush that wouldn't ignite. It was dirty, dangerous work, but the villagers were determined to rid Thời An of the menacing instruments of war.

I would have been hard pressed to find the courage to do what they did, walking precariously amongst the death-devices. The drive, determination, and courage of those Vietnamese peasants was once again an amazing thing to witness firsthand. Such heroes! I was glad I was able to help again, one more time, before I went home. No one wanted to see Vietnamese children become amputees by accidentally setting off one of the hideous devices.

At lunchtime I walked back to the teamhouse to find Mc-Fadden looking at me with a big grin on his face. "Congratulations, sir," he said, "Rạch Giá called. You are to be on tomorrow's Swing Ship, in route to the U.S. of A."

His announcement stunned me. "Really?" I said. "Holy Cow. Okay. Well, I guess I'd better get my stuff together then. Thanks, Sarge." I turned to walk back to my bunk, where my gear was.

"Hey Lieutenant, can I have a few words, off the record?" Mac asked. Mac knew we were together long enough to say any damned thing he wanted to say and he didn't have to ask. We'd been close even before the PBR ambush on the Cái Nhum river and his loyalty and support for me was a close second to Hogan. When he spoke, I turned and looked at him.

"LT, I've come and gone from this God-damned place three times now and one thing I've learned: Walk away from this place. Leave this damned shit-hole behind. You're goin' home where you belong. Go back and start a family, raise some kids, Hell, have some fun, join a country club. That's what it's all about. Don't worry about the rest of the guys here, they'll be fine. There ain't nothin' goin' on out here anymore anyway. This whole thing is winding down and everybody will be going home soon."

"Thanks, Sarge," I said, wondering if I could follow his advice. I took a look at my gear one more time. I was packed. Hell, I was overpacked.

Mac and I spent the rest of the afternoon tanning ourselves on top of the bunker. We were both so short we didn't give a shit if the commanding general himself flew in and spotted us. With less than twenty-four hours left in the field, it was a feeling hard to describe. I was actually going to make it out of there.

Elated as I was to have survived, to be going home to my wife and the rest of my family, I wasn't a part of *the team* anymore. I'd be set adrift from the rest of the men now, totally isolated from any of their concerns, questions, or problems. Their decisions involving Thời An would be their own now, not to be shared with me. Their knowledge of the history of the taming of Hóa Quản was limited only to what they had absorbed from Mac, Hogan, Winters and me. From that point on, their decisions concerning the Hóa Quản-Thời An area would have to be their own, based on fresh, current needs of both villages.

My time had passed. As a leper is cast from a village, the last day of the short guy becomes an unbelievable curse. Seeing me that short was so revolting and painful to the rest of the guys that they found it difficult to even conduct a conversation with me, much less seek advice. My pending departure came with the realization that they would have to shoulder the weight on their own, to make their own decisions and carry on the mission as I did when passed the torch by Lieutenant Darden. That, coupled with their own every-night thoughts about going home, made it difficult to even look me in the eye. It was a normal reaction and I knew the feeling.

I was more than expendable baggage. Going through their minds was this: Bring in somebody fresh on the team, somebody with a lot of time left in-country, somebody greener than me, somebody with eleven months of time left, somebody I can be shorter than. With every new guy came that great feeling: every new guy gets me shorter; every new guy gets me one day closer to home.

"Get this old guy out of here already... I can't wait to see him go!"

DECEMBER 27, 1969
Diary Entry:
*Spent morning working on paperwork and getting ready to leave on swing ship.*

Barker, Lloyd, and Binh were back in the village this morning supervising the clearing of the booby-trapped area as I wrote my final, melancholy diary entry above. The Swing Ship landed at the outpost around 10 a.m. and Mac helped me carry my gear out to the helipad. We threw the cumbersome duffle bag on the chopper, and I placed the Vietcông SKS rifle on board that I was taking home as a war souvenir. Standing next to the helicopter, Mac saluted me with a broad smile on his face. I saluted back, and then we shook hands with a tight grip.

"Remember what I said, sir!" Mac yelled, as I climbed on. "Promise me you'll forget about this place."

"I will, Mac, I will."

CHAPTER ELEVEN

# Return to Hóa Quản Village

I didn't keep my promise to Mac. If only I could have. How wonderful it would be if our minds were like computers. Open the "File Manager" on the screen of life, click on a selected file and hit "Delete."

But no. What's this? "Unable to Delete, Must Save... SAVE AS?"

Well, I don't want to save it. But okay, I'll just hit the red "X" and close the window then. It's on the hard drive someplace, but I'll just get it off the screen for now.

So, I put my diary away, and stored it in a fireproof filing cabinet. And life went on. Young, active, busy minds move along. I worked seventy hours a week, bought a home, experienced the miracle of childbirth, got the kids through college, helped them get established, got remarried, prepared for retirement and along the way arrived seven wonderful grandchildren!

And all the while, throughout the hectic, challenging, obstacle-ridden years, there was precious little time for remembrance, certainly no time to dwell on it—on *IT!*

But *it* always came back... uninvited and unannounced. Ghastly is what it is. Ghastly, ghostly and intrusive. The sound of a helicopter, the mildewy smell of a musty Boy Scout tent, the sight of an olive-drab entrenching tool at a flea market. And yes, as intrusive as sitting with *IT* at the dinner table on Thanksgiving. All of a sudden, I'm sitting with my "other family," and it's Thanksgiving, 1969, with Mac wisecracking, "Hey, Hogan, where's your freaking apron?" *Where are they now and what happened to them after I left?*

And so, I'm gone again. "In my mind I'm goin' to Carolina," sings James Taylor. Those innocent Carolina days at Fort Bragg with the other paratroopers of the 82nd Airborne in route to Vietnam, to Hóa Quản, to the teamhouse at Vĩnh Thanh, to Hogan reheating the contents of the Mermite cans. "And it seems like it goes on this way forever, you must forgive me... If I'm up and gone to Carolina in my mind."

For years I wondered if there was anything I could do about it. It was noticeable to my friends and obvious to my family.

"Oh well, that's all in the past now," my family would say, gently hinting, unable to understand why thoughts of Vietnam constantly pervaded my life, why I seemed to be the proverbial moth drawn to the flame. By avoiding the topic of Vietnam, by changing the subject, many thought they were doing me a favor. They were "helping" me forget the war.

"Sometimes I need a little time to myself," I used to tell my first wife. Then I'd be up and gone. After my divorce, close friends and family were still supportive, each wanting to help, willing to try to understand the periods of up and gone.

And then there was the anger. Arguments with my parents, my ex-wife, my children, my loved ones. Everyone argues, but I could take it nuclear, particularly with complete strangers. I started getting into bar fights. Drinking and working 78-80 hours per week seemed to help.

But there wasn't a day... not one... that some thought about Vietnam didn't haunt me. Not a single day. I called them "daymares."

Then I heard about the completion of a Vietnam Veterans Memorial in Washington, DC in 1982. I thought, maybe if I go there, I can get some closure. Maybe if I brought my diary along, I could look up the names I had recorded and make sure they all got home okay. That's the day I discovered Chuck Emery's name on The Wall.

When I told my folks about my trip to The Wall with my diary, my mom said, "You know, you really ought to consider writing about what's in your diary some day. I'd love to read about it, really."

The little diary I had purchased at the Menlo Park Shopping Center still sat tucked away in that fireproof filing cabinet. Whenever I came across it, it begged to be re-opened. Pages containing but a few words or meaningless sentences to anyone but myself screamed volumes to me. So compact, yet so powerful. It sat there, a compact little time-bomb. Either it had to go off or I would.

I started scribbling notes based on my diary entries. And as fate would have it, I won a sales contest to Hong Kong - only a short hop from Vietnam. "Maybe this is what I need," I told myself.

Time to take charge, time to face the demon once and for all!

MARCH 8, 1993

Thai Airways flight 680 departed congested Bangkok Airport at 10:40 a.m. A young Thai flight attendant asked if we'd like some juice or a pastry. "None for me," I smiled. Carolyn and I had purchased bottles of distilled Russian water at the airport in Thailand from a touristy stand with the catchy, Asian-emerging name of "Snak Ba, Snak Ba." The flight was a short hop to Ho Chi Minh City, rumbling onto the runway at Tan Son Knut airport at 12:15 p.m.

The trip had required much planning, international phone calls, a host of required shots, and a special "Internal Travel Permit," a *Giáy Phep Di Lai*, if you wanted to leave the city and visit the countryside. These were still the raw, dark days, before the lifting of the trade embargo and before re-establishment of diplomacy. Anything went. It was by their rules, or the answer was no. The communists were in charge. If you didn't like the rules, you didn't get to set foot "in-country."

I had to answer a lengthy questionnaire: Had I ever been to Vietnam before? Under what circumstances? What was the exact nature of the previous "visit" and for how long? And specifically, why did I now wish to travel to Hóa Quản Village? I answered all the questions truthfully. To not have done so invited trouble upon arrival.

Still, there were surprises upon arrival. "I need to collect both of your airline tickets, your visas and passports. I must turn them over to Saigon Tourist for safekeeping," Nguyen Vi said.

"Our passports?" Carolyn questioned, "Wait a minute! Our passports are all we have to prove we're U.S. citizens!"

"A formality," Vi smiled, "it is okay, trust me."

An unbelievable request, but I understood why. Surrendering our only identification was their assurance that we'd obey their rules, travel only where permitted and not go wandering off uncovering something embarrassing to the communist government. Or worse: getting ourselves in trouble, mugged, or killed by thieves.

Hanoi's negotiations with the U.S. for the lifting of the embargo were making excellent progress at that time and they were within a year of achieving it in 1993. It was not the time for Hanoi to have to explain an incident involving two U.S. citizens, one of which was a former enemy combatant during their American War. Absent a U.S. embassy to complain to or anyone in Ho Chi Minh City to turn to for help, we had a choice. It was do as they said or get back on another flight that afternoon. We reluctantly gave Nguyen Vi everything we had that proved we were American citizens, but insisted on retaining copies of same.

"Not a problem, Mrs. Amon," Vi said in perfect English. He immediately reminded me of Binh, my trusted friend and interpreter. He even looked like Binh and was about the same age that Binh had been back in 1969. I wondered to myself if that contributed to my trust in him about the confiscation of the passports, etc.

Vi helped us check into the *Huu Nghi* (Palace Hotel) on Nguyen Hue Boulevard, then hurried off to drop off the passports, visas, and airline tickets at the Saigon Tourist office on Dông Khai (formerly To Do) Street for "safekeeping." We agreed to meet him for breakfast the following morning.

Out on the street, we didn't have to walk far to be reminded of the communist police state: every major intersection was manned by two uniformed Vietnamese soldiers armed with AK-47's! At first, they took my breath away. Their weapons were loaded, banana clips protruding, ready to go! I attempted to take a picture of them, which evoked a scowling, immediate response from one as he pointed his finger directly at me and waved me off, silently gesturing: "No photos!"

I quickly found myself practicing my rusty Vietnamese language skills with some street vendors. "*Chào ông,*" (Hello), I began, as Chuck Emery and I had done so many years earlier. Carolyn was able to communicate with some in French.

Upon learning we were Americans and not Russians, crowds gathered to converse and practice their English. When I told them I was a former advisor, many shook my hand, some recanting their days as ARVN soldiers. Their eyes searched mine, hoping perchance to recognize the face of some young lieutenant or sergeant who had assisted them when they were wounded or needed help.

One former South Vietnamese captain, a *Dai Úy*, related how, after the war, he was sentenced to a re-education camp in the north for six months. The six months became eight years in exile from his family in Saigon. He was now relinquished to peddling a cyclo, a bicycle-driven cart, the highest profession he was allowed to attain because of his connection with the Americans during their American War. His shabby clothing and sun-weathered face were a far cry from his once honorable appearance as an ARVN officer. Our popularity on the street wasn't sitting well with the two on the corner brandishing the AK-47's. They glared at the camaraderie we were enjoying, so we decided to move along.

Further down, along Nam Kỳ Khởi Nghĩa Street, we came upon Reunification Hall, formerly the Presidential Palace. It was the scene of communist tanks crashing through the wrought-iron gates on the morning of April 30, 1975. The building had been preserved exactly as it was on that morning, when a communist soldier ran up the stairs and confronted South Vietnamese General Minh in the second-floor reception chamber. As the VC officer burst into the room, Minh said to the Vietcông in charge, "I have been waiting since early this morning to transfer power to you."

"There is no question of your transferring power," replied the VC officer, "you cannot give up what you do not have."[29]

Past Reunification Hall sat the American War Crimes Museum on Võ Văn Tần Street. Housed in the former U.S. Information Service building, the hideous display was not for the faint of heart. Perhaps the venue has changed since 1993, but it was something I had to see for myself. I wanted to know what the present government was telling the world in that museum, however shocking - and it was.

At the entrance was a sign reading, *"Nous accusions...* We, the victims, accuse the United States." Inside, lofty walls framed blown-up photos measuring eight feet square, prominently displaying that which had previously been published many times in the western world: a Vietcông prisoner intentionally being thrown from the open doorway of a helicopter in flight, napalm victims running from a village, scenes from the infamous village of Mỹ Lai. On display for all to see was a bullet-ridden U.S. Army 1st Infantry Division fatigue shirt with crimson bloodstains, displayed under a glass panel on the wall, irreverently still bearing the name of the soldier who wore the shirt. Below the shirt was an assortment of all the hand-held infantry weapons we carried as advisors, taken from the field and displayed exactly as found: a muddy M-79 grenade launcher, a broken M16, its muddy stock shattered by a bullet, a rusty officer's side arm: an old Army .45 pistol, just like the Remington Rand Model 1911A1 that I wore.

# Return to Hóa Quản Village

If one wanted more, larger spoils could be found at the Tunnels of Củ Chi: a downed UH-1D helicopter withering away in the elements, the Plexiglas pilot's side window riddled with AK-47 rounds.

Nearby was the Vietnamese communists' version of Arlington National Cemetery. Neat rows of white grave markers fell in place at a 45-degree angle from the main gate, each one the resting place of a Vietcông soldier killed in battle. In contrast, the grave sites of former ARVN soldiers were neglected, weed-infested, desecrated areas forgotten by all except immediate family. It was said the burial areas for the ARVN's were sometimes used for the grazing of water buffalo, whose dung marked the broken grave-stones.

Vietcong National Cemetery.

Originally, I came for adventure. It became much more than that. So, why had I come back? Did I really have to punish myself with all the morbid reminders?

Yes. And I wanted more. I wanted to see it all again. I needed to close the cover on the diary, close the file in my head titled "Vietnam." There wasn't anything Vietnam could do to me anymore that would cause any more pain than it had already caused - or so I thought.

Come on, Vietnam, is this the best you can do? Bring it on.

## MARCH 9, 1993

As promised, Vi met us for breakfast at the top of the Palace Hotel. Afterward, he had our driver take us to the Foreign Exchange Bank on Nguyễn Thị Minh Khoi Street. He cautioned patience as we began the process of converting $300 U.S. dollars into Vietnamese dông. I executed forms which had to wend their way from window 6 past countless rubber-stamping clerks, initialing along the way, until finally emerging, fully approved, at window 18.

"Be glad you are not Russian, Bob," Vi told me, "they come here to cash checks payable in rubles and have to wait hours!" Our three crisp $100 bills were a different story. A teller at the window handed me my approval papers and a wad of currency larger than a brick. My converted $300 was more than the average annual wage in Vietnam in 1993, about $215!

By 9:30 a.m., we were parked in front of the Saigon Tourist Office again to pick up our visas and internal travel permits from the Immigration Police. Vi emerged from the bureaucratic nightmare with the visas and permits in hand, all stamped "Tourist" in red.

Anyone with "Tourist" on their paperwork was under intense scrutiny and usually allowed no further than major cities like Cần Thơ or Rạch Giá. Allowing us to travel to a remote village like Hóa Quản was unheard of, but an exception was made because we didn't balk at their fees. Vi jumped into the car, reiterating, "I asked again about your ID papers. They say they will return your passports and airline tickets the day you leave. We must come back to pick them up on that date."

"Super, how trusting," I murmured to Carolyn, who raised her eyebrows as the car sped off for the six-hour car ride into the Delta. They wanted to be sure we'd return on time and be on the plane out of the country.

National Highway 1 was a paved two-lane road with no center line. The Army Corps of Engineers paved it in the '60's, and in 1993 it was still holding up well. There were few automobiles traveling the road, but an abundance of every other means of travel, including ox-carts. Our driver sped up. Within 4 hours, driving at 60 m.p.h. and leaning on the horn the entire time, we crossed the mighty Mekong and Bassac Rivers by ferry.

The other side of Cần Thơ revealed what had been the site of the American Army base, the place Chuck and I reported to on our first morning in the Delta when we received our initial briefing as advisors at Eakin Compound. I stared out of the speeding car at the weed-infested, dilapidated area. My eyes searched for the six-foot high "WELCOME TO EAKIN COMPOUND" sign but alas, it had been torn down since the war's end. The communists took special pride in eliminating any reminders of their American War. I tried to envision the medivacs I had summoned: the choppers arriving at the air strip here at Cần Thơ delivering the wounded like Quang, Dzu and Vinh, being carried on stretchers into the hospital and tended to by American nurses and doctors. It was no use; it was all from another time.

The box lunches prepared at the Palace were gone by the time we passed through Cần Thơ, and we had washed them down with our distilled Russian water. Now it was time for a rest stop. Vi knew of only one somewhat suitable place along that stretch of the highway, an open-air roadside Vietnamese "cafe" owned by a former ARVN soldier. It was the Vietnamese equivalent of an American Drive-In.

The "facility" was a fly-infested, filthy outhouse at the back of the building. Upon learning I was a former advisor, Mr. Ba ran out of the cafe and hugged me, engaging me in immediate conversation.

"I was ARVN soldier," he said, practicing his English, "many battles, wounded two times, many decorations, many American friends." He searched my face as others had done the day before in Saigon, wanting to possibly be reunited with an advisor he had known.

"Things not good here now," he said quietly, "much better when we friends with United States. Government we have now Numba Ten, not good for people." His outspokenness was courageous, but I didn't want Vi, a Ho Chi Minh City official, to get a hint of what he was saying. I decided to keep the conversation light, for his sake.

"The people of Vietnam are very poor now," I said, "it makes us sad."

"Communism very bad, government keeps the people down," Ba said. He went on to relate how his children would never be permitted to leave the rice fields even though they were smart children. Their destiny was to work in the fields for the rest of their lives, no matter what their level of intelligence or personal drive to excel. Only a handful of the luckiest could break free of the communist grip. A tiny percentage were allowed a trip to Saigon for tests if in the top of their class, but only if they received a political recommendation, which almost certainly meant a bribe.

"Do you know Captain Williams from El Paso?" Ba asked.

"No," I shook my head, "I'm sorry, I don't."

"He was good advisor," Ba stated, "the best, he was *my* advisor." When he finished, he gave me another hug, and I noticed a tear in his eye.

"I tried," I said, "we tried."

"We both try for freedom," he said, as I offered him money for the use of his facility. He waved me off and would have none of it.

We continued into town to our hotel and had a dinner of Rạch Giá steamed shrimp and a plate of Chinese fried rice. Ants climbed the walls of the restaurant as Carolyn and I sat dining. Later, we discovered gecko lizards patrolling our room and more ants in our bed. I did my best to comfort Carolyn, who accepted the conditions in stride. We tried to get some sleep as we had a busy day ahead.

My mind raced. I was beginning to like Vi because he reminded me so much of Binh. I even told Vi of my relationship with Binh.

"Perhaps Binh lives in Rạch Giá," I mentioned to Vi. "He would be in his late 40's. I wonder if he would be hard to find!"

Vi gave me a warm smile but shook his head, "Binh is such a very popular name, it would be next to impossible, Bob!" Twenty-four years earlier, Vi could very well have been an interpreter like Binh, working for U.S. advisors. We talked about that and he agreed. "Back then, yes. But things have changed," he said, "or maybe they are the same, just a different time."

"Yes," I agreed, "in a different time."

"Tomorrow we go to Hóa Quản Village," he said. "Are you ready, Bob?"

"I think so, Vi." I said. "I think so."

### MARCH 10, 1993

At the front of the hotel, our bags sat in the early-morning heat next to the much larger, overstuffed suitcase we had lugged halfway around the world. The extra suitcase contained hundreds of items we knew would be priceless in the village: toothbrushes, toothpaste, aspirin, soap, Band Aids, peroxide, Q-Tips, Tootsie Rolls, Life Savers, etc. It was a mini-MEDCAP!

A van pulled up in front of the hotel and Vi climbed out with another Vietnamese gentleman who was approximately my age.

Carolyn waits until the van is loaded with
our suitcases and "tour guides."

"Mr. Amon," Vi said, "This is Mr. Hanh." I shook Hanh's hand, wondering why he was along and why we needed the van. Hahn appeared to be approximately my age.

"Mr. Hanh is the Deputy Director of Kiến Giáng Tourist," Vi announced. They explained that Kiến Giáng Tourist was a subsidiary of the governmentally controlled Saigon Tourist. Neither of those were privately owned companies, but rather, Hanoi communist government bureaucracies with innocent-sounding names of privately-owned travel agencies. Hanh had achieved his appointment to Deputy Director after becoming a senior communist party official in Kiến Giáng Province. He was accompanied by a Mr. Thuông, our "tour operator."

Several other "tour guides" arrived, which explained the need for the van. Our whereabouts would be carefully supervised by our "guides." But they were also along for our protection. Hanoi didn't need any ugly incidents hindering the re-establishment of relations with the U.S.

In 1969, I had taken home my original topographical combat operations map as a souvenir, and I had it with me for the trip to Hóa Quản. After unfolding my map, I pointed to Hóa Quản and said to Hanh, "We are going here, right?"

"Yes," Hanh agreed, as he took out his own map and opened it on the floor to show me. "We go here. But name has changed. Was Hóa Quản, now called Thôi Quan."

Former VC Thuong (left) and Hanh (right) determine the route to Hoa Quan.

Interesting, I thought. Hóa Quản and Thời An had grown and were now considered the same village, with a mix of both names: Thôi Quan. I squinted at his old map, an interestingly crude version of my military map. I wanted to compare the two, to be sure we were talking about the same location. He noticed my obvious curiosity over his map, and I saw a smile emerge.

"This map very old," he said.

"So is mine," I said, "I was using mine in 1969."

"So was I," Hanh smiled again, as I shot him a curious look. The map he was showing me was one of two maps Hanh saved "from the old days." At the end of the day, he presented one of them to me as another souvenir.

"What were you doing with this map in 1969, Hanh?" I

asked.

"I was with the Vietcông in Kiến Giáng Province." He smiled. "All over this area, mostly in Kiến Binh District." I stared at him in disbelief. His admission stunned me, and it must have been quite obvious to him.

"Come, let's talk on the way. I remember you, we talk. We will drive to Bến Nhứt, here," he pointed, "then we must go by sampan."

"That's the route I thought we'd take," I said, amazed at the similarity of our thoughts. *But what was that he said about remembering me?*

The Toyota van was driven by a young man who introduced himself to me as he helped load the baggage: "My name is Duc," he said in perfect English. "I am pleased to meet you."

At the tailgate of the van and out of earshot of Vi, the only other fluently English-speaking Vietnamese, Duc confidentially revealed his feelings concerning the United States and the people currently in power in Vietnam.

"My uncle was killed by the Vietcông," he said. "My family hates the communists." Later in the day, at times when he was certain Vi couldn't hear him, he cornered me with questions about the United States. Duc was a young man concerned about the future of his country, troubled by what he saw and distrusting of anyone connected with the current government.

Some of his remarks could even be considered treasonous by some in our entourage. He told me his family was waiting for the opportunity to leave Vietnam for the United States, hence his emphasis on learning English.

"People who live under communism very sad," he continued, "have sad faces, long faces all the time, like the Russians have. Never smile, not happy because they are not free. Vietnamese love Americans. Americans smile, they are happy people!"

I couldn't help but smile at his oversimplification.

"See?" he said. We both laughed.

I immediately liked Duc, but was concerned that he might be overheard, so I turned my attention back to Mr. Hanh, the former VC.

Hanh and I took a seat in the van and used Vi as an interpreter to continue our discussion about what we were both doing in 1969. "I read your application for internal travel in Kiến Giáng," he said, "and I saw the picture of you with the monks in the village. I remembered you from 1969, so I approved the internal travel permit to go to Hóa Quản today." I thanked Hanh, and now I knew who had approved our trip to such a remote place. *But again, what's this about remembering me?*

How could the former Vietcông remember me after all these years? I was in disbelief. There were many advisors through the years. "This can't be!" I told myself. As he continued though, he authenticated facts to me that only someone who was there could have known.

"You were the tall one. You went to Vĩnh Thanh and then came back to Thời An. You had three black men on your team. I remember you."

"Actually, I think only two of us were black," I said, but thinking his recollection was way too much of a coincidence.

"No, you had three," he reiterated. "I remember."

After Carolyn and I returned home, I dug out my diary, and sure enough, he was right! There were actually three African Americans on my team for a while: Parson, Lloyd and Hogan! And he not only knew of the outpost in An Xuyên being overrun, he claimed he was there, confirming what "Coal Bin Willie" Wilson warned our team about in my diary entry of April 2, 1969!

Our conversation in the van went like this:

Amon: *"Hanh, do you remember an outpost in An Xuyên being overrun in 1969, when two U.S. advisors were killed?"*

Hanh: *"Yes, I was there. I was with the U-Minh 10 Battalion."*

Amon: *"What? You were there? Two advisors were killed and two were taken prisoner, right?"*

Hanh: *"Yes. We killed two and captured two. One was wounded."*

Amon: *"What happened there?"*

Hanh: *"We had many men and overran the position after a heavy attack. We killed two Americans and made the others come with us."*

Amon: *"Do you know their names? What did you do with them?"*

Hanh: *"We took them into the jungle and beat them for information. They were scared and didn't know much. I don't know their names."*

Amon: *"Then what did you do with them? What became of them?"*

Hanh: *"We were ordered to put them in a sampan and send them toward the U-Minh Forest. It was not my position to know where they took them. I never saw them after that. I came back up to Kiến Bình after that."*

Amon: *"And you say you remember me? Are you sure?"*

Hanh: *"I am very sure. I saw you several times in the village. We watched you and tried to kill you and anyone on your team. You and your men had a price on your heads. I could have made money if I had shot you!"*

Years after that incredible conversation, an acquaintance obtained some declassified POW documents. Since he knew I had served in the Delta, he sent me the following Refugee Report, a 1983 interview in Thailand with a former Vietnamese ARVN officer who had been a prisoner of war not far from our Vĩnh Thanh outpost (see adjoining map). It's possible the two Americans that Hanh took prisoner were the ones seen by the ARVN 2LT in the following report and located on the map on the following page.

# Return to Hóa Quản Village

JOINT CASUALTY RESOLUTION CENTER
LIAISON OFFICE
AMERICAN EMBASSY
APO SAN FRANCISCO 96346

1 1 Jul. 1983

Reference: T83-085
FROM: JCRC-LNB                                            10 June 1983

SUBJ: Refugee Report, Alleged U.S. Prisoners in Kien Giang

TO: Commander, JCRC
    Barbers Point, HI 96862

Source: Source ; DPOB: Source DATA
Source, SD a former ARVN 2Lt with the 21st Infantry Div.,
is currently residing in Source DATA
Thailand, where the interview was conducted on 25 May 83. Map:
Series L7014, 1:50,000, sheet 6028 I, Mar 68.

Information: In September or October 1976 while Source was being
held in jail in the Khu Tru Mat Ngoc Hoa Prison (WR4889) in old
Chuong Thien Province, he saw two caucasian prisoners. Source
was being held in a building near the Thac Lac (O Mon) Canal.
One morning a boat with several persons in it came from the southwest and docked by the prison. The people in the boat disembarked
and were taken into a nearby building to spend the day. Among
this group were two caucasians who, a guerrilla guard told Source,
were Americans. They were, according to this same guard, being
taken from the U Minh Forest area to North Vietnam. When entering the building in the complex used for field grade officers,
these alleged Americans passed within five meters of Source. They
were wearing clothing which looked as though it was made from
flour sacks. Both "Americans" had long hair and beards. This
group of people stayed in the prison for only one day, and left
that evening. Source did not see them go, but was told by an
acquaintance that they had left toward the northeast in their boat.

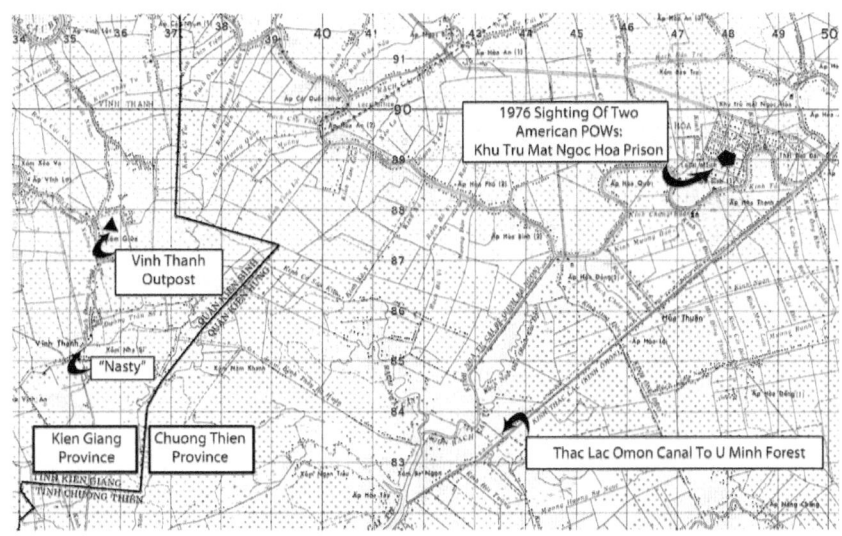

At Bến Nhứt, our entourage disembarked the van and climbed into a large sampan for the canal ride to Hóa Quản Village. Continuing our conversation in the moving sampan, I told Hanh, "No one on my team was shot by the Vietcông."

"I know," he said, "you were lucky."

"You were too," I said. "I'm glad I didn't have to shoot you."

"And I am glad for the same," he said, "because we can be friends now." Hanh went on. "The war is over. Time to forget the past." We shook hands and looked into one another's eyes. I smiled and nodded my head.

"Bob," Vi called back from the front of the sampan, "do you know where you are?" I noticed high ground to my right. It looked unfamiliar, but I knew the approaching intersection in the canal had to be none other than Hóa Quản.

"The pagoda is this way!" I said, pointing to my right.

"Yes," Vi said, "you know this place."

"Thời An is that way!" I yelled to Hanh. He nodded his head.

"What about here?" Vi pointed to his right, as we made the right-hand turn.

"My God, this is where the outpost was! It's gone! What is that building now?" I asked.

"Now the school!" Hanh called back, above the purr of the outboard motor at the rear of the sampan.

# Return to Hóa Quản Village

School in Hoa Quan where the outpost once stood.

"Vi, don't forget, I have the donation for the school," I said.

"Yes, okay," Vi replied, "but first we have to check in at the village police station; the village office."

I noticed that the mature coconut trees and nipa palm that once shaded the "lemonade stand" alongside the canal were gone, the price of expansion as Hóa Quản grew. A flimsy wooden bridge appeared before us. Seconds later the motor cut back and there, on the left, still standing, was one of the old, open-air, masonry abodes built by the French in the early '50's. It was a landmark to us even in 1969, because the Vietcông had used it for shelter one afternoon just prior to my arrival. During an ensuing firefight with 21st ARVN Division, the ARVN's had no compunction about blowing a few large holes in it with some LAW's (Light Anti-tank Weapons) to roust the VC out of the building. It remained in that condition throughout my tenure at Hóa Quản. And here it was again.

"This was the village chief's office in 1969," I told Vi.

"Today it is the police station and the office of the *Xã Truóng*, the Peoples' Committee of Hóa Quản. Mr. Ba Vĩnh is now the Chairman of the Peoples' Committee here," Vi said. Hanh waved to an emaciated man standing near the building. At his side was another man from the era. The two were not old men, but both looked well-worn beyond their years.

Hanh climbed out and approached them, having visited the week before on his "dry run" to discuss what would be taking place when we arrived. Carolyn and I followed Vi, eying the building. Over the years, someone had finally taken the time to patch up the blown-out holes with some mortar.

"Mr. Amon," Vi said, making the introductions, "this is Mr. Ba Vĩnh, Chairman of the Peoples' Committee of Hóa Quản and his assistant, Mr. Chuông, Deputy Assistant Chairman of the Peoples' Committee." Neither man smiled - the "long faces" Duc had joked about. Clearly, they weren't too excited about our visit.

I decided to make the first ovation, reaching for the chairman's right hand. "Might as well get off to a good start," I thought. As I extended my right hand, Ba Vĩnh offered his left in half-hearted fashion. I shook the left hand, nodding briefly, and then shook Chuông's extended right hand. When I looked back at Vĩnh, the lower right sleeve of his black pajama top swung in the breeze. He had no right hand! Most of it had been amputated just below the wrist!

"Mr. Vĩnh lost part of his hand in the American War," Vi announced. This prompted a stupid question on my part.

"He was also with the Vietcông?"

"Oh, of course! He was highly decorated!" Vi replied. I nodded to Vĩnh to acknowledge that and to pay my respect. My smiling eyes met his, but received a deadly, stern reply.

Was he putting on a "tough guy" show for the people in the village, for his superiors like Vi from Saigon, or did he still really harbor a grudge? Perhaps his wound was caused by someone on my team or by one of my 168 Company soldiers. The thought was sobering.

"Lovely," I thought. *We're not off to a good start here!*

The inside of the Office of the Peoples' Committee was furnished with a large wooden table and approximately ten chairs.

The near-handless Vĩnh sat at the head of the table. Assistant Chuông predictably sat immediately to his right. Carolyn and I grabbed seats square in the middle of the table. I had a reason.

"Duc," I said, pointing to the immense suitcase he had carried in for us, "*Xin, cho tôi* (Please, give me)!" I plopped the huge suitcase in the middle of the table and unzipped the zipper. I remembered how I sweated the X-ray machines at the airports, and the strange look of the inspectors who were curiously studying all the contents, including the many toothbrushes.

I opened the suitcase, revealing the contents. Speaking directly to Vĩnh through Vi, I told him I would like to pass the contents of the bag out to the village. Party Chairman Vĩnh shook his head with a scowl, mumbling something to Vi, "Not possible, Bob," Vi said, "Mr. Vĩnh says leave it with him and he will make sure it is evenly distributed to the people in the village."

By now children and teenagers clung to the open bars on the windows, staring at Carolyn's blonde hair, at the two American strangers in their remote village. They chattered excitedly about the contents of the suitcase, spotting the candy. Word in Hóa Quản had gone forth throughout the village: There are two crazy Americans with all kinds of free gifts in a suitcase! Come and see, they're at the office!

Chairman Vĩnh barked at the people gathered at the windows. He was annoyed with them for eavesdropping and made clear his displeasure. Minutes later they were back again, tenfold, peering inquisitively through the bars, listening to the translation. I concluded he had intended it to be a private meeting to accomplish something pre-planned; more than just a private "get acquainted" sitting. I didn't understand why he had isolated us in that room, but then, where else could we go that was more private than that open-windowed room?

Assistant Chuông was also not amused at the amount of attraction our arrival and the contents of the suitcase had spawned. He lit a Vietnamese cigarette, placed his elbow on the table, and using his smoking hand to support his chin, sat there alternately puffing and glaring at us in an obvious scowl. We had somehow unwittingly broken the tone of their intended private session.

Without as much as a "thank you" for having humped the fifty-pound suitcase half-way around the world for the benefit of the people in his village, Vĩnh spoke to Vi, who in turn translated.

"Mr. Amon, it is Mr. Vĩnh's understanding you wish to make a donation to the school?" he asked me. It dawned on me: the reason for the private meeting in his "office."

"Yes, Vi," I said, "you know I have $300 in dông, I want to give it to the school."

"Very well," Vi replied, "Mr. Vĩnh requests that you give the money to him directly for safekeeping, and as with the suitcase, he will make sure it is properly allocated."

"Yeah, right," I thought. *Do these guys take me for being that stupid? Crazy, a little, for even returning here, but not stupid.*

I had to figure out what to do. I remembered my new friend, the freedom-loving Duc, our van-driver and baggage-handler. I wondered what he was thinking. I raised my eyebrows as if in contemplation, looked at the ceiling, and glanced over in Duc's direction. My eyes met his. He had been standing against the wall, not privileged enough, not communist enough, to sit at the table with the senior party officials. It only took seconds to confirm what I was thinking.

Duc's eyes were waiting for mine to arrive. He had no expression on his face whatsoever, but his eyelids flared when my eyes made contact with his. Privately presenting the senior party official the money intended for the school would be a big mistake.

I quickly weighed the amount of leverage I had to work with. I still had the money in my pocket and the two hard-core communists, Vĩnh and Chuông, had been eying the contents of the suitcase like dogs eying a T-bone. The more public I made this and the more aware the entire village was of the amount of the donation to the school, the less likely were the chances of the $300 being split between Vĩnh, Chuông, Hanh, and Vi.

Suddenly, Chuck Emery's voice rang out in my now subconscious stupor: "Bob, what are they gonna do? Send you to Vietnam?"

I decided to give Mr. Vĩnh a lesson in negotiating with a capitalist. "Vi," I said, "tell Mr. Vĩnh I need the suitcase, so I'll have to empty the contents right here on the desk in his office. It's fine with me if he wants to distribute the items. But I'd like to present the money directly to the school teacher at the school in some sort of ceremony over there. I want to make sure the money goes directly to the school."

Negotiating with the communist Chairmen of the Peoples' Committee.

Vi translated, while civilians from Hóa Quản continued to encircle the building, packed like eavesdropping sardines against the open windows of the building, listening to every word.

When Vĩnh and Chuông heard the translation, they were furious. A public transfer of the cash was the last thing they needed, not wanting the parents of the school children of the village to know the exact amount of the donation and it's intended purpose. After much discussion of objections among themselves, Vĩnh turned to Hanh for advice. I looked over at my new Vietcông buddy and gave him a big smile, "*Duoc* (possible)?" I asked.

Hanh nodded back, choosing to smile back rather than meet Vĩnh's searing gaze. A glance at Duc confirmed the plan. I received a nod of approval. "Can we stop at the pagoda while we're up here?" I asked Vi. "I'd like to take some pictures, and I have many photos with me from 1969, in case anyone from the village is interested in seeing them."

I wanted to get away from the "office," having endured enough glares and "long faces" from the Chairmen of the Peoples' Committee.

We left Vĩnh in the building to comb through his booty and walked north toward the pagoda. I moved along, chatting with Carolyn and Duc in the hot sun. It seemed impossible that I was now walking along the same path I had traversed so many times before, walking to the pagoda with Hogan, with Guerrero, with Hungl, and Dai Úy Hoa. To our left, in the open paddy, was the scene so many years ago of the gunship incident. I was still concerned that someone in the village might remember the American gunships killing their fellow civilians. "Bob," Vi said, breaking my trance, "do you recognize the building ahead?"

The form of a building emerged beyond some nipa plants. I walked faster now. There, on the left, there it was: the pagoda at Hóa Quản - unchanged, undaunted, just as I remembered it! My eyes fixed on the sight. It was older, yes, dilapidated, yes. A decaying, inviting, enchanting Vietnamese masterpiece in need of repair and something: paint, at least. It didn't matter.

And all of a sudden, I wasn't a touring, returning visitor in 1993. I was back in 1969!

Parson was seated next to Binh. I could see it all quite clearly. It was the morning of the MEDCAP: the pathetic leper was before us now, getting dapsone from Parson. And the lady with the elephantiasis!

"There's the little boy with the gangrene," I cried out to my subconscious. "Grab him! Come back you, come to me, I'll help you, give me one more chance." To the right of the pagoda were three muddied bodies, drying in the sun. I walked over, breathless! I stood there on the same spot on the now crumbling, poorly mixed concrete. The three bodies were at my feet: no respect, no remorse, lit cigarettes in their mouths: foul-smelling, stink-of-death Vietnamese cigarettes.

*What did I do to you? I desecrated you. I took your picture after you were just killed minutes earlier. And I am sorry. I am so sorry! I deserve punishment. Come on, Vietnam, punish me!*

I entered the pagoda. The sight of the monks and the smell of the cigarettes sent my heart racing. I scanned the walls, the ceiling, it was on me now, all the memories, vivid and fresh: sitting with Dai Úy Hoa at the funeral service. Here, I sat here. I opened up my 1969 photo album of Hóa Quản, and placed it on a long table just inside the doorway. Civilians packed the building and descended upon the photos like vultures.

Elderly monks and village people flipped page after page, pointing and grabbing my arm. They were ten deep trying to get to the album. One man found his wife, now dead fifteen years. Another identified a picture of himself as a young man. They found friends and neighbors, some of which had moved away, some who had been consumed by the war.

An old man in black satin pajamas approached and shook my hand, wanting to know if I remembered him. I didn't remember him exactly, but I did remember a man twenty-four years earlier who I had seen wearing black satin pajamas in the village, thinking to myself at the time that it seemed rather strange to me. Now he stood in front of me, the black satin well-worn from many a canal-washing. I politely told him I did remember him. He identified himself as one of the PSDF, the Peoples Self Defense Force I had trained and armed! Carolyn stood back, firing away with both of our cameras.

As the younger monks waited patiently for the elderly to finish satiating themselves on the old photos, I wandered outside to meet with others who remembered our advisory team. They were not only there to say hello, they were shaking my hand and thanking me for coming back, and for what we tried to accomplish in Hóa Quản in 1969.

I turned as Vi introduced me to one of the young monks. The monk was holding the photo album in his hand and had a strange look on his face, as if he had something to tell me.

Showing my photo album to a crowd in the village.

Some of the crowd knew what he was about to say and had followed him out of the pagoda into the sunlight, forming a circle around us, softly chattering and waiting to see the results of the discussion. Carolyn continued taking pictures.

In the sweltering heat of the late morning, the young monk pointed feverishly to one photograph in particular.

"My father," he said through Vi, "my father." It was a photo of myself and Lieutenant Hungl, the platoon leader with the 168 Company, my first and most favorite counterpart of all. The monk was identifying his father standing next to me in the picture taken a generation before.

"Your father?" I asked excitedly, "this is your father?"

"Yes," Vi translated, "his name is Hungl."

"Yes, I know," I replied. "Vi," I asked, "Where is he?

Does he live nearby? Ask his son can we go visit him now, I'd really like to see him today!" Vi again translated to the young monk, who sadly shook his head.

"No," Vi said, "that is not possible, he is dead."

"Dead?" I said, "your father is dead, Hungl is dead?"

"Yes," Vi replied for the monk.

"I'm so sorry. Tell him I'm so sorry. When did he die?" I asked.

"He died in January 1970." he answered.

*January of 1970? I returned to the U.S. by January of '70.* Tears started to well in my eyelids. *I cannot cry in front of all these people, please don't let this happen.*

But I had to know. "Vi, ask him how he died," I said.

"He was shot," Vi replied, "he was shot by the Vietcông." I had the answer I asked for but dreaded. The monk reached up to give me a hug. In full view of everyone in the village both of us couldn't control the emotions that came crashing down upon us as I looked back into the young Cambodian eyes. We wept, embraced, and together, with what little time we had, remembered his father and the brave soldier, my friend, Thiếu Úy Hungl.

One of the young monks pointed to this photo of myself and LT Hungl in 1969.

The moment I learned this monk is LT Hungl's son.

The short sampan ride to the school is a foggy memory at best. Presenting the money to the schoolteacher was a hazy kaleidoscope of 1969 and 1993. I knew I had accomplished what I intended. I was aware enough to know that the immense crowd of parents and students had witnessed the public donation. It was like being on morphine. I felt like Quang must have felt. I was numb. I felt my soul ascend from the flesh and bone of my insignificant physical being. As if on film, I watched the smiling schoolteacher gratefully accept the donation from me.

# Return to Hóa Quản Village

The schoolteacher on my right and Vinh on my left.

The exorcism having begun, I had to have it continue. Light up those Vietnamese cigarettes!

The pain of learning the circumstances of Hungl's death, and the look on his son's face as he had to explain it overwhelmed me. I wandered alone outside the school building, looking not at the schoolyard, but at the fields of fire.

*In my delirium I wasn't at the schoolhouse any longer, my spirit left the schoolhouse for the outpost. The outpost is still there, see?*

*Quang's wife is on her knees behind me now. She's in the dust, arms raised skyward, her mouth wide open in a horrific scream to the heavens, with no sound coming forth. Even the medivac landing in front of me is silent. See all the pretty yellow smoke Quang? You're gonna be okay.*

*Hey, Binh, let's get them all on board!*

*That's it, Hogan, help me with point-man Dzu. And don't forget the new Chuẩn Úy. Oh, Binh, you're back with the little boy! Get him on too. Got to get him to Cần Thơ to fix the gangrene. Put the leper alongside, and the woman with elephantiasis next to her, I can save her too. I can save them all!*

*Six farmers approached from the village, walking abreast and holding hoes and blackened cooking pots filled with crabs and rice, their black pajamas soaked in blood. What's this, Binh?*

*I found them in the village, Trung Úy, I told them they could come too.*

*Yes, yes, of course. Let's get them on.*

*They were all here now, in the yellow mix of the chopper swirl. Even Chuck Emery appeared out of nowhere, smiling at me through his glasses.*

"It's okay, Bob," he was saying, "the adventure's over now. Write a book and tell them we were honorable and had good intentions, that we tried our best to keep Vietnam a free country! And tell them what it was like at the 'Rice Roots' level."

*With a wave, he climbed on board and disappeared into the smoke. Everything disappeared. Chopper, smoke and all.*

*But Hogan was still standing next to me. The whole team was there, Winters, Parson, Guerrero, Lloyd, McFadden, and Binh: they formed a circle around me.*

"Lieutenant," Mac said, glancing at the others, "remember the talk we had on your last day?"

"What talk, Sarge?" I asked.

"Remember what we said, about forgetting this place?"

"Yes, I remember," I replied. "I will, Mac, I will."

# EPILOGUE

LTC Bill Stanberry was not in Rạch Giá when I passed through on my way home from Vietnam in early January, 1970. At that time, he was still one of only three officers in Vietnam who was rated fluent in Vietnamese. Because of that fact, he was hand-selected by General Peers in late December, 1969 to report to Quảng Ngãi Province to aid in the investigation of one of the largest publicized massacres of unarmed civilians in the 20th century. His translation of the testimony provided by the district chief of Sơn Tịnh District is now part of the congressional records on the notorious Mỹ Lai Massacre investigation, which involved the slaying of hundreds of civilians.

Stanberry's successor and replacement, Colonel Richard Ellison from Hampshire County, Massachusetts, was killed on Feb 16, 1971 along with SSGT Leslie Karnes from Sikeston, Missouri. They were riding in a Boston Whaler in route from an outpost that was being constructed not far from Hóa Quản Village. A north Vietnamese reconnaissance unit operating out of the U-Minh Forest observed the Boston Whaler heading south and ambushed them on their return to Rạch Giá. Karnes was posthumously awarded the Silver Star for his heroism that day.

Colonel Stanberry retired from the U.S. Army as a "full-bird" colonel after twenty-eight years of service to our country. Colonel Stanberry and his wife, Martha, adopted Colonel Tài's oldest daughter, Nguyen Thị Kim Mai, in 1971 at the age of fifteen. Mai resides in California. The Stanberrys were also instrumental in getting Colonel Tài's youngest daughter, Cức, into the United States. Bill Stanberry went on to establish Stanberry Realtors and Stanberry Associates and has multiple offices in and around Austin, Texas. The successful company is now run by Sharon, Bill and Martha's daughter. The Stanberrys have six grandchildren.

Bill and Martha Stanberry graciously invited Carolyn and me to visit them at their home in Austin, Texas in July, 2019.

During our many hours of fun-filled conversation and recollection, much of the timeline and information in this book was validated by the colonel and he enthusiastically offered to write the Foreword for this book. But more importantly, I got to know the colonel in a way I could never have imagined while serving under him. At that time, he was my commanding officer who greatly outranked me and was fourteen years my senior. After sharing thoughts and personal recollections after fifty years, I'm proud to say that we all became wonderful friends.

Colonel Stanberry let me read and examine many maps and documents he still had from the era, including an Officer Efficiency Report (OER) written on him by John Paul Vann in January of 1970. Vann gave the colonel a perfect, unblemished report. This highest of OER ratings is known among Army officers as a "walk on water OER."

"In your book you wondered why I brought all those dignitaries to your remote outpost for your briefings, Bob," the colonel said to me on the second day of our visit.

"Yes, sir," I said, "I did."

"You made me look good, that's why," he said, tongue in cheek and with a smile. We all had a good laugh.

Colonel Stanberry's counterpart, Colonel Nguyên Van Tài, the former Saigon history professor and province chief of Kiến Giáng, did not fare so well during and after the war. Tài's oldest son, an ARVN lieutenant, was killed in 1968. Colonel Tài was able to get his second son, Hai, out of the country before the collapse of the Republic of South Vietnam. That son became a Geneva banker. His third son, Thanh, is still in Vietnam.

After the Stanberrys adopted Mai, Colonel Tài was captured when the communists took over Kiến Giáng Province. For his cooperation with the Americans during their American War, Tài was imprisoned and tortured for fourteen years in a Hanoi "re-education camp." During this time and at Colonel Stanberry's request, Ambassador William Colby tried to get Tài released, but to no avail. Colonel Tài was eventually freed by the communists in 1989 and returned to what remained of his family in

Saigon. He passed away in 1998.

John Paul Vann was buried in Section 11 at Arlington National Cemetery on June 16, 1972. Two days later, President Richard Nixon posthumously awarded Vann the nation's highest civilian citation, the Medal of Freedom. In 1988, Neil Sheehan published the very detailed Pulitzer Prize-winning book about Vann's life, *A Bright Shining Lie: John Paul Vann and America in Vietnam.*

Chuck Emery's sister, Helen Emery, first visited Carolyn and me at our home in Florida in the fall of 2018. We've since become close friends and remain in touch. Her unselfish and much-appreciated contributions to this book helped put all the pieces together, some of which have been revealed and some of which will remain private, for Chuck's sake. Our mutually beneficial visits have been quite therapeutic for both of us and have helped with closure. Helen is now retired and lives in a beautiful little lakefront community in central Florida.

Chuck Emery should have been on a plane going home on September 27, 1969. Instead, he volunteered for a six-month extension and was killed the very next day. Chuck is buried in Section 2L, Site 7248 at Long Island National Cemetery in Farmingdale, Long Island. His name appears on the Vietnam Veterans' Wall in Washington, DC on panel 17W, Line 15.

Bob and Carolyn Amon with
Martha and COL Stanberry – July, 2019.

Helen Emery and Bob Amon in St. Augustine, FL – Oct, 2018.

## ACKNOWLEDGEMENTS

I often tell people that Carolyn and I got married for better or for worse. I couldn't do any better and she couldn't do much worse.

I admit that while the latter part of the self-deprecating punchline is tongue-in-cheek, the first part is spot-on. I know today that Carolyn is truly my one and only, "the love of my life," as I've often told her, who also happens to be my best friend. And yes, I couldn't have done any better than marrying her.

I've never considered myself a gifted writer. I'm a simple man who's most comfortable writing that way. *How hard can it be to write about my war experience when I've got my diary entries as a chronological guideline?*

The answer is, it's hard. Damned hard. Hardest thing I've ever put into words. Honey, you were there for me through my darkest of writing self-doubts, always encouraging and helping me get the words just right. But the other side of the equation was your awesome and tireless emotional support and understanding. You even agreed to accompany me back to Vietnam *before the lifting of the embargo*. And why? Most people would have thought that to be downright crazy. Unnecessarily dangerous even.

You did it because you so unconditionally loved me enough to know that I needed to go there and then dump the words out on paper. What an unselfish, kind act of love! Thank you so much, "Sweets," for all the selfless and generous hours you spent on the manuscript. But especially for tolerating my periods of "up and gone."

I also wish to sincerely thank the following, in no special order:

My mother and father, Effie and Bob Amon Sr. My mom kept a map of Vietnam on the wall and watched Walter Cronkite every night for the entire year, worrying herself into migraines until I came home. After encouraging me to write this book based on my diary, she actually took an early unedited copy of the manuscript to her local book-of-the month club and read a segment out loud.

"My son is writing a book about his experiences in Vietnam," she bragged to them.

Once a month while I was in Vietnam, my dad went to the ACME in Rahway, NJ and sent me oversized "care packages." At the end of his life, with his physical health waning, his mind remained crystal clear and his pride in me unwavered. As I sat next to him on his deathbed, he introduced me to every nurse taking the next shift.

"This is my son, Robert," he'd say. "He served in Vietnam."

A thank you to my sisters, Kathy and Peggy, who have always been proud of my service and supported my early ambitions to write this book.

Our kids and grandkids require a special shout out for their inspiration. Thank you, Jeff and Joanne, Kim and David, Tracey and Jackie for your support and especially for instilling in our grandkids an appreciation for all our veterans. Fisher, Nathan, Courtney, Colton, Wyatt, Melody and Michaelyn, you probably don't know what an inspiration you've been for this book, so I need to tell you here. It delights Grandma and Grampa that you've already demonstrated, at such early ages, a keen perspective of our freedoms and appreciation for those who help defend them. Please don't ever lose that devotion and respect for all who wear our uniform. If Grandma and I had only known how much fun you are to be with, we'd have had you first!

Don Garrido, my boyhood friend and fellow Eagle Scout, you require a special thank you. Thanks so much, Don, for the countless hours you put into the early manuscript. A special thanks to Dr. Michael James, PhD, LPC, LCADC, ACS.

Many thanks to Zach Corbin for his generous contributions while reviewing the work. And nothing could have replaced the fastidious oversight of my publisher, Ed Wilks.

To my cousins, Dana and Jamie, and their respective husbands, Tom Phipps and Steve Tucker: thanks so much guys. This book has been enriched by your helpful suggestions and ideas. Our St. Augustine barnstorming sessions continue to bring fond memories. And certainly no one could have been more supportive than Ginny Moffat and her husband, cousin Gary. You guys always had my back.

I am very much obliged and indebted to Helen Emery, Chuck Emery's sister, for her starkly honest input and clarification of the painful questions surrounding Chuck's military records.

It was apparent to us the first time we met you, Helen, that you're a very brave and honest woman. Not surprisingly, you possess the same candid qualities exhibited by your brother. Carolyn and I wish to remain close friends with you for many years to come. God bless you and your family for your sacrifice.

Colonel Stanberry, thank you so much, sir, for your incredibly generous offer to write the Foreword for this book. Your keen memories of Kiến Giáng Province and clarification of enemy movement were things I'd either forgotten or couldn't have known at the time. It was wonderful to get the bigger picture and hear first-hand the reasoning behind why my particular team was selected to carry out missions in hostile areas of the province. Words cannot express the happiness Carolyn and I feel about our reconnection and friendship after fifty years.

And thank you, Mrs. Stanberry (Martha), for so graciously inviting us into your home in Austin for what became two days of non-stop fact-checking and interesting reminiscence. Carolyn and I are forever indebted and look forward to many years of continued friendship.

Finally, I have to forever thank the people of Vietnam, especially the citizens of Hóa Quản Village, whose warm welcome and forgiving ways helped me heal my soul and find closure.

Their American War is over for them, as it is for me.

They've moved on.

And so have I.

## REFERENCES

1 The National Archives and Records Administration, (2008) [Online]. Available: http://www.archives.gov/research/military/vietnam-war/casualty-statistics.html [2014, August].
2 Ray A. and Stephen P. Bows, Vietnam Military Lore, 1959-1973: Another Way To Remember (Hanover, MA) 1988.
3 Neil Sheehan, A Bright Shining Lie (New York: Random House, 1988), 178.
4 Wikipedia, "Hoa Hảo," [Online]. Available: http://en.wikipedia.org/wiki/H%C3%B2a_H%E1%BA%A3o [2014, August].
5 Sheehan, A Bright Shining Lie, 199.
6 Daniel Robinson, Joe Cummings, Vietnam, Laos and Cambodia - A Travel Survival Kit (Berkeley, CA: Lonely Planet, 1991), 473.
7 "Brugia malayi" (Wikipedia) [Online]. Available: http://en.wikipedia.org/wiki/Brugia_malayi [2014, August].
8 Dud: Derogatory Vietnam War-Era slang for a person of worthless value; refers to ordnance or rounds that fail to perform or explode.
9 Sheehan, A Bright Shining Lie, 178.
10 Ibid., 192.
11 Ibid., 733.
12 The National Archives and Records Administration, (2008) [Online], [2014, August].
13 "The Faces of the American Dead in Vietnam: One Week's Toll, May 28-June 3," Life Magazine, Vol. 66, No. 25 (June 27, 1969), 20-32.
14 "The Wall-USA, Casualty Summaries," (1997, National Archives) [Online]. Available: http://www.thewall-usa.com [2014, August].
15 Sheehan, A Bright Shining Lie, 513-518.
16 Klick: Military slang for one kilometer or .62 miles. Unclear in origin, the term was used mostly during the Vietnam War.

17 UPI. "Red Regiment Poses Threat to Delta Area." The Norwalk Hour, August 25, 1969, 1-2. Accessed September 24, 2019. https://news.google.com/newspapers?nid=1898&dat=19690825&id=yR9JAAAAIBAJ&sjid=LQYNAAAAIBAJ&pg=6031,2395846
18 Sheehan, A Bright Shining Lie, 732.
19 Ibid., 733.
20 Ibid., 735.
21 Ibid., 730.
22 Ibid., 786, 787.
23 Earnest Hemmingway, For Whom the Bell Tolls, 1940 (from the writings of John Donne, Meditation XVII, 1623.
24 DA Individual Deceased Personnel File: Emery, Charles Henry Jr., 05346761, Form 10-249: Certificate of Death Overseas, 30 Sep 69.
25 DA Individual Deceased Personnel File: Emery, Charles Henry Jr., 05346761, AGPZ Form 80: Report of Casualty, 30 Sep 69.
26 DA Individual Deceased Personnel File: Emery, Charles Henry Jr., 05346761, Form 41: Record of Emergency Data, 8 Feb 69.
27 Servicemembers' Group Life Insurance – a $10,000 policy provided free of charge by the Veteran's Administration for active duty personnel serving in Vietnam.
28 "Short:" Vietnam-era military slang for someone whose tour of duty was almost over; Someone with a "short" time to go. Also: "short-timer."
29 Robinson, Cummings, Vietnam, Laos and Cambodia - A Travel Survival Kit, 140.

## CONTACT THE AUTHOR

To contact Robert Amon, or for more information about Rice Roots, including sample chapters and additional photos, please visit the official website for this book:
www.RiceRoots.com

Robert (Bob) and Carolyn Amon are enjoying retirement and reside in Beach Haven, New Jersey in the summer and St. Augustine Beach, Florida in the winter.

This enables them to remain close to their four children and seven grandchildren.